LOST SOULS

What is the state of contemporary American morality? From their original conception in Christian scripture to their assimilation into Western culture, the 'Seven Deadly Sins' – lust, greed, envy, pride, and all the rest – have guided human morality, steering human behavior and psychology away from evil and toward a full embrace of the good. But their hold on modern life is increasingly tenuous. Indeed, one may observe that these days, deadly sin is far more common and more commonly practiced than its virtuous counterparts – humility, charity, kindness, industriousness, and chastity. Without greed, there is no economy; without anger, no politics; and without pride and envy, surely less motivation and competition would exist.

James D. Wright carefully examines the complexities and ambiguities in modern society in the context of the seven deadly sins and their corresponding virtues. Are we all lost souls, condemned by our immoral deeds, or are the trappings of older sin deteriorating? Is it time, finally, to reconsider the classifications of evil and good?

Wright uses each chapter to consider how the social sciences have operationalized each 'sin', how they have been studied, and what lessons have been learned over time. He reviews recent trends and contemplates the societal costs and benefits of the behaviors in question. *Lost Souls* emerges, then, as a meditation on contemporary sin, concluding that the line between guilt and innocence, right and wrong, is often very thin.

James D. Wright is an author, educator, and the Provost's Distinguished Research Professor Emeritus in the Department of Sociology at the University of Central Florida. He has published 28 books and research monographs, and more than 300 journal articles, book chapters, essays, reviews, and polemics.

James D. Wright's *Lost Souls* is a remarkable reflection on the shifting moral landscape of contemporary America; wherein, the seven deadly sins of lust, gluttony, greed, sloth, anger, envy and pride have seemingly been transformed into virtuous ideals. It is a must read for those of us grappling with the moral foundations of the Trump era.

Darren E. Sherkat, Southern Illinois University

James D. Wright gives a clear view and analysis of contemporary culture and morality with insights in every chapter. His writing is so engaging – and often funny – that you don't realize how much you are learning about sociological theory and social history until after you have finished a chapter. Every chapter illuminates Biblical injunctions and modern norms, social science research and its interpretation, and contemporary society.

Murray Webster, Professor of Sociology,
University of Charlotte

This erudite and fascinating book summarizes a broad swatch of sociological research as it shows convincingly that what some might regard as sinful may also be socially necessary.

Arne L. Kalleberg, Kenan Distinguished Professor of Sociology,
University of North Carolina at Chapel Hill

LOST SOULS

Manners and Morals in Contemporary American Society

The Seven Deadly Sins in a Secular World

James D. Wright

Routledge
Taylor & Francis Group

NEW YORK AND LONDON

First published 2018
by Routledge
711 Third Avenue, New York, NY 10017

and by Routledge
2 Park Square, Milton Park, Abingdon, Oxon OX14 4RN

Routledge is an imprint of the Taylor & Francis Group, an informa business

© 2018 Taylor & Francis

The right of James D. Wright to be identified as the author of this
work has been asserted by him in accordance with sections 77 and 78
of the Copyright, Designs and Patents Act 1988.

Library of Congress Cataloging-in-Publication Data
A catalog record for this book has been requested

ISBN: 978-1-138-48179-4 (hbk)
ISBN: 978-1-138-48180-0 (pbk)
ISBN: 978-1-351-01161-7 (ebk)

Typeset in Bembo
by codeMantra

"Be patient, my soul: thou hath suffered worse than this."

Thomas Holcroft (1745–1809), British author

This book is dedicated to my dogs Barnie and Belle and my cat Indiana, who were constant companions throughout the writing process, all of them sound asleep in the various nooks and crannies of my writing studio. To Belle, your admiration of me is wholly undeserved. To Barnie, not every falling leaf or passing vehicle needs to be barked at. To Indy, please stop walking across my keyboard when I am trying to write.

CONTENTS

ILLUSTRATIONS

Figures

Table

PREFACE

It will come as a surprise to many readers that the seven deadly sins are not specifically Biblical in origin, although they have served for centuries as principles of Christian ethical education. The Big Seven, as we currently know them, are lust, gluttony, greed, sloth, anger, envy, and pride, and these specific seven offenses were first listed as such by the monk Evagrius Ponticus, who identified the seven as base urges that pious men were expected to overcome or sublimate. Evagrius's student John Cassian brought the Big Seven into Western (European) culture with his publication *The Institutes,* which dates to around 420 AD. So, while their origins are clearly religious, they are not specifically Biblical.

The Bible is not bereft of lists of Dos and Don'ts, lists numbering anywhere from six to 17. Leading the list, of course, are the Ten Commandments that Moses brought down from the mountain. Elsewhere in the Old Testament, we have the "six things that the Lord hateth" from the Book of Proverbs: "A proud look, a lying tongue, and hands that shed innocent blood, a heart that deviseth wicked imaginations, feet that be swift in running to mischief, a false witness that speaketh lies." A seventh – "he that soweth discord among brethren" – is listed as an abomination. (Quotes from the King James Version, Proverbs 6: 16–19)

Still another list, this appearing in Paul's Epistle to the Galatians, and thus from the New Testament, numbers 17 vices, including most of the traditional Big Seven: adultery, fornication, uncleanliness, lasciviousness, idolatry, sorcery, hatred, variance, emulations, wrath, strife, sedition, heresies, envy, murder, drunkenness, revelry, "and such like." (Galatians 5: 19–21). The quoted material is from the King James Version (hereafter, KJV). The Common English Bible lists "fighting" instead of "variance" and "obsession" instead of "emulations." In yet another translation, "variance" is rendered as "dissension."

A final revision into the currently accepted Big Seven was undertaken by Pope Gregory I in about 590 AD. Gregory's version was adopted by Dante in his *Divine Comedy* (1320 AD) and also by Chaucer in *The Canterbury Tales* (begun in 1389 AD) Today, they are part and parcel of the Catholic catechism used to teach young people how to shun evil, embrace good, and lead a pious life.

It may also surprise many readers that there is a parallel listing of seven "holy virtues" (sometimes referred to as "contrary virtues"): humility, charity, kindness, patience, chastity, temperance, and diligence.

A sociologist analyzing Western societies today would, without question, conclude that deadly sin is far more common and more commonly practiced than holy virtue. One might even conclude that sinfulness – lust, gluttony, greed, envy, pride, and all the rest – have become hallmarks of postindustrial, postmodern society. And that, specifically, is the theme of this book. Without greed, there is no economy; without anger, no politics; without lust, well, not much of anything these days. Christian teachings to shun the Seven Deadlies fly squarely in the face of pretty much everything contemporary American society (indeed, Western society at large) urges people to do. Either the Christians have gotten things all wrong or eternity is seriously overpopulated with lost souls.

A third possibility, of course, is that the realities of modern life are complicated and cannot be morally assessed by reference to a few ancient, outdated, absolutist proscriptions. The modern world is far too subtle and nuanced for that, a point to which I return again and again in the following pages. Where in the continuum from charity to rapacity, for example, does sinfulness set in? At what point does self-interest become greed? When do relaxation and rejuvenation turn into sloth? What, for that matter, is the distinction between normal sexual appetites and sinful lust? Moderns will not be bludgeoned into righteousness by a set of absolute principles; our moral choices are full of ambiguities and are rarely clear-cut. One need not be a moral or cultural relativist to understand that the choices with which we are presented are complex and contradictory. Lists of "thou shalt" and "thou shalt not" provide very uncertain guides to behavior in our complicated modern world.

Indeed, the sheer number of these Biblical listings of sins of varying severity suggests either that God was not of one mind about proper human behavior or, far more likely, that God's various interpreters had (and have) different ideas about what particular behaviors are most objectionable –to the writer perhaps, if not to God Himself.[1] Thus, one finds throughout Christian teachings various, often tortured, explanations of why things appear on one list but not another. Which of the Seven Deadlies, for example, rules out idolatry? Which of the Ten Commandments rules out gluttony? There are certainly some commonalities across all the listings – anything lustful, for example, gets you on everyone's naughtiness list –but there is also a great deal of variation from list to list in what is sinful and what is only –shall we say? –ill-advised.

It is fairly common in commentaries on the Christian catechism to see the Seven Deadlies defined as "base" or "capital" sins from whence all other sins derive. They are depicted as the roots of a giant tree, and all the other sins and vices are the trunk, branches, and leaves of the tree. Trim away one branch and it will grow right back. To eliminate all sin thus requires that the entire tree be uprooted. In other words, all things noted as sinful either in the Bible itself or in various commentaries on the Bible derive ultimately from the Seven Deadlies. Such, in any case, is a common thread of argumentation.

Another common thread is lengthy exegeses on definitions. Just what *is* pride, for example? Or greed? Or sloth? Consider the craftsman who is proud of his work and sells it at a sufficient profit that he can take a day off. Do these simple behaviors commit three of the Big Seven? Clearly, this is different from the factory owner who pays miserable wages and charges as much as the market can bear in order to support his lavish lifestyle (of which he is noisily proud). But different *how*? Lengthy tomes have been written around just these sorts of points.

Obviously, depending on definitions, any list of sins can be made compatible with any other list. Take as an example the essay by Ed Friedlander, "The Seven Deadly Sins."[2] Discussing pride, our author observes,

> There is no reason you should not enjoy your own genuine abilities and genuine achievements. Pride is not a sin when it merely involves taking satisfaction in a job done well – nobody ever hurt anybody else over this. But we make ourselves and others unhappy by demanding attention and recognition, or by not asking for help and guidance when we need it.

OK, that seems reasonable, but in this version, the criterion seems to be making people needlessly unhappy. What Biblical authority exists for this criterion? And if that is the real issue, then why do we refer to "pride" as a deadly sin but not "making people needlessly unhappy"?

What about greed?

> A free market has proved to be the most effective way to make a nation prosperous. The profit motive, which medieval Christianity distrusted, is not the sin of greed. In fact, when Gordon Gecko proclaims that 'Greed is good,' he's merely proclaiming (though for a bad purpose) this fact of life. We get into sin when we equate our worth as people with our financial assets. There is no reason to go without the basics that you need to live a healthy life. But today, entire cultures define your worth in terms of your possessions and earning power, and reject you if you're not making money.

Again, that sounds OK, but what do cultural definitions of "worth" have to do with individual avarice, acquisitiveness, voracity, or related sins of a materialistic life? Do these redefinitions not make the true meaning of the Seven Deadlies less clear and not more?

As if these redefinitions were not enough, Friedlander provides further explication by illustrating the Seven Deadlies with reference to the television comedy *Gilligan's Island*. I quote at length:

> Most obvious is the Professor, who fits PRIDE to a T. Any man who can make a ham radio out of some wire and two coconuts has to be pretty cocky. His character was later revised and given a series of his own, called "MacGyver."
>
> For the sin of ENVY we need look no further than Maryann, who may have worn those skimpy little tops, but could never achieve Ginger's glamour. (As an interesting and completely irrelevant side note, a nationwide survey of college students a few years ago revealed that the professor and Maryann were voted the most likely couple to have 'done it' on the island.)
>
> And who could doubt for a moment that Ginger is LUST incarnate? Sure, the kids were supposed to think she was ACTING, but we all know what being deprived episode after episode was doing to her. You know and I know that glazed look wasn't boredom, my friends.
>
> What kind of person takes a trunk full of money on a three-hour cruise? Mr. Howell gets my vote for GREED.
>
> We are now left with three characters and three Deadly Sins. We have Gilligan, the Skipper and Mrs. Howell to whom we must match GLUTTONY, SLOTH and ANGER. As you can see, there is a Gilligan problem here.
>
> Certainly we can further eliminate Mrs. Howell from this equation by connecting her with SLOTH. She did jack shit during her many years on the island and everybody knows it.
>
> This leaves ANGER and GLUTTONY, either of which the Skipper had no shortage. He was, after all, a big guy with the tendency to hit Gilligan with his hat at least once an episode. After much consideration, I have decided that he can easily do double-duty, covering the two remaining Deadly Sins.
>
> So here we have the Seven Deadly Sins trapped in an endlessly recurring Hell of hope followed by denial and despair, forced to live with each other in our TVs until the last re-run ends. And who is their captor? What keeps them trapped there? Gilligan. Gilligan is the angry devil who always wears red. Ingenious.

On the other hand, Friedlander has done an admirable job translating the Seven Deadlies into contemporary vernacular:

Traditional Name	Contemporary Meaning
Pride	Ego-tripping
Envy	Entitlement
Anger	Abuse, violence, racial or sectarian hatred
Sloth	Whining
Greed	Materialism
Gluttony	Addiction
Lust	Many synonyms

The Bible is pretty clear about what happens to people who commit any or all of the seven deadly sins. Considering that they are *deadly* sins, one presumes the consequences to be dire and, indeed, eternal damnation of the soul is said to be the sinner's fate. First Corinthians advises: "Do you not know that the unrighteous will not inherit the kingdom of God?" And Paul says in his epistle to the Romans: "For the wages of sin is death, but the free gift of God is eternal life in Christ Jesus our Lord."[3] In Ezekiel, it is written that "the soul who sins shall die." Further, committing any one of the Seven Deadlies is to commit them all: "For whoever keeps the whole law but fails in one point has become accountable for all of it" (James 2:10).

Clearly, no human has gone to his grave having never committed any of these sins, leading to the expectation that Heaven must be empty save for a few saints and angels.[4] John, however, adds a critical proviso: "If we confess our sins, He is faithful and just to forgive us our sins and to cleanse us from all unrighteousness." Ah, yes, the ultimate "out" of every Catholic schoolgirl: You can do anything you want as long as you confess your sins before taking Communion at Sunday Mass. Many high school boys have exploited this very point for their own sexual gratification. Granted, the Church expects sinners to be "truly sorry" for their misdeeds and to promise they won't "do it again," but enforcement of these standards seems pretty lax.

★ ★ ★ ★ ★ ★

I am by no means the first sociologist to contemplate the seven deadly sins or the larger issue of evil in society. But our ranks, although noble, are relatively thin. The first American sociologist to pay any professional attention to the problem was Edward Alsworth Ross, whose *Sin and Society* was published in 1907. Ross was an interesting character; one of the first American sociologists, a political progressive, but a firm believer in eugenics, the idea that social improvements only result from genetic improvements, from inducing people with desirable traits to reproduce at higher rates and inducing those with undesirable traits to reproduce less or preventing them from reproducing at all. Ross was a firm proponent of involuntary sterilization for "defective" persons. Even at the turn of the (20th) century, these were very controversial ideas, and Ross was fired from Stanford University because of these views and his tendency to express his hatred of other races in strong, crude language in public presentations. This was Stanford's first "academic freedom" case and led to the founding of the American Association of University Professors, still a staunch defender of the rights of University professors. As for Ross, he left Stanford for Nebraska and ultimately made his way to Wisconsin where he finished his career.

The first chapter of Ross's book discusses "New Varieties of Sin." Sin and evil were effectively equivalent and defined as "conduct which harms another." In the modern world, most of the "conduct which harms another" was, according to Ross, corporate conduct and resulted from the lack of accountability in and control of the corporate world. Thus, the book opens with a lament:[5]

> The sinful heart is ever the same, but sin changes its quality as society develops. Modern sin takes its character from the mutualism of our time. Under our present manner of living, how many of my vital interests I must intrust to others! (…) I rely upon others to look after my drains, invest my savings, nurse my sick, and teach my children. I let the meat trust butcher my pig, the oil trust mould my candles, the sugar trust boil my sorghum, the coal trust chop my wood, the barb wire company split my rails.
>
> But this spread-out manner of life lays snares for the weak and opens doors to the wicked. Interdependence puts us, as it were, at one another's mercy, and so ushers in a multitude of new forms of wrongdoing.

So in modern society, evil arises because the morality of the marketplace supplants the morality of the individual, and the market is based mainly on greed. In this line of analysis, predatory capitalism was the root of all evil (not "the love of money," as St. Paul would have had it, although these may well be the same thing). Most of the book is thus a turn-of-the-century diatribe against the more abusive depredations of the robber barons, banks, monopolies, trusts, and the other institutions of the bureaucratized corporate economy. These entities corroded the social fabric; undermined primary social bonds; created atomized, anomic individuals; and destroyed the religious and familial traditions that had in earlier societies held evil and vice in check. In a particularly lyrical and memorable passage, Ross says:

> The springs of the older sin seem to be drying up. Our forced-draught pace relieves us of the superabundance of energy that demands an explosive outlet. Spasms of violent feeling go with a sluggish habit of life, and

are as out of place today as are the hard-drinking habits of our Saxon ancestors. We are too busy to give rein to spite. The stresses and lures of civilized life leave slender margin for the gratification of animosities. In quiet, side-tracked communities there is still much old-fashioned hatred, leading to personal clash, but elsewhere the cherishing of malice is felt to be an expensive luxury. Moreover, brutality, lust, and cruelty are on the wane. In this country, it is true, statistics show a widening torrent of bloody crime, but the cause is the weakening of law rather than an excess of bile. Other civilized peoples seem to be turning away from the sins of passion. The darling sins that are blackening the face of our time are incidental to the ruthless pursuit of private ends, and hence go without prejudice. The victims are used or sacrificed not at all from personal ill-will, but because they can serve as pawns in somebody's little game. Like the wayfarers run down by the automobilist, they are offered up to the God of Speed. The essence of the wrongs that infest our articulated society is betrayal rather than aggression. Having perforce to build men of willow into a social fabric that calls for oak, we see on all hands monstrous treacheries – adulterators, peculators, boodlers, grafters, violating the trust others have placed in them. The little finger of Chicane has come to be thicker than the loins of Violence.

How charming and naïve this all sounds from the vantage point of a century later! Without gainsaying the "monstrous treacheries" inflicted on the world by corporate greed, misconduct, and outright criminal behavior, one would be hard-pressed to make the case that today's world is bereft of "explosive outlets," spite, "the gratification of animosities," malice, brutality, lust, or cruelty – a great deal of it perpetrated by individuals against one another. "Older sin" – specifically, the seven deadly sins – does not seem to have "dried up," as Ross anticipated. To the contrary, at least to the skeptical observer, these seem to be prominent, almost defining, features of the modern world. Modern sin, far from "lacking the familiar tokens of guilt," reeks of them. And it is these older sins, not the newer malfeasances of the banks and corporations, that are discussed in this book.

To avoid misinterpretation, I am not arguing that "the man who murders with an adulterant instead of a bludgeon" or "cheats with a company prospectus instead of a deck of cards" has committed a lesser evil than an ordinary murderer or a sleazy card shark, only that this book (for the most part) is about the latter, not the former. I have no quarrel with George Bernard Shaw, who wrote in his play *Major Barbara* that "The greatest of evils and the worst of crimes is poverty." Indeed, I borrowed that very line as a title to one of my books.[6] But our focus here is on the misdeeds of individuals. Readers interested in an up-to-date insider's look at the evil corporation would be well-served by Nafei (2009).

On the other hand, Ross's insistence on modern commerce as the root of much contemporary evil does sound reminiscent of Gandhi's Seven Social Sins and, in particular, his admonitions against "Wealth without Work," "Politics without Principle," and "Commerce without Morality," all points that we take up in detail in our concluding chapter, where we argue that Gandhi's ethical philosophy provides a more sure-footed moral basis for the operation of modern society than Pope Gregory's Seven Deadlies do.

The next scholar to take up a sociology of evil in a serious way was Stanford Lyman, whose book *The Seven Deadly Sins: Society and Evil* was published in 1978 and is the inspiration for the present work. Unlike Ross, Lyman is more concerned with personal wrongdoing than with corporate evil, although the alienation and atomization of the modern world that results from corporate Weberian rationality, bureaucratization, and brazen manipulation is ubiquitous in the background of the work.

Like many other moderns, Lyman's intention was to resurrect a sociology of evil per se as a proper subject for sociological inquiry. His book is organized into seven main chapters, each taking up one of the Seven Deadlies (much the same as this book). Each chapter considers the historical origins of a particular deadly sin; the changing definitions of the sin in works of theology, philosophy, and literature over time; and concludes with a consideration of the status of the sin in the modern world and in modern thought and literature. The chapter on sloth, for example, considers sloth as it is taken up by Homer, Chaucer, Spenser, and Shakespeare; its appearance in the literatures of psychoanalysis and Buddhism; its treatment in the works of Weber, Arendt, Aquinas, Freud, Camus, Marx, and Chekhov; etc. More contemporary scholars whose work is cited in the chapter include Georg Simmel, Robert E. Park, the psychoanalyst Franz Goetzl, Bruno Bettelheim, David Matza, and Kenneth Burke, among numerous others. The chapter (and the book as a whole) is a literary and historical *tour de force*, majestic in its aspirations, compelling in its realization.

But for all its erudition, in the end, we find that we have learned relatively little about sloth in the modern world – how widespread it is, which groups are most slothful and which least, how sloth is distributed within society, what social functions or dysfunctions sloth or indolence might entail. We are told in the conclusion that "the sin of sloth, like all the others, is still with us" and that we have witnessed a "twofold despair – a deep feeling of the worthlessness of work coupled with an apprehensive dread of the deadliness of leisure." But no real empirical evidence is adduced in favor of any of these propositions. Is sloth, "these days," indeed more common than industriousness? Lyman shows no interest in such questions. So in the end what we have is not a sociology of evil but a history of values – a piece more philosophical than sociological.

A still more recent entrant in the sociology of evil is Edwin Lemert's *The Trouble with Evil: Social Control at the Edge of Mortality,* published in 1997. Lemert's intention was to show that a sociology of evil is indeed possible – that "evil can be subjected to sociological analysis, (...) it can be studied with the existing methods of social science" – a proposition to which we too are committed. Clearly, a great deal of early 20th century sociology was concerned with the so-called "social evils" – with prostitution, drunkenness, gambling, and related activities of the dissolute and downtrodden. At times, these concerns dominated the research work of the early Chicago School and, thus, explicate the founding of American sociology. By mid-century, the principal evils of concern were those that existed on a much wider scale – Nazism, Communism, and McCarthyism at the level of whole societies; and their corollary and supporting mass belief systems – racism, anti-Semitism, authoritarianism, xenophobia, ethnocentrism, misogyny, paranoia, and mistrust. In the 50s and 60s, large literatures sprung up around all these topics, literatures that in essence *defined* sociology for my generation of scholars.

In recent decades, these kinds of concerns have receded into the sociological background. Lemert asks why. Surely part of the answer is "the prevalence of cultural relativism as a predominant perspective," although female genital mutilation, jihad, holy wars, and various other cultural practices have caused more than a few scholars to back away from extreme relativistic views. Still, few contemporary sociologists would accept that the value system of any one culture or people is inherently superior to any other, so terms such as bad, immoral, sinful, or evil have generally been expunged from the discipline's vocabulary. William Ryan exhorted all of us to stop "blaming the victim" in his 1971 book of the same name, and ever since, it has been considered bad form to hold anyone who could claim victimhood status accountable for their victimized condition (see Felson, 1991, for a particularly insightful discussion of "blame analysis"). Sin and evil can only be defined from the viewpoint of an ethical system, and who's to say that any one such system takes precedence over any other? Such notions seemingly require an absolute moral framework, and most sociologists are uncomfortable with that idea.

To the extent, then, that modern sociologists take up issues of sin and evil at all, it is under the guise of the rather antiseptic term "deviance." But the very concept of "deviance" is itself problematic (Liazos, 1972). Deviance is that which "deviates" from the normal, but these days, what's "normal?" At one time, the standard curriculum of a course in deviance could be characterized as "nuts, sluts, queers and perverts." Most courses would also have a unit on crime and criminals. But all this and more has evaporated in a rush to political correctitude. "Nuts" are now the dispossessed victims of mental illness and community indifference. "Sluts" are exploited sex workers. "Queers" have evolved into the Lesbian, Gay, Bisexual and Transsexual community (LGBT) and demand an end to "heteronormativity." "Perverts" are – what? – people whose preferred activities differ from those of white, middle-class Protestants. Even criminals are now often seen as powerless victims of a racist criminal justice system. As one of my former students said when she was asked to teach her department's course on deviance, "There's nothing left to teach." The apotheosis of this *tendence* in the modern world is the oft-quoted aphorism "One man's terrorist is another man's freedom fighter." Not even mass slaughter such as that witnessed on 9/11 or in Paris and Brussels 15 years later can be unambiguously and universally understood as *evil*.

Clearly, society is only possible if peoples' behaviors can be controlled. Anarchy is the alternative. The law and value-socialization are the two principal mechanisms by which this has historically been accomplished; call these "social control" and "self-control," respectively. A general drift in modern society is away from mechanisms of self-control and toward mechanisms of social control (e.g., Janowitz, 1978). Basically, we now rely on the police and the vast criminal justice apparatus (along with mental health professionals and the larger therapeutic community) to do what family and religion used to do. But none of the Seven Deadlies, however ill-advised, is *illegal*. If gluttony were against the law, the prisons would be filled with the obese and the besotted. If greed were illegal, Wall Street would empty into the nearest federal penitentiary. If pride were a criminal offense, the entire self-esteem industry would have to be dismantled.

At one time, society relied on values imparted in the family, at school, and at church to restrain the excesses of its citizens. But the family, we are told, at least in its traditional sense, is dying out; educational institutions no longer teach values; and on the religious side, the major recent trend has been the sharp increase in the proportion of the population claiming no religious preference (known in religious research circles as the "nones"). Some have argued that as a result of these large-scale social forces, the prevalence of most of the seven deadly sins has increased over the past decades – not always for the same reason, perhaps, but with the same effect, namely, a more dissolute, materialistic, and sexualized society.

And maybe that is not such a bad outcome. John Green remarks in his excellent book *The Fault in our Stars*: "Some tourists think Amsterdam is a city of sin, but in truth it is a city of freedom. And in freedom, most people find sin." Clearly, most people in the West these days seem to value freedom a good deal more than they value piety. Indeed, freedom *of* religion has clearly come to include freedom *from* religion. The very religious, traditional values embedded in the Seven Deadlies are out of touch with the general drift of Western society in the last century. (Or such in any case is another point we pursue aggressively in later chapters.)

Lemert makes the excellent point that all of the sociologists who have written on evil, while they "do not quite endow man the social animal with original sin, make it clear that given certain socio-psychological circumstances, he is prone to evil" (and presumably, she too). The general idea here is that anyone is capable of evil, indeed, of monstrous evil, but for the restraints imposed by socialization, religious teaching, and such other sources of self-control to which people are exposed. So evil is inherent in human nature and is only restrained by social norms. Thus comes the more or less standard conclusion that the alienation and anomie (normlessness) endemic in modern mass society is ultimately what makes (or allows) evil to flourish.

A positivistic social science of evil, Lemert tells us, would symbolize evil as a "social problem," i.e. as something that transcends both human volition and personal psychopathology. It is not enough to note that people eat gluttonously and, therefore, become obese. One must also "situate" gluttony in its broader social context: the shift from agricultural to industrial to postindustrial society, the marketing of food by corporate agribusiness; the symbolic identity of obesity and success (as in the term "fat cat"), the success of soda companies in marketing sugary sodas as fun and healthful, the portion sizes foisted on the public by restaurants and food companies, and so on. Gluttons are not just fatsos who can't shove back from their plates – they are victims of a social system that encourages and rewards gluttony. But does this not take us back, more or less, to Ross's insistence that the banks, corporations, marketers, and evil businessmen are the ultimate source of evil? Is this not just another way of excusing people for their sinful behaviors? Indeed, does this not deny even the possibility of individual sin or, for that matter, personal responsibility?

In the old days, young people would explain their misdeeds with the excuse "The Devil made me do it!" (a line made famous by the comedian Flip Wilson on his weekly TV show). Indeed, this was Eve's excuse for the original sin: "The serpent deceived me, and I ate" (Genesis 3:13). Today, it is the tobacco companies, agribusinesses, adroit marketers, advertising agents, Anheuser Busch, gun manufacturers, and greedy businessmen who "made me do it" (and who, not coincidentally, must therefore be made to pay huge sums for making people do stupid things). No one, it seems, is to be held responsible for any of their transgressions. Even the hard-core druggie is the victim of the neighborhood dealer, who is in turn a victim of unfortunate social circumstances. Once the concept of sin goes out the window, personal responsibility for practically *anything* goes out with it. So part of my agenda in this book is to resurrect empirical analysis rather than excuse making as social science's fundamental calling.

I am not one to write abstruse essays on "Sociology, Sin and Evil." Many other social scientists have taken up these questions, but not, generally, in the way that I intend to. We shall be content with common, ordinary-language definitions of our subject, and we will use those definitions to look at issues such as how much sin there is in today's society, what behaviors and social conditions or characteristics are associated with sin, and what consequences flow from sin. And for every sin there is a complimentary virtue whose extent, social correlates, and behavioral consequences are also explored. We leave larger philosophical and theological questions to those with the talent and taste for such things. (The concluding chapter, however, is a partial departure from this stricture.)

In preparing to write this book, I came across a website: www.Bibleinfo. com. It seems to be written for younger people because it avoids extensive theological disputation and textual exegesis and speaks to matters of Christian ethics in simple, straightforward language. The entry on the seven deadly sins found in this source provides the very definitions we seek:

List of the Seven Deadly Sins:

1. **Envy** = the desire to have an item or experience that someone else possesses
2. **Gluttony** = excessive ongoing consumption of food or drink
3. **Greed (or Avarice)** = an excessive pursuit of material possessions
4. **Lust** = an uncontrollable passion or longing, especially for sexual desires
5. **Pride** = excessive view of one's self without regard to others.
6. **Sloth** = excessive laziness or the failure to act and utilize one's talents
7. **Anger (or Wrath)** = uncontrollable feelings of anger and hate towards another person

These, then, are the practical definitions we will use throughout the remainder of the book. As for the corresponding virtues, and using the above ordering, they are admiration, temperance, charity, piety, humility, industriousness, and kindness – all of which also exist widely in the modern world.

Bibleinfo.com provides the useful information that

> these seven deadly sins are completely and totally forgivable by God, but this doesn't give free license to commit these sins. Biblically, the only sin that cannot be forgiven is complete rejection of God's grace which is outright rebellion against God, also known as blasphemy against the Holy Spirit.

Also,

> Each one of these sins has its root in the desire for more and the human need for *excess*. Each sin goes against the root of Christianity which is: love for God, love for our fellow man, and love for our bodies.

Clearly, *excess* is the key. It is not sinful to be sexually attracted to your spouse; it is *excessive* lust that is problematic. It is fine to eat rich, pleasurable food, but never to *excess*. No one suffers eternal damnation of the soul because they take the occasional vacation; it is the *excessive* failure to act that gives one problems. So in the end, the centuries-long brouhaha over the Seven Deadlies, what they mean, what they imply, and how they can be avoided boils down very simply to this: Moderation in all things – presumably, even moderation itself from time to time!

I lived in New Orleans for 13 years. At the time, there was a Mexican restaurant right on St. Charles Avenue, and in the men's room, there was an advertisement for a Mexican beer that bore the advice *Nada con exceso, todo con medida* ("nothing to excess, all in moderation"). Can it really be that a sign in the men's room of a Mexican restaurant in New Orleans in fact contains the key to a virtuous life? There's no end to the irony.

Carrie Kirby, a writer for www.wisebread.com, a website for people who want to "live large on a small budget," recently posted an essay concerning "Why Scientists Say You Should be *Committing* the Seven Deadly Sins," the theme of which is that all (well, most) of the Seven Deadlies can be good for you in one way or another.

Take pride. Are we not always being admonished to take pride in our school, our work, our nation, "even our ethnicity?" So really, what's the problem? Psychologists have learned to distinguish between *hubris* and *authentic pride* (sometimes rendered simply as bad pride and good pride), the latter symbolized by the phrase "pride in a job well-done." The distinguishing characteristic of hubris is that it is unjustified, excessive, unearned – the pride that "goeth before the fall." Authentic pride is a social virtue; hubris is a personal psychopathology.

Then there's greed. Ivan Boesky, the real-life inspiration for the character Gordon Gekko in the film *Wall Street*, proclaimed that "greed is healthy," and there is a sense in which this is clearly right. As Kirby puts it, "We're biologically programmed to go out and get what we need." Greed, in short, is the great motivator that makes people and whole societies productive. It's what gets us out of bed in the morning, the ultimate solution to sloth. How many successful communes can you point to? How many complete failures? A communications professor is quoted as saying "Unrestrained greed is detrimental to society; unrestrained disapproval of greed is detrimental to society. People attempt to find a balance between biological imperative and social necessity."

Envy? When your coworker gets a fat raise and you don't, it makes you envious, and that envy drives you forward to do a better job. Anger? As the rock group *Tears for Fears* had it, "Shout! Shout! Let it all out!" Anger is cathartic. Seething unexpressed anger is what sometimes explodes into murderous rage. Lust? One study showed that if college students were "hooking up" (having casual, non-committal sex) for the right reasons, such as the fun of it all, they felt better about themselves; not so for those hooking up for the wrong reasons (i.e., revenge sex, mercy sex, coerced sex), whose subsequent emotions were negative. Sloth? Studies have shown that even brief breaks improve performance, and the National Sleep Foundation acknowledges that most workers would "really benefit" from occasional short naps now and then. The rejuvenating effects of weekends and vacations are too obvious to bear mention, although there is a documented phenomenon of "leisure sickness," and leisure time does not appear to be recuperative to the same degree in all people (e.g., Blank et al., 2015)

That leaves gluttony, the only behavior among the Seven Deadlies that does not admit of moderation. Surely, early in human evolution, gluttony conferred survival value. It is regularly overlooked that from the dawn of time up to 20 or 30 years ago, the problem was getting adequate calories *into* the human diet, not getting them *out*. In the same spirit, a little gluttony would do wonders for persons suffering from anorexia or bulimia and would also be a pleasant change of pace for the roughly one in seven American households who are food-insecure (Wright, Donley, and Strickhouser, forthcoming). Sure, a Thanksgiving or Christmas feast is often gluttonous, but the social value derived from such occasions probably offsets the personal damage of overeating, most of all if this degree of gluttony only happens once or twice a year.

In short, what is sinful and what is not are no longer always obvious. What seems to be sinful from one perspective can be seen as socially necessary from another. It is easy to show, and we will show, that Americans apparently commit the traditional seven deadly sins on a more or less regular basis. But the underlying moral realities are subtle, and what might seem sinful from one perspective is often proper behavior from another. The line between guilt and innocence, between sin and salvation, is often thin.

★ ★ ★ ★ ★ ★

The remainder of this book unfolds in seven main chapters and a conclusion, one chapter for each of the seven deadly sins (and its corresponding virtue) and a conclusion that briefly summarizes what we have learned then considers an alternative set of moral principles (Gandhi's Seven Social Sins) that seem far more appropriate for the modern world than the original seven. Each chapter considers how the social sciences have operationalized each "sin," how they have been studied, and what has been learned. Where the appropriate data are available (not often), we also review trends – whether certain behaviors have become more or less common over time. Another recurring theme concerns the costs and benefits to society of the behaviors in question, and which predominates. (For example, alcohol consumption poses certain social and economic costs to society but also produces certain benefits. Are the costs reasonable given the benefits?)

J. D. Salinger once wrote: "We're all just lost souls, hoping for a tomorrow that will be better than today." As I take pains to document in later pages, we are not *all* lost souls. A great deal of human decency, kindness, and rectitude remain. At the same time, in our secularizing age, a better tomorrow is probably as close to Heavenly Salvation as most of us can ever expect to come.

Notes

1 Throughout, I follow the convention of referring to the Deity as male although I can think of no good reason why God could not be female. Female deities are numerous in pre-Christian religions.
2 Retrieved 12-29-2015 from www.pathguy.com/seven_sins.htm
3 Paula Poundstone offered this clarification: "The wages of sin are death, but by the time taxes are taken out, it's just sort of a tired feeling."
4 Or maybe not so empty, since there seems to be about 10,000 saints recognized by the Catholic Church. (An exact count has never been made, so far as Google is aware.)
5 All the Ross passages quoted in these pages are from the online version of *Sin and Society*, retrieved 12-30-2015 at: www.brocku.ca/MeadProject/Ross/Ross_1907/ Ross_1907_toc.html
6 Joel A. Devine and James D. Wright, *The Greatest of Evils: Urban Poverty and the American Underclass*. Hawthorne, NY: Aldine de Gruyter Publishing Company, 1993.

ACKNOWLEDGMENTS

My gratitude to my friends Ray Stringer and Deirdre Flanagan who spotted a few errors of fact and whose reactions to the book resulted in an evening of stimulating conversation; to my colleagues Darren Sherkat, Amy Donley, and Rachel Rayburn for reading and commenting on earlier drafts; to my friend and critic Michael Overington who still does not believe that this book is publishable; to my colleague Murray Webster, whose critical reading and commentary resulted in a much improved book; to anonymous reviewers whose constructive criticisms also resulted in a better book; to Mandi Barringer for numerous helpful comments and her excellent work on creating the index; to Mary Curtis and her staff at Transaction Publications, who are always delightful to work with and who patiently steered this manuscript through the shoals of their buyout by Taylor and Francis; to Tyler Bay and his staff at Taylor and Francis, who have been delightful; to the outstanding production crew at CodeMantra who were also delightful, and most of all to my wife Chris, whose understanding and tolerance make my writing possible.

1

GREED

The Basis of Capitalist Society

"Greed is a central element in human existence. It is also frequently mentioned as a factor in many recent organizational and financial scandals. Thus, it was surprising to discover that empirical research on greed is rare" (Wang and Murnighan, 2011). The five or six years that have passed since this was first written do not cause us to change the conclusion. For all the attention greed has received as a causative agent in recent financial and other societal catastrophes, research remains embryonic.

There is, of course, no lack of commentary on or condemnation of greed as a force in society. It is a simple matter to identify numerous essays on topics such as "Why Greed Begets More Greed," "Greed in Today's Society," "Effects of Greed in the World Today," "In Greed We Trust," and like titles. The *Huffington Post* even has a website that collects their recent postings on the topic.[1] In the press and popular mind, there is a general understanding that "these days" banks, corporations, and super-wealthy people epitomize greed and its general social destructiveness. But very few of these essays derive their content from serious social science research.

What Is Greed?

In the Preface, we defined greed as "an excessive pursuit of material possessions." Clearly, one can be "greedy" with one's time, affection, or attention, but at its base, greed is about lusting after more and more material goods for their own sake. The interesting term in this definition is not "possessions" but "excessive" because what constitutes excess can only be defined in reference to an extant standard of living.

Consider: Early in 20th-century America, an automobile was "excessive" and ownership of one was a matter mainly of status and, therefore, greed. A horse and buggy would get oneself and one's family around quite adequately; conveyance by horse remained commonplace into the 1940s. Then, postwar affluence and the suburbanization that affluence and the GI Bill made possible turned cars into necessities. Later, the large-scale entrance of women into the paid labor force made two cars a necessity for many families. Today, many new suburban homes have three-car garages since the kids need transportation of their own too. So, just where (if at all) in the continuum from no cars to three or four or more cars does car ownership become "excessive" and, therefore, greedy? Is even one car "excessive" in a world of seven billion people but only one billion cars on the road? The vast majority of the world's population gets by without one.

Taflinger (1996) says that acquisition becomes excessive when it becomes harmful, but this doesn't help us very much since the dividing line between harmful and harmless must be rather arbitrary too. Alfred Adler's (1927) book *Understanding Human Nature* says that

> greed is closely related to envy, and the two are usually found together. We do not mean the form of greed that expresses itself in the hoarding of money. There is another, more general form that expresses itself chiefly *in a reluctance to give pleasure to other people*. Such people are avaricious in their attitude toward society and toward every other individual. The avaricious person builds a wall about himself to keep his treasures safe.

This probably gets us closer to a usable notion, namely that "greed" becomes a vice when the acquisition of money or material things becomes an end in itself rather than a means to some other end. Here, "excessive" implies pointless, nonproductive acquisitiveness, or avarice. To be greedy is to hoard resources, to keep them from other people, whether the hoarding serves some larger purpose or not.

There is little doubt that some amount of greed is hardwired into the human organism and serves many useful purposes. As Taflinger expresses it,

> Every person needs a degree of wealth to survive: you need to buy food, pay the rent, and get clothing, transportation, haircuts, cable TV. Without money..., you could starve or freeze to death, something that is definitely harmful. In addition, the more wealth you have, the better the quantity and quality of the things it brings you can get. Again, how could a desire for wealth, and thus the things it gets you, be harmful?

Greed, in this line of analysis, is essential for survival, is hardwired into the biology of the species, and will never disappear from human affairs. These facts being true, what point is served in treating greed as sinful?

The answer lies in the fact that humans are social and cultural beings as well as particular individuals, and while greed may always profit the individual, and, thus, be inevitable, it does not necessarily profit the larger society or culture. Greed, for example, necessarily creates social inequalities (some, after all, will be more successful in being greedy and others less so), and these inequalities generate unrest, displeasure, envy, rebellion, and revolution. Greed creates the haves and have-nots and, thereby, the entire history of dissension between the two. Marxian class conflict is really just the conflict between those who have succeeded in being greedy and those who have failed, is it not?

Societies, Taflinger reminds us, exist to manage conflict among their members. Society creates law, methods of social control, religion, government, and even families to allow people "to get along without fighting each other in response to their biological urges." The conflict created by greed is to concentrate resources in too few hands. So, without greed, there would be nothing to fight over, and society and its institutions would be pointless. Greed is inherent in the very notion of "growth" and "progress." It is therefore essential to our notions of the "social." But clearly, greed must also be controlled if whole societies are to prosper.

Greed and Capitalism

Many have argued that greed underlies modern capitalist economic systems. Walter Williams makes the case in his essay for *Capitalism Magazine*, "The virtue of greed."

> You can call it greed, selfishness, or enlightened self-interest; but the bottom line is that it's these human motivations that get wonderful things done… Free markets, private property rights, voluntary exchange and greed produce preferable outcomes most times and under most conditions.

Others agree that greed is indeed the basis of capitalist society but bemoan rather than celebrate that fact. Schumaker (2004) is a leading example. He grants that evolution has programmed us to be greedy but is not convinced that a greedy society is also a happy one.

> As human beings continue to be reshaped by consumer culture into restless, dissatisfied, and all-desiring economic pawns, greed is being redefined as a virtue and a legitimate guiding principle for economic prosperity and general happiness. In the process, it is steadily eating away at the cornerstones of civilized society and undermining the visions, values and collective aspirations that made us strong.

The economist Lester Thurow is quoted approvingly: "altruism does not seem to be congruent with the way human beings are constructed. No one has been able to construct a society where communal altruism dominates individual greed." At the same time, "greed locks us into discontent, which in turn keeps us motivated and itchy for change." Still, as Richard Easterlin and many others have shown, increasing personal wealth and the excessive consumption it makes possible do not seem to promote human happiness. The result is a collective state of unhappy consciousness, the so-called Empty Self of modern life.

A survey referenced by Schumaker found that almost 90% of Americans agree that "humans always want more, it is part of human nature." True, but at the same time, "more and more mental-health professionals are saying that greed is not nearly as good for people as it is for economies, with some warning that greed is beginning to overwhelm conscience, reason, compassion, love, family bonds and community." A greedy society and economic system, that is, may well excel in producing material goods, profits, and great wealth, but in so doing may also erode spiritual values, communitarian outlooks, and social bonds. Greed, although inevitable, extracts an unwholesome price.

To be sure, people can and do act altruistically and charitably, a point to which we return later in this chapter. So, it is clearly not the case that people will only do "good" things if they are paid to do them or punished if they don't. And one can draw a distinction (although a thin one) between self-interest and selfishness. As Snowdon (2015) puts it, "Selfishness implies indulging oneself at another's expense, but free-market transactions only take place when two self-interested parties see a mutual benefit." So the pursuit of self-interest per se is not necessarily greedy or avaricious so long as self-interest does not lead to another's unhappiness.

At the same time, if you look up self-interest in the dictionary, selfishness is the first listed synonym, and Snowdon himself admits that "in a free market it makes no difference whether the entrepreneur is impeccably well-intentioned or unashamedly self-serving," or in other words, it makes no difference to the free market whether greed or simple self-interest is the driving motivation. In the end, both increase profit and, thus, benefit the whole economy (if not its individual members).

Not all analysts agree that greed is the basis of capitalism. Indeed, there appears to be a minor industry among conservative economists in denying that capitalism is based on greed. The Snowdon book is one example. Another is the essay by Jay Richards, "Greed is not Good, and It's Not Capitalism," published by the American Enterprise Institute, a well-known conservative think tank. Still a third, "Greed is Not Good (But Self-Interest Is)," by Wesley Gant appeared in an online outlet called *Values and Capitalism*. But for every such piece that Google turns up, there is another along the lines of "Pope Francis: Greed has Hijacked Capitalism" or "8 Ways the Prophets of Capitalist Greed Justify Their Success and Your Slide Toward Poverty" or "4 Ways Greedy Capitalists Rig the System to Profit Off Our Misery."

From the latter:

> Self-indulgent capitalists have turned much of America against its own best interests by promoting a winner-take-all philosophy that reaps great rewards for a few people at the expense of everyone else. To the neo-liberal, vital human needs like health and education are products to be bought and sold.

So whether capitalism depends on greed seems to depend on one's political ideology more than reason or evidence. Much seems to depend on whether selfishness and self-interest can be easily and sharply differentiated.

Interestingly, many of those arguing that capitalism does *not* depend on greed have overt religious motivations. The conundrum for these conservatives is that they believe in free market capitalism as the best means of organizing the economic affairs of a nation, but they also believe in traditional Christian morality with equal fervor. Traditional Christian morality defines greed as a deadly sin, so if capitalism requires or glorifies greed, then it must be rejected as a fundamentally immoral social and economic system. Alternatively, if capitalism is based on greed but is also the best way to organize economic affairs, then greed cannot be a sin. So, the only position left is that capitalism is not based on greed after all.

A recent work by Jay Richards, *Money, Greed and God* (2009), questions the initial premise that capitalism is based on greed. To the contrary, Richards argues, capitalism is fully compatible with Christian morality. The argument proceeds along five lines:

1. *Although individuals in capitalistic systems may be greedy, that does not mean that capitalism is based on greed.* This seems thin and unconvincing. Capitalism depends on the accumulation of capital, which, in turn, demands profit, which means charging more for goods or services than their corresponding costs. Further, accumulated capital is to be reinvested so as to increase output and with it even more profit, which leads to further reinvestments and more profits – an endless cycle of capital accumulation. This does not seem to differ very much from individual greed – the incessant quest for wealth as an end in itself. If greed does not define capitalism, it is at least hard to imagine a successful capitalist regime without greedy individuals (i.e. individuals seeking to maximize their own self-interest even if it has to be at the expense of others).

2. *Ah, but selfishness and self-interest are not the same.* As I noted earlier, in my dictionary and most others, selfishness and self-interest are treated as synonymous. And while the two can perhaps be differentiated depending on whether accumulation comes at the expense of others (in Marxian economics, this is axiomatic), the differentiation is by no means sharp.

Besides, this seems a mighty thin thread from which to hang matters of such world-historical importance. The argument that capitalism is based on individuals acting to maximize their self-interest but not on selfishness, and is therefore compatible with Biblical morality, seems specious.

3. *Exchanges in capitalism are mutually beneficial.* I buy meat because I want it; the butcher sells me meat so he can make a profit. Both of us benefit from the transaction. Just what does this have to do with the morality of the transaction or the system within which the transaction is conducted? I'm greedy: I want more meat at the lowest possible cost. The butcher is greedy: He wants to sell me more meat at the highest possible profit. That we both believe we have maximized our self-interests in the transaction only means that we are both greedy (I seek to maximize my interests at the expense of the butcher and he seeks to maximize his at mine), not that neither of us is.

4. *Capitalism channels selfishness to good ends.* Here the argument is that since there are many butchers that I could frequent, and they compete among themselves for my business, the ensuing competition assures that they will all offer high-quality meat at reasonable prices. Shady practices, spoiled meat, or high prices would drive my business somewhere else; butchers are all forced into good practices because they have to compete for my business. Alas, the history of capitalist excess belies this line of argument. Consider, e.g. the decades-long struggle for safe milk; the unsanitary practices in the meatpacking industry prior to Upton Sinclair's (1906) expose; or the contemporary cases of price-fixing, manipulation, and other monopolistic practices. And what fuels these and a thousand similar capitalist excesses? Greed. That both parties benefit in some ways from capitalistic exchanges does *not* imply that all benefit *equally* or that the exchange is conducted on some basis other than greed.

5. Finally, *capitalism encourages generosity.* Yes, but in the very limited sense that the greedier one is, the more profit or wealth one accrues, the more is available to be given away. Besides, as Alfred Adler reminds us,

> Almost everyone in today's civilization shows traces, at least, of greed. The best the average person does is to veil it, or hide it behind exaggerated generosity, which amounts to nothing more than giving of alms, an attempt, through gestures of generosity, to bolster one's self-esteem at the expense of others.

In the end, Richards's arguments attempt to gloss over the rather obvious relationship between greed and capitalism. Capitalism was theorized by Adam Smith as an economic system based on the assumption that everyone would behave economically according to their own self-interest. Selfishness (greed) is therefore central to the capitalist economic system. So either greed is indeed a deadly sin and capitalism is therefore sinful or capitalism is the best system yet devised to organize the economic doings of a nation, in which case, greed is not a sin. You can have it either way, but not both ways.

The Nobel economist Milton Freidman was unequivocal in his celebration of greed. "The world runs on individuals pursuing their separate interests," he wrote. "Is there some society you know that doesn't run on greed?" Alas, no. While one longs (desperately at times) for an economic and social system based on charity and kindness, not on greed, merciless exploitation, and endless accumulation, history provides no compelling example of such a system.

Eskow (2016) has pointed to "Six signs our culture is sick with greed." (1) There is still no shame in profiting mercilessly from Wall Street fraud and shenanigans. Fraud settlements against a company, say J. P. Morgan, are announced and boom! The stock price goes *up*. "What is astonishing is the lack of shame" among banking and corporate executives whose companies have committed so many crimes, or the celebration of those very crimes as outstanding opportunities to make more money. (2) These "greedy CEOs still have credibility in the media," often sought out for their expertise in "fiscal responsibility." One recalls John Stewart's dressing down of Jim Cramer – the nation's leading spokesman for capitalist greed – on the *Daily Show*. Said Stewart, "I can't reconcile the brilliance and knowledge that you have of the intricacies of the market with the crazy bullshit I see you do every night."

Nos. 3 through 6 on Eskow's list: (3) These days, business schools teach would-be executives how to "rip people off" through misleading ads and dubious (although highly profitable) marketing practices. (4) Even popular music idealizes greed. From Kanye West: "Money can't buy everything, it's true, but what it can't buy I can't use…." From Snoop Dogg: "I'm not selling out, I'm buying in." (5) "Insight and spirituality are being commercialized…" (6) "… and so is kindness to our fellow human beings." In Eskow's mind, it all adds up to a sickness of the soul. "We can't afford to live in a world where our only aspiration is to accumulate wealth, irrespective of how it's accumulated…" But the fact is, whether we can afford to live in such a world or not, it is the predominating feature of the world that we do live in.

I cede the final word in this matter to Suranovic (2011) and his essay, "Is Greed the Problem with Capitalism?," where *Washington Post* columnist Steven Pearlstein is quoted as follows: "In a capitalist economy like ours, the basic premise is that everyone is motivated by a healthy dose of economic self-interest…. Without some measure of greed and the tension it brings to most economic transactions, capitalism wouldn't be as good as it is in allocating resources and spurring innovation." Suranovic calls this the "central idea" behind Adam Smith's theory of capitalism. He explains:

> Smith is arguing that the economic system provides for our wants and needs because, first and foremost, people are trying to help themselves, and they do so by producing and selling meat, beer, and bread to others.

These market outcomes are not achieved because of charity. We do not appeal to other peoples' humanity when we seek our sustenance, but rather to their self-interest, or in this case their greed.

Whether greed is essential to capitalism or just a common convenience, it is clear that the consequences of greed for society as a whole are both positive and negative. Greed propels society forward and maximizes economic growth, while at the same time posing the potential for a great deal of social unrest because of the inequality that greed creates. What else can greed be credited with (or blamed for)?

Costs and Benefits of Greed to Society

Social Cohesion. One purely theoretical but extremely interesting recent analysis of greed and social cohesion is that of Roca and Helbing (2011). Setting aside the game-theoretic mathematics (which are both arduous and tedious), these researchers found that moderate levels of greed promoted social cohesion:

> Moderate greediness causes individuals' dissatisfaction, making them explore other strategies and/or positions and experience the benefits of being cooperative in a cooperative neighborhood. As long as those benefits are sufficient to satisfy individuals' aspirations, cooperation and agglomeration [of people] coevolve and create a stable population with a high level of cohesion.... In comparison, a model society of individuals with low levels of greediness is unable to realize social benefits. It lacks the drive to develop effective cooperation and agglomeration, because non-greedy individuals become easily satisfied with whatever payoffs they obtain and thus, maintain their strategy and position. In consequence, neither cooperation nor agglomeration emerges in such a society.... At high levels of greediness, finally, individuals are so difficult to satisfy that they keep exploring other locations and strategies, thereby destroying cooperative clusters.

Model societies with low levels of greed lacked drive and motivation; the un-greedy were content with what they had and were unwilling to sacrifice for the common good. So some degree of greed is necessary not just to propel the economy forward but to promote social cohesion and a sense of community as well. Too much greed leads to individual dissatisfaction, social discontent, and a lack of social cohesion.

Bloated Consumerism. One of the serious downsides of greed is reflected in the now-common aphorism "He who dies with the most stuff, wins." Our collective obsession with accumulating more and more stuff is reflected in any number of ways. For several years, the mini-storage industry was among the fastest growing sectors of the American economy. Many families have now accumulated so much stuff, it no longer fits in their houses. In suburban neighborhoods, one can drive past house after house with two-, and sometimes three, -car garages and yet find that all the household vehicles are parked in the driveway. Why? Because the garages are so full of stuff, the cars no longer fit.

In many suburban neighborhoods, there is an annual ritual, the "community garage sale." On these occasions, excess stuff spills out onto tables set up in the driveways, items are carefully priced, endless streams of buyers pass by, many haggle, and at the end of the day, a great deal of stuff has been redistributed. I have often wondered how much of the stuff I see on garage sale day is stuff accumulated in prior garage sales. Could we call that "stuff squared?" Maybe "recycled stuff?"

Whatever we call it, accumulating stuff seems to be a national obsession. When I ask people recently back from, say, Italy what they did on their vacation, the answer is frequently "Shop!" Not "toured the Vatican" or "motored down the Amalfi coast" or "sipped cappuccino at a sidewalk café in Piazza San Marco," but "Shopped!" Buying more and more stuff has become a national sport.

The obsession with stuff is often fed by credit, and in the process of accumulating more and more stuff, many families get into deep credit card debt. Right now, according to one source, the average American household is carrying $15,355 in credit card debt.[2] Debt service currently consumes nearly a tenth of household income. Part of the proliferation of debt is that the cost of living has risen much faster than personal incomes in the past decade or so, and credit card debt is used to make up the difference. But another part is sheer greed to possess things you cannot quite afford.

The desire to consume more housing than one can afford, and the willingness of (shall we say?) greedy banks, savings and loans, and finance companies to fuel the desire, gave us the housing crisis of 2007 and led to the Great Recession of 2008, the effects of which still linger. The quest for bigger and better but still affordable housing has moved families deeper and deeper into the suburbs and away from downtown, leading to longer commutes, more congestion, and more air pollution and greenhouse gasses. Indeed, Census reporting on commutation now includes the category of "super-commuter," people who drive 90 minutes or more to get to work – three hours a day for the round-trip! The desire for more, bigger, and flashier cars fuels the world's automobile industry but has also led to the proliferation of 6,000-pound SUVs ferrying 125-pound housewives to and from the grocery store. These monstrosities can cost as much as $80,000 and up and sometimes only average 10 miles per gallon or even less around town. Being classified by the EPA as light trucks, not cars, exempts them from the EPA's miles-per-gallon standards so their owners are free to guzzle all the gasoline they can afford. Thus, we begin to see some of the social, economic, and environmental costs that greed entails.

The economist Robert Frank (2011) has written about "expenditure cascades" that result when greed goes unchecked – the well-known problem of "keeping up with the Jones's." Your neighbor Jones shows up in a spiffy new Cadillac Escalade (list price: $73,000). Not to be outdone, the next thing you know, you're in the showroom buying a Lexus LX (list price: $89,000). Across the street, Smith (also not to be outdone) comes home one weekend in his brand new Mercedes G-Class luxury SUV (list price: $119,000). The same thing happens with houses, home theater equipment, swimming pools, and European vacations – everything has to be flashier, newer, and spiffier than what the Jones's have acquired. The debt resulting from these expenditure cascades increases the likelihood of bankruptcy, destroying families (via the pressures resulting from financial insecurity).

One analyst (Seltzer, 2012) goes so far as to describe today's rampant, insatiable greed as an "addiction" – not so much an addiction to getting rich as to getting *richer* and *richer still*. The stuff you can own if you are rich is rather beside the point. "Greed or wealth addicts are hardly focused on depleting or disbursing their fortune but on *acquiring* and *maintaining* it." Greed addicts come to possess in abundance all the things that money can buy – big, fancy houses, cars, yachts, and penthouse apartments – but are often bereft of the things money can't buy: Love, emotional intimacy, happiness, and peace of mind. "Of all the things one might be addicted to, nothing tops the greed-laden pursuit of wealth in its audacity, manipulativeness, and gross insensitivity to the needs and feelings of others, not to mention its extreme, short-sighted, irresponsible covetousness."

Significantly, as noted earlier, once past the level of poverty and outright destitution, more money and more stuff does not seem to make people appreciably happier. The classic study of the topic was by Richard Easterlin and was published in *The Public Interest* in 1973. Dozens of elaborations on the basic argument and findings have been published since. Basically, what Easterlin found was that yes, people with more money are also happier, but not by very much. And it was not absolute affluence but rather relative affluence that made the difference. As long as you felt you were better off than your neighbors, you were happy. The latest entrant in this line of research is a study that found that the *belief* that money could buy happiness was most widespread among the young and declined pretty regularly with age. Whether this reflects wisdom or disillusionment, I leave to readers to decide.

Greed also fuels a great deal of fraud, scams, and outright crime, all of which have been abetted by the information technology revolution. Stories air daily about loan modification schemes, stolen identities, credit card fraud, shady time-share deals, efforts to scam seniors, and on down a dismal list. All of this is motivated by the strong desire to get something for nothing and at another's expense – the very definition of greed.

Public Perceptions of Greed and Business

It is fair to say that Americans in general disapprove of greed and are quick to blame greed for all manner of social ills. Still, direct evidence on these points is rare. Daniel Kahneman and his associates (Kahneman et al., 1986) found a reluctance on the part of consumers to patronize companies that generate profits by taking advantage of their customers, for example, by price gouging. In a related study, Bhattacharjee (cited in Ariely and Gruneisen, 2013) found that most people see the "mere act of profit seeking" itself to be bad for society. In this study,

> More profitable firms were regarded as less deserving of their winnings, less subject to competition and more motivated to make money regardless of the consequences. Furthermore, when asked to compare two hypothetical organizations that were identical aside from their "for-profit" or "nonprofit" status, people perceived for-profit firms as less valuable and more socially damaging than the nonprofits. Thus, the perception of greed as harmful extends to the mere act of profiting, which is of course the only way that capitalist markets can function.

The distrust of greed as a business motivator seems to be based on a basic desire for justice, which is to say that many perceive greed (successful greed, that is) as unjust. Another study cited by Ariely and Gruneisen found that more than 60% of a sample of Americans supported caps on compensation for the highest earners regardless of their net contribution. Public opinion surveys also consistently show majority support for a more equitable distribution of income. Sure, those who contribute more should earn more, but only up to a limit, beyond which fairness kicks in as the more important criterion.

A remarkable series of studies by Wang et al. (2011) provides further insights into the origins of "greed-worship" in America. In one experimental study involving a money allocation task, a significant predictor of how much money a participant kept for him or herself was being an economics major or having taken multiple economics courses! A related study by the same authors found that having been educated in economics predicted more positive attitudes about greed. A similar study of MBA students is needed but would, one assumes, find the same general patterns.

Greed and the Global Financial Crisis

Kenway and Fahey (2010) ask "Is Greed Still Good? Was it Ever?" within the framework of the global financial crisis. Greed, they note, "is endemic. Accumulation (savings and investment) and profit have been one central feature of the history of the capitalist economy" (p. 719).

Central too, particularly during economic booms, have been emoscapes [emotional landscapes] of exuberance and ideoscapes [political or ideological landscapes] about constant growth and the spreading of prosperity. But a critical reading suggests that such exuberance is likely to be avaricious and callous and that the notion of unremitting growth is delusional as well as environmentally dangerous.

In point of fact, while greed may indeed be endemic to capitalism, growth is not. The Great Depression of the 1930s was the first global crisis in capital accumulation. And how was that crisis resolved? It was not by the recommitment of capital to the productive process, but through a variety of "regulatory reforms, the provision of state supported education, health and welfare, and the promotion of a mixed economy" (p. 719). State spending (often in the form of military spending) created new investment opportunities, but by the 1970s, that too had proved inadequate, and a new era of "stagflation" (high unemployment *and* high inflation) was ushered in: Another crisis, this one resolved by "financialization," a money-to-money proposition where capital was invested in the financial-insurance-real estate (FIRE) sector rather than in the production of goods and the creation of jobs. "Financialization involves a situation where 'the traditional role of finance as a helpful servant to production has been stood on its head, with finance now dominating over production'" (Foster and Magdoff, 2009: 100; Kenway and Fahey, 2010). And the limits of financialization as an accumulation strategy were sharply revealed in the late Great Recession.

All the while, the rich (the greedy?) have gotten richer and richer while the working and middle classes struggle. Thus, we have a proliferation of McMansions on the one hand and homelessness on the other; second and third homes for the few, second and third jobs for the many; luxury cruises and related leisure time affections for the rich, staycations for average Jills and Joes.

Of course, the greed-is-good ideoscape and the greed emoscape are not restricted to the financial and corporate worlds, they infected and intersected with the broader consumer culture that has become so central to everyday life for everyday people. Greed, corporatism and consumerism have become the sacred trinity of our times. Greed is defined as an overwhelming desire to have more of something than is actually needed. Consumer culture is based on a similar emotional imperative.

(2010: 721)

And so, capital accumulates to generate more capital and to consume more and more "than is actually needed." If that is not an economic system based on greed, then what is? "Greed creates a must-have, must-have-more and must-have-now atmosphere." Greed creates what Kenway and Fahey call casino capitalism. The rich are in the back room playing high-stakes poker while the rest of us pour our few quarters into the slots.

Who Is Greedy and Who Is Not?

A series of studies by Piff et al. (2012) suggests that "higher social class predicts increased unethical behavior." Two theories are at issue. On the one hand, people with lower levels of resources to begin with might "be more motivated to behave unethically to increase their resources or overcome their disadvantages." On the other, the increased resources, freedom, and independence enjoyed by the wealthy might lead to self-absorption, excessive emphasis on the self, and a greater willingness to behave greedily or unethically to advance one's own position in society. Results from seven separate observational and experimental studies strongly favor the latter point of view.

Two of the seven studies were "naturalistic field studies," i.e. behavioral observations. The first study "investigated whether upper-class drivers were more likely to cut off other vehicles at a busy four-way intersection with stop signs on all sides." Social class was inferred from the make, age, and appearance of a driver's vehicle. Overall, 12% of all drivers cut through the four-way stop out of turn (cut off other drivers). "A binary logistic regression indicated that upper-class drivers were the most likely to cut off other vehicles at the intersection, even when controlling for time of day, driver's perceived sex and age, and amount of traffic." Lexus, BMW, and Mercedes drivers were more likely to cut in out of turn than the Ford and Chevy drivers.

A related study focused on cutting off pedestrians at a crosswalk. Although California law requires that vehicular traffic yield to pedestrians in the crosswalks, 35% of the drivers in this study did not. And again, "upper-class drivers were significantly more likely to drive through the crosswalk without yielding to the waiting pedestrian" (who was a study confederate).

The third study was a survey posing different scenarios to assess tendencies toward unethical behavior. In each scenario, an actor was described as unrightfully taking or benefiting from something, and respondents were asked how likely they would be, under the same circumstances, to take the same advantage. Social class was self-reported. "As hypothesized, social class positively predicted unethical decision-making tendencies, even after controlling for ethnicity, sex, and age." By their own assessment and admission, persons who describe themselves as of a higher class are also more likely to engage in ethically dubious behavior.

And so it goes. Study 4 showed that higher-class individuals took more candy that would otherwise go to children than lower-class individuals; Study 5 showed that higher-status persons were more likely to lie to a job candidate than lower-status persons; higher-status persons in this study were also more likely to believe that greed was justifiable and moral; Study 6 found that social class also positively predicted the likelihood of cheating in a game of chance and more favorable attitudes about greed; Study 7 showed that if you prime lower-status individuals with a "greed-is-good" message, they adopt more favorable attitudes about greed themselves. However the topic is approached, the results are the same: Status and greed go hand in hand.

Pay It Forward

Pay It Forward was a 2000 movie starring Haley Joel Osment, Helen Hunt, and Kevin Spacey. The plot premise was pretty simple. Osment is given an assignment by his teacher (Spacey) to enact a plan that would make the world a better place. What he comes up with is "pay it forward," the basic idea of which is that rather than "pay back" a favor that someone does for you, you "pay it forward" by doing equally magnanimous favors for three others. Each of them does likewise, and so on, and eventually there is a social network of good deeds and a better world. The concept clearly entails a voluntary reorganization of the affairs of humankind on the basis of kindness and generosity rather than greed.

The "pay it forward" concept has sparked a small but intriguing experimental literature (e.g., Gray et al., 2014; Yang et al., 2015). In one series of studies, participants were given six dollars and then asked to decide how much of the money to give to another participant. What was not given away could be kept. The interesting wrinkle is not what the first person decided but what subsequent participants decided to do with the money. First, the good news: People who were treated fairly were likely to treat the next recipient fairly. (Here, "fair" means an even split: I keep three bucks and give the other three to the next person.) Then the bad news: People who were treated greedily paid the greed forward much more often than people who were treated generously paid the generosity forward. In general, people responded to both greed and generosity by being equitable. Apparently, bad behavior leaves a stronger impression on us than good behavior does. Gray and his co-authors interpret this to mean that negative emotions exert a greater influence on us than positive emotions. And thus, greed triumphs over generosity!

Subsequent studies elaborate on the basic experiment in various ways. Willer, Flynn, and Zak showed, for example, that people with a stronger sense of solidarity with the community were more likely to behave generously. Likewise, Yang et al. found that socially close others were more likely to be treated generously than distant others. What all studies find, pretty unequivocally, is that if A stiffs B, B is going to stiff C, and on down the line. Greed begets more greed. Alas, if A is generous to B, B is about as likely to stiff C as to be generous or equitable. Generosity does not beget more generosity. As a determinant of human affairs, then, greed seems more powerful than generosity or equity.

The Prisoner's Dilemma

The generic version of the "Prisoner's Dilemma" is this: Two gang members are arrested for assaulting a man with a deadly weapon. They have no opportunity to communicate with each other after the arrest. The police lack enough evidence to convict both men of assault with a deadly weapon and hope to get both of them imprisoned for a year on a lesser charge (simple assault). But both men are simultaneously offered a "deal." They can either betray the other by testifying that the other committed the crime or "cooperate" with the other guy by remaining silent. The plea offer is:

If both betray the other, they both get two years in prison.

If one betrays and the other remains silent, the betrayer goes free and the silent partner does three years.

If both remain silent, they are both convicted on the lesser charge and both do one year.

Clearly, the best overall outcome is achieved when both remain silent; the worst overall outcome is if both betray the other. Empirically, the standard outcome is that both players are greedy, both betray the other, and both do two years. Cooperation would lead to a better overall outcome; greed gives both players a 50–50 chance to go free. Greed predominates.

There are dozens of variations on the basic game and various strategies that game theorists have concocted, some of which do lead to optimal outcomes, that is, to cooperation even in the face of no information or communication (see e.g. Axelrod, 2006). So it cannot be said that the Prisoner's Dilemma demonstrates the impossibility of cooperation, only that in conventional, non-contrived situations, greed rules the roost. (As it happens, cooperation strategies depend critically on the likelihood that the participants will meet again – thus showing the importance of social distance, social networks, and feelings of community solidarity in fostering cooperation.)

The Tragedy of the Commons

A final example of the predominance of greed in human affairs is offered by the so-called "Tragedy of the Commons" (Hardin, 1968). Stated succinctly, the tragedy is that in some situations, individuals acting individually in their own best interests do things that are contrary to the best interests of the whole. The original "commons" was common grazing land in the British Isles (thus, "commons" in the sense of the Boston Commons). Absent effective regulation or moderations inflicted on behavior by some sort of price mechanism, everyone would graze their livestock on the common grazing land and overgrazing would be the rapid result. The individual pursuit of self-interest can therefore rapidly deplete common resources – grazing land, fish stocks, the oceans, the atmosphere, and pretty much all natural resources owned publically. In such situations, maximizing individual self-interest does *not* maximize the collective good.

Free access and unrestricted demand for a limited (finite) resource sooner or later lead to overexploitation. Benefits accrue to the exploiters, but costs are borne by all. Axelrod (mentioned earlier) and many others have noted that even self-interested individuals sometimes cooperate when cooperation serves both individual and collective interests; here again, a community orientation is a key predictor of cooperation in various experimental "tragedies." Clearly, some common resources have been used widely and successfully for centuries, so "tragedy" is not the invariable result. Still, whether the issue is fish stocks or virgin timber, regulation has historically proven necessary to sustain the resource and prevent overexploitation. It therefore falls to governments (the "Leviathan" in Hobbes's terms – "to keep them in awe...") to intercede in the behaviors of self-interested individuals. This, in short, is the collectivity (government) attempting to discipline individual greed. Absent proper and well-enforced regulations, as long as there is still a profit to be made, the coal companies would mine right down to the very last seam, and crabbers would hunt their prey into extinction.

Research has demonstrated that a host of factors foster cooperation in so-called "commons" dilemmas. The most comprehensive review of psychological factors is by Kopelman et al. (2002). Ostrom et al. (1994) have also studied how real-world communities manage public resources. A critical factor appears to be collective awareness of the threat of resource depletion. And once again, community orientations and dense social networks foster cooperation.

What about Charity, Altruism, Volunteerism?

Despite the predominance of greed in the pantheon of human motivators, people freely donate money to charitable organizations; volunteer time, energy, and treasure for causes they believe in; "loan" money to relatives knowing full well they will never get it back; give blood, bone marrow, and their own organs to anonymous recipients; and behave in numerous other selfless, prosocial, altruistic ways. How can this be if people are always acting so as to maximize their own self-interest? What's the "self-interest" in giving your money away?

One line of argument says that prosocial behavior really does not exist, that everything is done to maximize self-interest, and that no other motivation for behavior can be identified. However selfless an act might appear to be, the actor always derives some benefit that exceeds the cost of the selfless act. Vexen Crabtree (2006), a self-described Satanist, points to such benefits as neuro-chemical rewards ("the feel-good factor"), personal pride (creating a positive self-identity), social rewards (a desire to be seen as a "good person" within one's social network), and the "want of power over others" (helping others is one way of affirming one's power over those others). These are the non-tangible but quite real utilities people derive from apparently selfless acts. Other similar motivators might be wishing to be thought well of, accumulating social and cultural capital within one's social network, repaying prior obligations, and perhaps even increasing the odds that St. Peter will judge kindly when you finally show up at the Pearly Gates.

Clearly, it is possible to conjure up hypothetical selfish reasons for any apparently selfless act, save possibly throwing yourself on a live grenade to spare the lives of everyone else in the foxhole. But in the end, what does the conjuring accomplish? If Joe donates money to a homeless program because it makes him "feel good," all that tells us is *why* Joe is an altruistic person, not that he isn't one. If you begin with the *assumption* that all behavior is self-serving, then it becomes so. But what does this accomplish other than rendering all humanity venal and, thereby, salvaging the premise that all behavior "must" result from greed? Surely, we do well to distinguish between motive and consequence.

In her Presidential Address to the Midwest Sociological Society, Roberta Simmons (1991) argues that this line of reasoning effectively trivializes prosocial and altruistic behavior.

> In my view, altruism has nobility and should not be trivialized. Nor should it be discounted even if not 'pure.' Even if society reinforces the altruistic act through praise, which enhances self-esteem and happiness, the helping act should not be minimized. An aggressive species, we also help the weak, for which we should be proud.
>
> *(1991: 15)*

Altruistic behavior has been an object of interest to sociologists ever since Auguste Comte, who coined the word sociology and the word altruism (in French, *altruisme,* derived from *autrui*: "other people") in about 1852. For Comte, altruism is "the definitive formula of human morality." In a later passage, Comte spoke about human "instincts of benevolence" as the ultimate source of happiness. Far from somehow being contrary to self-interest, Comte viewed altruism as the essence of humanness. Thus, his famous motto: "Live for others."

Durkheim too wrote at length on altruism, most notably about altruistic suicide, by which he meant self-sacrifice for the good (mostly survival) of others or of the community at large – the type of suicide committed when the soldier jumps on the grenade. (Contrary to what many believe, altruistic suicide was described by others prior to Durkheim, indeed, even before Comte coined the term. But that is a tale for another day.) Altruism for Durkheim was more generally a set of social norms commanding that members of society give primary consideration to the welfare of their fellows, not just to their own well-being – a set of social expectations that keep people focused on the greater good. These normative prescriptions for behavior are inherent in Durkheim's notions of social solidarity.

Philosophers from Nietzsche to Ayn Rand have held opposing views, of course, many of them flatly denying that there can be reasons for behavior other than self-interest. But there is no denying that the world witnesses and benefits from a great deal of apparently selfless behavior. Simmons herself studied kidney and bone marrow donors, both of which require donors to undergo painful, high-risk procedures (kidney donations more so). Most of the kidney donors she studied were donating their organs to a family member, but the bone marrow donors were registered with the National Bone Marrow Registry, so donations would almost always go to complete strangers. Clearly, powerful social norms would dictate donating a kidney, say, to saving the life of a sibling, but all this means is that social norms often compel altruistic behavior (or, in other words, that altruism is somehow part of what it means to be a social species).

Sure, donors are "are driven by concern for the victim, and are also happy that they could help. The desire for happiness is sometimes interpreted as an egoistic motive" (Simmons, 1991: 5). But again, to say that people behave selflessly because of a concern for others or because it makes them happy to do so only tells us *why* they are altruistic, not that they aren't. Somehow, it seems downright mean-spirited and demeaning to declare that there must always be egoistic motives behind every apparently selfless act. And if such a conclusion follows inevitably from theoretical first principles, it seems that those principles are what need skeptical investigation. As Simmons tells us, "altruism is one process that helps to glue society together." It is at least in part how society as a whole negotiates the tension between individual and collective needs.

If one accepts that selfless behavior is at least a theoretical possibility and stops looking for the selfish motives that "must" lie behind every altruistic act, there is a fairly large social science literature on the topic and a lot of interesting findings. First, as was evident even when Simmons was writing (early 1990s), the major social psychological mechanism that produces altruism is *empathy* – the inclination, willingness, or, perhaps, ability to understand and share the feelings of others; not pity, not guilt, not domination, but empathy. The more empathetic one is in the face of another's need, the more one "feels the pain" of the other and is compelled to help. This is the "empathy-altruism" hypothesis that has been around since the 1980s and much evidence exists to support it.[3]

Another finding that dates back 40 years and has been replicated scores of times is that altruists are generally happier and enjoy stronger feelings of self-worth than others. "Stronger feelings of self-worth," of course, come dangerously close to pride; so as is often the case when discussing the Seven Deadlies, winning on one means losing out on another. Still, if you are down in the dumps and feeling worthless as a human being, giving some money away or volunteering at the local soup kitchen often makes you feel better. As I say, the positive effects of charitable acts on self-esteem and overall happiness are documented in dozens of studies (see, e.g., Choi and Kim, 2011; Sargeant and Woodliffe, 2007; Thoits and Hewitt, 2001).

Correlates of Prosocial Behavior

Bekkers and Wiepking (2007) have produced by far the most comprehensive and far-reaching review of the research literature on "Generosity and Philanthropy," a review covering some 500 studies in all the social sciences and all the world's regions. To bring some order to this vast reservoir of information, two types of knowledge are discussed: (1) Who gives what? and (2) Why do people give?

Concerning the first – Who gives what? – let's begin as our authors do, with religion. The expectation, of course, is that more religious people would be more generous with their time and money than the irreligious, and, superficially at least, that is what the data show: "Positive relations between church membership and/or the frequency of church attendance with both secular and religious philanthropy appear in almost any article in which this relation was studied" (p. 6). There are exceptions, of course. An Australian study and a handful of American studies report no relationship between giving and religion, but these studies are rare. It is also the case that in experimental situations, religiosity and giving are not strongly related, but in the real world, apparently they are.

One recent study of children (Decety et al., 2015), based on 1,170 children from six countries, found (in contrast to much other research) that children raised by religious parents were *less* likely to be charitable in a so-called "Dictator Game."

What explains the correlation between religious participation and giving? One likely explanation for at least part of the effect is that regular church attenders are asked more frequently and, thus, give more often. Another is that attendance at religious services and donating to charities or causes are both part of an underlying orientation to community. A third line of explanation is that religious people are more pious or hold other charitable religious beliefs more deeply and, therefore, give more. There is at least some evidence for and against each of these explanations.

Other commonly reported correlates of charitable giving, volunteering, and other prosocial behaviors include education (students of economics excepted!), home ownership, perceived financial well-being, age (older persons give more), being married, having children, and certain other factors. Concerning gender, "Most studies find no reliable differences [in altruism] between males and females" (p. 15). Various personality traits are also associated with these behaviors, including emotional stability, empathy, and extraversion. Finally, there is some evidence that cognitive ability is positively associated with giving.

The relationship of giving with income is of special interest. In general, people with more money give more money, as would be expected. But when charitable giving is calculated as a percentage of income, it is the poor who are most generous (Piff et al., 2010, 2012).

Bekkers and Wiepking also consider the reasons why people give, which fall into eight broad classes: (1) awareness of need; (2) solicitation; (3) costs and benefits; (4) altruism; (5) reputation; (6) psychological benefits; (7) values; and (8) efficacy. Many of these are obvious, but a few merit comment. With respect to awareness of need, for example, it appears that objective need is less important than subjective perceptions of need. To illustrate, Lee and Farrell (2003) found that panhandlers were given more money the needier they appeared to be; Bielefeld et al. (2005) found that donations to (nonreligious) causes were higher in areas with the most income inequality; etc.

An often overlooked factor in analyzing who gives and who doesn't is "Who gets asked?" Any solicitation increases giving, but some types of solicitation are more effective than others. "A large majority of all donation acts occurs in response to a solicitation" (p. 8). Giving also increases when it is easy and convenient to give, and decreases otherwise.

Much of the Bekkers-Wiepking paper is devoted to the various psychological benefits people derive from their prosocial behavior: "warm fuzzies" (the "joy of giving," the "warm glow" that many experience when they are charitable); enhanced self-image (pride?), reputation within one's social network; reduction of cognitive dissonance; etc. Values also make a difference, for example, the value people often ascribe to efforts to "make the world a better place." Other values associated with charitable giving include altruism, humanitarianism, egalitarianism, post-materialism, and social responsibility, among others.

Finally, people are more likely to donate if they believe that doing so will make some difference in the cause they are supporting.

Conclusions

One of Rene Bekker's conclusions about charitable donations is that "a more coldly rational approach to life reduces giving." And therein lies the rub. Self-interest rationally considered is the cornerstone of modern capitalist economies (which, frankly, is the only kind of economy there is); aggressive pursuit of self-interest, however, leads inevitably to accumulation; accumulation generates massive inequalities; and these inequalities generate a need for governmental programs and charitable giving to nonprofit social service organizations. If capitalism does not cycle between crises of accumulation, as Marx and his followers believed, the system certainly walks a fine line between being overwhelmed by greed or hobbled by social inequality – between reckless accumulation for the sheer hell of it and compassionate recognition that the losers in the Giant Greed Game need help.

How much help? That is hard to say. According to the Urban Institute (McKeever, 2015), in 2015, there were nearly a million and a half nonprofit public charities registered with the Internal Revenue Service, to whom some $1.73 *trillion* were donated. The nonprofit sector accounted for just less than one trillion dollars in gross domestic product, about 5% of the total. Add in another two trillion or so in Federal expenditures on social safety net provisions (Social Security, Medicare, Medicaid, and other health insurance programs; various food programs; and other safety net provisions), and we come up with an annual downside cost in the vicinity of $4 *trillion,* a bit more than a fifth of the entire American economy (which generated about $18 trillion in 2014). Call that the "greed tax rate" – the amount of money we have to spend to take care of the basic needs of those who are not so good at being greedy.

It seems obvious that there is way more greed in American society than there is charity and more selfishness than selflessness. Far from being sinful, greed is what makes the economy tick. History, alas, is full of failed attempts to erect economies on some other basis.

That being said, it is true that the existence of sociology as a discipline is largely due to the bounty of prosocial behavior that characterizes much social interaction. Between the unrestrained greed of the economist and the neurotic fixations of the psychologist lie the normative prosocial behaviors studied by sociologists. Both Comte and Durkheim understood that the social fabric is held together by a web of shared understandings and behavioral norms imparted through socialization. This insight remains sociology's most profound and unique contribution. People behave in prosocial ways not because they profit directly from so doing and not even because it helps them get into Heaven, but because in the end, other-directedness is the only certain protection against Thomas Hobbes's "warre of all against all."

Whether "pure altruism" exists or not is still debated, but whatever the resolution, a great deal of apparent altruism can be seen everywhere. And while altruism may well be motivated by a desire to feel good or to be thought well of by others, it is hard to see the behavior as "greedy." As Simmons says (1991: 10), "altruistic behavior should not be discounted simply because one reacts with positive emotions to the experience."

When it comes to volunteering and charitable giving, President Woodrow Wilson said:

> You are not here merely to make a living. You are here in order to enable the world to live more amply, with greater vision, with a finer spirit of hope and achievement. You are here to enrich the world, and you impoverish yourself if you forget the errand.

It's a sentiment Americans (and many others) have always taken to heart. The great French observer of American manners and morals, Alexis de Tocqueville, was astonished by the volunteer associations and organizations that gave breath and spirit to American civic life. Today, each year, some 60–65 million American adults (one out of four) volunteer their time and effort in churches, schools, civic clubs, and like organizations. (Alas, three out of four do not.) The annual volunteer hours add up to about eight billion. As already noted, charitable giving and volunteering is a multi-trillion dollar yearly enterprise. In many social and human service agencies, volunteers and charitable donations are not just an asset, they are a necessity.

As we have seen, social scientists have created a large research literature around the questions of who gives and who volunteers. The two tendencies are positively related in that those who do either tend to do both. (The same people are also blood donors, have library cards, and attend church regularly.) Volunteering is *not* strongly related to labor force participation – full-time workers are as likely to volunteer as those not even in the labor force. In general, the relationship of volunteering to age is curvilinear: Low among the young and old and peaking in middle age, although there has been a recent upturn in volunteering among younger people, especially college students ("millennials"). Donated dollars increase with income, as would be expected, but as a percentage of expendable income, low-income people give *more* than upper-income people. The most important predictor of volunteering is social networks. Consistently, in study after study, those with the most extensive social networks, the most organizational memberships, and the most prior volunteer experience are the most likely to be volunteers.

All true, of course, but still... I am unable to shake off the passage in Kurt Vonnegut's *God Bless You, Mr. Rosewater* that will stand as a conclusion to this chapter:

> Thus did a handful of rapacious citizens come to control all that was worth controlling in America. Thus was the savage and stupid and entirely inappropriate and unnecessary and humorless American class system created. Honest, industrious, peaceful citizens were classed as bloodsuckers if they asked to be paid a living wage. And they saw that praise was reserved henceforth for those who devised means of getting paid enormously for committing crimes against which no laws had yet been passed. Thus the American dream turned belly up, turned green, bobbed to the scummy surface of cupidity unlimited, filled with gas, and went bang in the noonday sun.

Notes

1 www.huffingtonpost.com/news/american-greed/.
2 www.nerdwallet.com/blog/credit-card-data/average-credit-card-debt-household/.
3 In fairness, there is also some contrary evidence. Einolf (2007) used survey data to examine correlations between a measure of empathetic concern and 14 different prosocial behaviors. Statistically significant correlations were found for 10 of the 14 behaviors, but "substantively meaningful" correlations were found for only three. Empathy may not be as important in driving helping behaviors as was once thought.

> The findings of this article do not contradict... assertions that empathic thoughts and feelings are an important motivator of altruistic action in particular experimental situations, or... that empathy is an important part of moral development. But the current findings... indicate that individual differences in the personality trait of empathic concern may have little or no relationship to most real-life helping behaviors.
>
> *(2007: 1277)*

2

GLUTTONY

The Sociology and Economics of Overconsumption

An anagram of United States of America is Dine out, taste a Mac, fries.

Where better to begin our discussion of gluttony than with Diamond Jim Brady (1856–1917), a businessman, financier, and philanthropist in what Mark Twain described as America's "Gilded Age" (roughly 1870–1900). Most of Brady's extensive fortune was derived from selling supplies to the railroad industry. He is remembered for many things: He was, for example, the first person in New York City to own a car, and he had a penchant for collecting and wearing fine jewelry (his collection of precious stones and jewels would be worth about $60 million in today's dollars). But above all, he was and remains famous for his gargantuan appetite (almost certainly exaggerated in surviving accounts, but still prodigious by any standard).

According to John Mariani (1991), Brady would consume more food at breakfast alone than would be required by a normal person in an entire day: "eggs, breads, muffins, grits, pancakes, steaks, chops, fried potatoes, and pitchers of orange juice." He would allegedly

> stave off mid-morning hunger by downing two or three dozen clams or oysters, then repair to Delmonico's or Rector's for a lunch that consisted of more oysters and clams, lobsters, crabs, a joint of beef, pie, and more orange juice.

The evening meal might consist of "three dozen oysters, a dozen crabs, six or seven lobsters, terrapin soup," and a steak, with "a tray full of pastries and two pounds of bonbons" to finish up. Later in the evening, allegedly, Brady would snack on "a few game birds and more orange juice."[1]

Fast-forward to the early years of the 21st century and the recent publication by the National Institutes of Health, *Overweight and Obesity Statistics*, where we learn that according to Federal definitions, more than two out of three American adults are at least overweight, more than one in three are obese, more than one in 20 are *morbidly* obese, and about a third of all children and adolescents are overweight or obese. Moreover, trend data going back to 1962 confirm that the proportion of fatties has been increasing.

In short, whether gluttony is indeed a deadly sin or not, it has apparently become America's national pastime. And not just America. Worldwide, more than half of all adults are overweight. And while America apparently leads the list for adults, Mexico, Australia, New Zealand, and several Western European nations are not far behind. As for children, Greece, Italy, New Zealand, and Slovenia have higher rates of child obesity than we do (OECD, 2014). Diamond Jim's meals were certainly excessive, but not so much more excessive, it appears, than the diets of an increasingly large fraction of the developed world's population.

What Is Gluttony?

Earlier, we defined gluttony as the "excessive ongoing consumption of food or drink," but clearly, one can be gluttonous in other ways. "He's a glutton for punishment" is a common ordinary-language phrase. We also often say, "She's a glutton for work." And if gluttony is the "excessive consumption" of more or less anything, then we could speak of someone being a glutton for houses or cars or antiques or clothes or plastic surgery or anything else that can be consumed to frivolous excess.

Gluttony is sometimes difficult to distinguish from the other deadly sins. Greed could be conceptualized as a "gluttony" for money or material things, lust as a "gluttony" for sexual pleasure, envy as a "gluttony" for status, and so on. And we will discuss later in the chapter some aspects of gluttony that go beyond food and drink. But we will at least start with gluttony in the traditional sense.

In his discussion of gluttony (1978: 212–231), Sanford Lyman remarks, "Although gluttony is a recognized sin, it is rarely considered a social problem," this because gluttony "stems primarily from its location in the personal and individual aspects of life" (p. 215). How times have changed! While at one time, perhaps, it was considered someone's personal business what they swallowed by the mouthful or poured down their throat, there is now a small (OK: Not so small) army of regulatory watchdogs (some official, many self-appointed) whose business it is to monitor what people eat and drink and grunt disapprovingly whenever the items being consumed depart from their sense of the acceptable. What I have in mind here is the calumny a pregnant woman can expect when sipping an innocent glass of white wine in a public place, or the disapproving looks one receives from one's lunch companions when ordering a bacon double cheeseburger while everyone else at the table is grazing on their salads or even, these days, the disapproval that comes when you are caught eating plums imported from Chile ("Do you not *care* about your carbon footprint!?!")

Today, it seems, what people eat and drink is *everybody's* business. We have lengthy and highly elaborate rules about what children in the schools are and are not allowed to eat, many of which are known to have as their principal effect increased plate waste. The Federal government publishes dietary guidelines; private organizations such as the American Association of Retired Persons fill up their newsletters with advice on healthy eating. Charitably, much of this obsession would be described as a new food-focused moral Puritanism. Less charitably, we have been set upon by food Nazis – people, perhaps, who are gluttons for doling out unwanted advice.

At the level of Federal officialdom, the Naggers-in-Chief are the Centers for Disease Control and Prevention (CDC), the Surgeon General, and the Public Health Service, whose advice is never "moderation in all things" but rather total abstinence from anything that might carry even a wisp of risk. Consider, for example, the recommendation that pregnant women avoid alcohol altogether for the entirety of their pregnancy. Now, it is known that drinking while pregnant *can* lead to fetal alcohol syndrome (FAS), something women would surely want to avoid. But what is the risk of FAS to women in general? Less than one case per thousand live births. Among women who drink *heavily*, the risk jumps to 43 per thousand or about one in twenty – not trivial, but by no means a certain outcome. Teetotaling women, of course, have a 0% chance. But what, then, of women who have a single glass of wine during the nine months of their pregnancy? Women who have a glass of wine once a week? Once a day? Is there a dose-response curve here, where below a certain level of consumption, the risk remains zero?

While some sort of dose-response curve seems likely (clearly, one molecule of ethyl alcohol would not have any detectable effect), the fact is, no one knows if there is a dose-response curve or not. The CDC itself emphasizes in all its FAS publications that "There is no known safe amount of alcohol during pregnancy or when trying to get pregnant. There is also no safe time to drink during pregnancy" (Center for Disease Control, 2015a). But just because *we don't yet know* what a safe amount might be does *not* mean there isn't one, only that the appropriate research has not yet been done.

It is likely, moreover, that the appropriate research will *never* be done. A recent review by Clarren and Cook (2013) points out that adequate measures of dose are almost impossible to achieve since "generally, people do not know exactly how much alcohol they consume." Moreover, the rate at which alcohol passes through the placenta and enters into the fetal bloodstream is highly variable. Then too, different fetuses differ in their response, as indicated by the finding that fraternal twins (but generally not identical twins) often respond differently to alcohol in their systems. Finally, there is not a single "response" but rather a spectrum of non-specific disease clusters and developmental abnormalities.

> Based on the variabilities between mothers and fetuses, metabolism, [and] genetic interactions with environmental factors, it is very unlikely that 'absolute risk' for the harmful effects of alcohol consumption during pregnancy will be established and the question of 'how much is too much' will remain unanswered. Thus, the best advice is 'NO exposure equals NO risk.'

While this may or may not be the *best* advice (it requires women to forego something pleasurable for possibly no good purpose), it is surely the *safest* advice. What if your doctor told you something sensible, such as "If you are going to drink while pregnant, do so in moderation – not more than a glass or two of wine a week," you followed that advice, and then gave birth to an FAS baby? Lawsuits would quickly follow! If the same decision rule were followed in economic decision-making, however, all the money would be in cash under the mattress and none would be invested in the stock market. Some risk is not necessarily a bad thing!

By the way, the latest CDC recommendation is that sexually active women who are not using birth control should also abstain from alcohol entirely, just in case they have a drink or two before they realize that they are pregnant. Sixty or seventy years ago, pregnant woman were often urged by their doctors to put their feet up in the evening and have a glass of wine – it would be relaxing and, therefore, healthful. This is exactly what my mother was told when she was pregnant with me. To increase relaxation, she was also told to have a cigarette.

As for not being thought of as a "social problem," one would be hard-pressed these days to find a social problems text that did not include a chapter on alcohol and drug consumption or a lengthy discussion of obesity. How things have changed in the four decades since Lyman published his book!

Gluttony as Disease

For the larger part of human history, gluttony was understood as a personal or moral failing, a result of people not having the strength of will to control their own behavior. For the last half-century, we have become accustomed to thinking of gluttonous behavior as a *disease* and, thus, as a medical problem that we expect medical science to cure. This began with the 1956 American Medical Association declaration that alcoholism was a disease, a conceptualization subsequently transferred to the excessive use of drugs other than alcohol, then to compulsive over-eating (and since to many other things, including excessive sexual appetites, "addiction" to indebtedness, and a wide range of other gluttonous behaviors).

A key sign that something has attained the status of "disease" is the existence of a Twelve Step program to combat it – a Bad Behaviors Anonymous, if you will. One can now find countless organizations modeled on Alcoholics Anonymous—Sex and Love Addicts Anonymous, Crystal Meth Anonymous, Food Addicts Anonymous, Debtors Anonymous, Narcotics Anonymous, Over-eaters Anonymous, and probably many others. In virtually all cases, Step One of the Twelve is to admit that you are powerless to control your "disease," another giant step toward excusing all sorts of ill-considered behaviors and, thus, liberating gluttons of every description from taking any personal responsibility for their sorry, pathetic selves.

There is more to the medicalization of social problems, of course. In addition to a 12-Step program for everything, we also expect there to be a pill for everything. Indeed, the legal, legitimate, and socially sanctioned use of drugs has become so entrenched in our society that America could be fairly called a "drug culture" in that nearly everyone uses drugs of one or another sort for all kinds of purposes. When we are ailing and go to the doctor, we expect to be given a pill that will make us feel better. If we have trouble sleeping, we take sleeping medications. If we feel anxious, we want anti-anxiety drugs and if we feel depressed we seek anti-depressants. Millions of us get "up" in the morning with caffeine and come "down" in the evenings with alcohol. It has even been argued that mood-altering drugs satisfy an *innate* human need to suspend ordinary awareness, a need that we experience much like sexual tension. The use of drugs to make one feel better or to solve one's problems is deeply entrenched in our culture and expectations.

There is an emerging perspective in the field of addictions that the medicalization of addictive and compulsive behavior is wrong-headed, that these behaviors are *not* diseases (e.g. Albrecht, 2014; Heather, 1992). Heather concludes that

> the specific disease concept, associated mainly with the Fellowship of Alcoholics Anonymous, is contradicted by empirical evidence and unhelpful for preventive and treatment responses to problem drinking, especially for the effort to detect and modify problem drinking at an early stage. The more general disease concept shares these disadvantages and is also ineffective in engendering sympathetic attitudes towards problem drinkers among the general public.

A more useful approach is to "view problem drinking as the result of an interaction between the individual's personality and the social context in which he or she has learned how to drink" – in short, a "social learning" perspective instead of a disease perspective. Presumably, the same would be true of compulsive over-eating, excess sexuality, and so on. These are learned behaviors, not incurable medical disorders.

Excusing Gluttony

If we deny gluttons the excuse that they suffer from a disease, many other rationalizations remain. In his discussion of "Absolution from the Sin of Gluttony," Lyman discusses four: Accidents, defeasibility, biological drives, and scapegoating. The former are the excuses of happenstance: "I didn't realize how much I was eating." "The occasion demanded it." "Everyone kept ordering more drinks." Excuses of accident mitigate if not fully absolve the glutton from sin.

Excuses of defeasibility are more interesting in that they deny the freedom to behave otherwise: "I didn't know the food was fattening." "I couldn't control myself" and related failures of knowledge or will. Lyman remarks:

> Indeed, as experts disagree about the physiological and nutritive effects of cholesterol, carbohydrates, and calories, individuals not only find it hard to follow a proper diet but are also in a position to invoke their understandable ignorance as an excuse for excess.
>
> *(p. 227)*

Excuses of biological drive return us to the notion of gluttony as a disease. "I have a glandular disorder that makes me overeat, or a duodenal condition, or a metabolic malfunction, or bad genes." "Sorry, I was just born this way." Again, these excuses deny personal responsibility by depicting gluttony as biologically inevitable. In Lyman's wry words, these excuses "call upon [the glutton's] accusers to indulge his excesses until research finds a way to relieve him" (p. 227).

Then finally we have scapegoating, a convenient variant on "the Devil made me do it." "This is what people of my racial or ethnic background eat." "I am addicted to food because my parents always fed me when I cried." Here the glutton is pointing the finger at socialization and the food customs of his or her religion, ethnicity, race, national origin, or family background.

> When we turn to the realm of justifications we enter the kingdom of virtue regained... Justifications for gluttony do not deny that there is a sinful quality to voracious over-eating. Rather, they distinguish between the generally impermissible and the particularly allowable. In some instances, they show that the apparently gluttonous act is not only acceptable but required.
>
> *(p. 228)*

The Thanksgiving Day dinner is an obvious occasion when gluttony is required. The obligatory intoxication of New Year's Eve is another. One particularly poignant example mentioned by Lyman is the tradition of giving the condemned permission to be as gluttonous as they wish for their last meal.[2]

Capitalism Encourages Gluttony

Kenway and Fahey (2010) tell us that consumer culture is based on an emotional imperative to consume, indeed, to consume far more than is necessary for survival or even satiation. To a large extent, in the modern consumer culture, a person's worth is *defined* by his or her ability to consume. One philosopher has characterized the consumer culture as a "libidinal economy," an economy of desire. Each personal feeling, want or desire becomes something to be exploited for profit in this libidinal economy, a major purpose of which is to make people want or desire *more* – more food, drink, cars, housing, physical beauty, and opportunities to self-actualize, in short, more of *everything*. As Jay Richards has put it, "Consumerism is a form of gluttony, even idolatry, in which we make food, drink, and stuff our highest loyalty" (2012). Or in the somewhat more graphic words of Gwendolyn Foster, "Consumption. Excess. Gluttony. Hoarding. Waste. Massive debt. The pathologies of capitalism are our greatest export" (2012). She likens American consumerism to coprophagia – the eating of feces and dung. And while her general analysis is a bit over the top, the image of consumption as poop-eating is graphic and not entirely inappropriate. Witness, for example, some of the more highly-rated TV reality shows these days.

In short, "Every cultural message we receive is more about indulgence than it is about moderation. Capitalism encourages us to pamper and feed our every desire" (Bradley, 2014). Whether it is food and drink, or technology, or entertainment, "more" is always "better." The more we consume, the happier we think we are. Max Weber thought that asceticism was essentially "the spirit of capitalism" (Weber, 1905: Chapter 5). And there is a sense in which that is true (i.e. in the ascetic recommendation to reinvest rather than consume). But there is a larger sense in which it is preposterously false. Imagine what a capitalist economy would look like in a nation of ascetics, a nation full of people who seriously believed that moral virtue demanded avoidance of all forms of indulgence. All commerce would be choked to a halt.

Obesity as Gluttony

We opened this chapter with a few comments on the "epidemic" of obesity in this and other countries. But here, as everywhere, there is more to the story than meets the eye. To begin, what determines who is overweight or obese? How are such things measured? And how are the cut points established? Before we start wringing our hands over the epidemic of obesity, maybe we should be pretty certain what it is and how it is measured.

Typically, the measurement of interest is the so-called "Body Mass Index", or BMI, which is simply the ratio of your mass in kilograms to the square of your height in meters. Thus, a person 5'8" tall and weighing 200 pounds would have a BMI of 30.4 – right at the boundary between "overweight" and "obese."[3] BMI was first conceived and defined by the French social scientist Adolphe Quetelet – now a largely forgotten figure in the history of social science but one of the true founders of sociology as it is currently practiced (see Wright, 2009, for a discussion of Quetelet's contributions).

Rather obviously, this BMI ratio can take on any value; empirically, almost all BMI scores range from 15 (pathologically underweight) to about 40 (morbidly obese). But BMI = 40 is not the upper limit, not by a long short. The heaviest person ever documented was Jon Brower Minnoch, who died in 1983. At his peak, Mr. Minnoch stood 6'1" tall and weighed about 1400 pounds, which yields a BMI score of 185.5! Whitney Way Thore, the star of TV's "My Big Fat Fabulous Life," began the series at 5'2" and 380 pounds, for a BMI of 69.5. Even at her "target weight" of 250 pounds, her BMI would still be in the forties. Her comment on her BMI score? "I believe BMI is bullshit!"

Clearly, Mr. Minnoch and Ms. Thore are obese. But where in the BMI continuum does obesity begin? At what point can you be considered overweight? It turns out that the BMI categories were first developed and promoted by the World Health Organization (WHO) in the mid-1990s and subsequently adopted by public health and medical agencies around the globe (this despite a large number of issues and criticisms levelled at the BMI). The US adopted the WHO categories early in the 2000s specifically to facilitate international comparisons. In theory, the cut points in the continuum correspond, more or less, to points where the risks of, say, type 2 diabetes jump, but the risk data in fact do *not* show observable "jumps" corresponding to the BMI cut points for any disease entity. (In fact, the case for *any* causal relationship between obesity and any other disease entity, type 2 diabetes excepted, is surprisingly thin.) The cut points are not reflective of any scientific or medical knowledge or data; rather, they are the arbitrary decisions of UN bureaucrats in Geneva.

For the record, the cut points now used more or less universally are as follows:

BMI 18.5 or less: Underweight
18.5–24.9: Healthy weight
25.0–29.9: Overweight
30.0–35.0: Obese
Over 35: Morbidly obese

Thus, a 5'2" women has to weigh between 101 and 137 pounds to be considered healthy by these standards. At 138 pounds and up, such women are overweight, and if they hit 165 pounds, they are considered obese. So consider the case of plus-sized model Ashley Graham. Ms. Graham is 5'9" tall and weighs 201 pounds. Her BMI is 30. By the WHO standards, she is obese. But if you bother to Google up a photo of Ms. Graham in a two-piece bathing suit, descriptors such as "gorgeous" or "voluptuous" or "fabulous" would come to mind long before "obese."

Late Breaking News: Just days after the above was written, a new study on the BMI was published in the *International Journal of Obesity* (Tomiyama et al., 2016). These authors compared BMI categories to independent measures of cardio-metabolic health (blood pressure, serum cholesterol, etc.) for 40,420 participants in the National Health and Nutrition Examination (NHANES) surveys from 2005 to 2012. Results indicated that "nearly half of overweight individuals, 29% of obese individuals, and even 16% of obesity type II/III individuals [morbidly obese] were metabolically healthy. Moreover, over 30% of normal weight individuals were cardio-metabolically unhealthy." BMI is possibly useful as a preliminary screening tool but is taken way too far when it is used, for example, by insurance companies to set rates, by employee fitness programs to decide who will be required to participate, by transplant surgeons to determine eligibility for transplants, or by researchers and policy-makers to ascertain the extent of the "obesity epidemic" (all common practices at present).

Alas, however misleading and arbitrary the BMI cut points are, they are almost universally adopted in scientific studies, so there is little choice but to accept them and make do. But like practically every other arbitrary medical standard ("allowable" blood glucose levels, "safe" blood pressure readings, "acceptable" cholesterol levels, and on down a long list), these cut points are extremely conservative since medical science always strives to err "on the safe side."

Obesity: Prevalence and Correlates

We have numerous literature reviews of the prevalence and correlates of obesity on which to draw, the most recent and comprehensive of which (so far as I can tell) is Wang and Beydoun (2007). The following discussion is adapted largely from this review.

As reportedly earlier, about two-thirds of American adults are considered to be overweight or obese. The percentage considered obese has increased from 13% to 32% since the mid-1960s. Projections of these trends to the current year (2016) suggest that right now, 75% of US adults are overweight or obese, and 41% are obese. In short, "obesity has increased at an alarming rate" (2007: 6).

Obesity and being over-weight are not randomly distributed in the US (or elsewhere). In general, men are more likely to be overweight or obese than women, and these conditions tend generally to increase with age. The rule of thumb is that US adults gain about one pound per year, so a 60-year-old man can be expected to weigh about twenty more pounds than he weighed when he was 40, all else equal.

There are large racial and ethnic differences in weight, especially among women. African-Americans and Mexican-Americans are about 10 percentage points more likely to be overweight or obese than non-Hispanic whites; among women, the difference is about 20 points. Among African-American women over age 40, more than 80% are overweight or obese; half are obese. Extreme obesity is about twice as common among African-American women as among white or Hispanic women.

The associations of weight with race and ethnicity raise the possibility of large income and socioeconomic status effects, and in this, the data do not disappoint. In general, lower SES is associated with *higher* percentages overweight and obese. These effects are not equally obvious among all gender, age, and racial groups to allow the conclusion that in all cases and regardless of other factors, weight is negatively associated with SES, but this is true often enough to sustain it as an important generalization.

But wait! How is it that people at the bottom of the income distribution are more likely to be overweight or obese than people at the top? How poor can people be if they can afford to eat themselves into a state of advanced obesity? The answer, of course, is that healthy food is relatively expensive food; and likewise, cheap foods tend to be high in fat and carbohydrates, very "energy-dense," and relatively low in proteins and other nutrients. Eating well, in short, often costs more money than low-income families can afford to spend. (On this point, see Wright et al., 2018.)

So now we must confront the difficult question, If people are overweight because they cannot afford to eat a healthier diet, does the resulting obesity qualify as "gluttony" or not. Probably not: Seriously overweight but affluent people are clearly gluttonous, but seriously overweight poor people are more desperate than gluttonous – they weigh too much because their food choices are seriously limited. Thus, not all obesity can be allowed to count as "gluttony." That said, all studies show plenty of fatties in the middle and upper middle classes.

Obesity has also been increasing among US children. As of the Wang-Beydoun review, 26% of children under age six were already overweight or obese, and 14% were obese. The "epidemic" of child obesity has led directly to former First Lady Michelle Obama's Let's Move campaign, initiated in 2010, and a whole raft of other interventions designed to control weight among children and adolescents (see Flodmark et al., 2006, for an overview).

So clearly, overweight and obesity are on the rise across all significant social groups; of this, there seems to be no serious question. (Studies using measures other than BMI report the same general trend.) But why is this the case? Have Americans of all descriptions simply become more gluttonous? Or is the story more complicated than that, as it always seems to be?

Clearly, people gain weight when they consume more calories than they burn off. (It takes about 3,600 excess calories to add one pound of weight, the approximate caloric content of about six medium-sized chocolate milkshakes.) So increases in the overweight and obese categories imply either more calories being consumed, fewer calories being burned off, or both. And, of course, there is evidence for both effects.

Concerning the caloric burn-off, there is ample evidence of increasingly sedentary lifestyles and this must surely contribute to weight gain. (We return to the topic of sedentary lifestyles in the chapter on sloth.) Kids no longer run off after school to a neighborhood pick-up baseball game. Rather, they run into their rooms, fire up their computers, and spend their evening hours gaming or Facebooking and Twittering with their friends. More and more, schools have eliminated recess to increase the amount of instructional time in the school day, although it is widely recognized that this probably makes no sense.

Among adults, the term "couch potato" has become a metaphor for physically undemanding leisure pursuits. The average American adult now watches nearly three hours of TV per day. And "work" has come less and less to mean "physical labor" and more and more to mean spending eight hours a day at a desk or in front of a computer screen. People drive more and walk less; sit in movie theaters far more often than they go to the gym; shop in the supermarket for produce rather than tend a backyard garden. As a result, the average daily *need* for caloric intake has declined while the average daily intake has increased.

Factors involved in the excess caloric intake include eating out more often. At one time, eating out was a special treat, something families did every once in a while. Now it is part of our lifestyle and culture. Fewer and fewer households have someone in the home all day to prepare meals; more and more have every available adult in the paid labor force. After an eight hour day, not everyone is keen to come home, prepare, cook and serve a full meal, and then clean up. We don't have the time or energy for such things.

Alas, restaurant meals are on average more caloric than home-cooked meals. And there is also evidence that restaurant portions are getting larger (Young and Nestle, 2002). For some commonly consumed restaurant items, e.g. French fries, hamburgers, and soda, today's portion sizes are two to five times larger than in the past (Wang and Beydoun, 2007). Neilsen and Popkin (2003) found the same trend in home-cooked meals over the period 1977–1996, and there is every likelihood that the trend has continued since. So, whether in the home or out, people are apparently eating more while their need for calories is declining. A mere ten excess calories a day (for calibration, one teaspoon of sugar is about 15 calories) equates to 3,650 excess calories a year, and that in turn, adds up to one additional pound of body fat. So it is easy to see how obesity could become epidemic.

To be clear, gluttony is by no means the only factor involved in the "epidemic." Restaurant practices, food marketing strategies, increasing labor force participation of women, and even urban design decisions (not making it easy or even possible for people to walk or bike to where they need to go) are all causally implicated. That said, learning how to push away from the table and take a brisk after-dinner walk would go a long way toward halting the epidemic. And to the extent that people are unwilling to do these things, their own gluttony is at fault.

Moral Discourse, Gluttony, and Obesity

The Naggers-in-Chief and a horde of civilian true believers have sought to depict gluttony in moral terms, as "bad behavior" that leads inexorably to discomfort, disease, and premature death. Current medical guidance, abetted by worrisome pronouncements from the CDC, "includes advice on reducing behavioral factors that place people at risk" (Daneski et al., 2010). Daneski et al. contend that, far from being some 20th or 21st century development in the management of disease, this social construction of risk was anticipated in medical textbooks of the 18th and 19th centuries that discussed the link between individual behaviors and apoplexy (incapacity resulting from stroke). In both cases, the discourse voices "a number of judgmental and moral concerns [that] are articulated particularly around diet and exercise" – i.e. a moral discourse quite similar to today's alarms over the "obesity epidemic." Their Table 2 is instructive in that it lists "The history of stroke prevention," specifically, the year in which specific behavioral changes first appeared in the literature as means of preventing stroke:

Recommendation	Date first cited
Stop smoking	1890 (Constantin)
Regular exercise	18th-century texts
Diet and achieving satisfactory weight	18th-century texts
Reducing intake of salt	1952 (Davidson)
Avoiding excess alcohol	18th-century texts

Source: Daneski et al., 2010.

As today, 18th- and 19th-century authors were quick to blame apoplexy on lifestyle choices – on "gluttony, debauchery, and fiery passion in youth," as one writer described it. Said another, "luxury and slothfulness dull and weaken the body." Never mind that then, as now, the evidentiary basis for a link between obesity and stroke is pretty weak and unimpressive. Indeed, according to one author, no trials have ever provided evidence linking obesity to stroke (Curioni et al., 2006). The link has been widely assumed but never established.

"Despite the weak evidence base for the linkage between disease and unhealthy living, it has become a preoccupation of both policy makers and the news media" (Daneski et al., 2010: 738). In contemporary social problems terminology, the obesity epidemic has evolved into a "moral panic." Consider the statement from one-time Surgeon General Richard Carmona, who at the outset of the war in Iraq declared that obesity was a greater health threat than Saddam Hussein's weapons of mass destruction, or the statement of an earlier Surgeon General, C. Everett Koop, that excess fat was killing "a thousand Americans per day" (Abel, 2015). Never mind that no credible study has ever managed to link excess weight to excess morbidity or mortality (again, with the exception of Type 2 diabetes). As Abel puts it,

> Anyone who bothers to examine the evidence in the case against fat with a critical eye will be struck by the radical disconnect between the data in these studies and the conclusions their authors reach. This is actually a common occurrence in the world of obesity research.

Identical conclusions were reached in the extensive literature review by Campos et al., published in the *International Journal of Epidemiology:*

> Except at true statistical extremes, high body mass is a very weak predictor of mortality, and may even be protective in older populations. In particular, the claim that 'overweight' (BMI 25–29.9) increases mortality risk in any meaningful way is impossible to reconcile with numerous large-scale studies that have found no increase in relative risk among the so-called 'overweight', or have found a lower relative risk for premature mortality among this cohort than among persons of so-called 'normal' or 'ideal' [sic] weight.
>
> *(2006: 55)*

The outcome of moral panic around obesity has been "fat shaming," the principal idea of which is to make obese people sufficiently ashamed of their condition that they will eat less, exercise more, lose weight, and, therefore, become healthier. The common perception, in short, is that "weight stigmatization is justifiable and may motivate individuals to adopt healthier behaviors" (Puhl and Heuer, 2010). This is wrong on several counts: First, most overweight and obese people are *already* ashamed of their weight. But it turns out that the more ashamed an obese person feels, the *less* likely he or she is to exercise and the *more* likely to binge on food. Moreover, weight loss dietary regimens are rarely successful and people are generally not very successful at maintaining an exercise program either. The result of "fat shaming" is not healthier behavior; instead, "stigmatization of obese individuals threatens health, generates health disparities, and interferes with effective obesity intervention efforts" (Puhl and Heuer, 2010). Similar conclusions have been advanced by Link and Phelan (2001). They find that obese people who feel bad about their weight also tend to believe cultural stereotypes that associate being overweight or obese with gluttony, laziness, and lack of self-control. This calls to mind Lyman's comments about excusing gluttony on grounds of defeasibility: "I couldn't help myself. It is just the way I am."

Foodies: The New High Art of Gluttony

Myers (2011) has written a remarkable essay reviewing several new books by "foodies" that extol foodie culture. Among the books reviewed are *Blood, Bones and Butter* by Gabrielle Hamilton, *Spoon Fed* by Kim Severson, and *Medium Raw* by the insufferable Anthony Bourdain. The principal message of the essay is that "Gluttony dressed up as foodie-ism is still gluttony." The foodies, in short, are the New Gluttons of the 21st century.

A key point is that gluttony is not primarily about over-eating so much as it is about "an inordinate *preoccupation* with food," and if this is what we mean by gluttony, then contemporary foodie culture must be the most gluttonous culture in history. "These people really do live to eat." Indeed, a true foodie is literally obsessed with food, far more (for instance) than an overly fat person. "It has always been crucial to the gourmet's pleasure that he eat in ways the mainstream cannot afford. For hundreds of years this meant consuming enormous quantities of meat." The difference these days is that foodies voice "an ever-stronger preference for free-range meats from small local farms. He [the foodie] even claims to believe that well-treated animals taste better, though his heart isn't really in it." Thus, for the first time in the history of gourmandizing, today's foodie feels "more moral, spiritual even, than the man on the street." This moral logic, Myers writes,

> now informs all food writing: the refined palate rejects the taste of factory-farmed meat, of the corn-syrupy junk food that sickens the poor, of frozen fruits and vegetables transported wastefully across oceans—from which it follows that to serve one's palate is to do right by small farmers, factory-abused cows, Earth itself. This affectation of piety does not keep foodies from vaunting their penchant for obscenely priced meals, for gorging themselves, even for dining on endangered animals—but only rarely is public attention drawn to the contradiction.

The famous Berkeley restaurateur, Alice Waters, says that "the most political act we can commit is to eat delicious food that is produced in a way that is sustainable, that doesn't exploit workers and is eaten slowly and with reverence." One of the authors Myers reviews notes that a signature item on the *Chez Panisse* menu is "grilled rack and loin of Magruder Ranch veal," which, Meyer remarks, "is environmentally sustainable only because so few people can afford it." Foodie culture, self-proclaimed as virtuous, truly sociable, and humane, turns out to be just "mindless, sweating gluttony." The foodie Tom Kliman writes approvingly about a friend:

> I watched tears streak down a friend's face as he popped expertly cleavered bites of chicken into his mouth … He was red-eyed and breathing fast. "It

hurts, it hurts, but it's so good, but it hurts, and I can't stop eating!" He slammed a fist down on the table. The beer in his glass sloshed over the sides. "Jesus Christ, I've got to stop!"

If that isn't a bald-faced celebration of sheer gluttony, then what is?

Gluttony and Death: Burials of the Morbidly Obese

Obesity may or may not shorten one's life span but it certainly complicates the disposal of your body once you are gone. Indeed, it is no exaggeration to say that the obesity epidemic has created something of a crisis for the death care industry, affecting everything from the initial pick-up of the body down to lowering the casketed remains into the ground or incinerating them in the crematorium.

Persons of more or less average weight can be lifted onto a gurney by two men, slid into a standard ambulance or van, and transported to the funeral home. Persons in the four hundred pound and up range require special accommodations: More men to transfer the body to a gurney, special heavy duty gurneys that can handle the weight, and special vehicles that are capable of transporting large loads. In cases of severely overweight people, flatbed trucks are often needed. One case involved a 750 pound woman who died at home. The coroner's office had no truck large enough to transport her to the morgue, so a towing company was called. The towing company hooked a chain to the mattress on which she was lying, dragged her and the mattress into the front yard, then used the wrecker's hoist to lift the mattress and body into the bed of a heavy-duty pick-up truck (see Emergency Physician's Monthly, 2009).

Alas, the troubles of the morbidly obese have only begun once they are removed from the site of death and taken to the mortuary or coroner's office. Embalming the corpse requires about a gallon of embalming solution for every fifty pounds of body weight – say, four gallons for a 200-pound corpse. A 600-pounder therefore requires about twelve gallons of embalming fluid, plus four or five bottles of cavity fluids just to sterilize the body. As one environment-friendly embalmer put it, "it pains me to see this much formaldehyde being pumped into the earth."[4]

Then there is the matter of the outsized coffin. Normal coffins can handle moderately overweight persons, but for the morbidly obese, this is another matter. Coffins as large as a queen-sized bed are sometimes required. Casket companies specializing in these gigantic burial boxes have sprung up, for example, Goliath Caskets, which custom-builds caskets up to 52 inches wide and capable of handling thousand-pound bodies.[5] Needless to say, these huge custom-built caskets are expensive – with all the frills, they can cost as much as a new car. And, of course, moving the casketed body around the mortuary is another problem. Often special lifts are required.

Then comes burial day. One item from Australia has pointed out that "Obesity makes pallbearing too dangerous" (Power, 2014).

> One of the oldest rites of respect for the dead, the shouldering of the coffin by pallbearers, is being phased out as too risky as obesity takes its toll on the funeral industry. As Australians become heavier, the funeral industry is being forced to change traditions, introduce automation to reduce the risk of injury and upsize everything from coffins to graves.

More and more funeral homes, it appears, are changing burial procedures to accommodate severely overweight people. Among the measures being adopted are conducting all services at graveside to minimize the handling of the body, fully automated coffin trolleys that remove the need for pall-bearers, routinely stocking extra-extra-large coffins, and automating the removal of the casket from the catafalque to the hearse.

Outsized coffins require outsized burial plots, of course. A normal gravesite is three feet wide by eight feet long, but some cemeteries now offer extra-large plots (4' wide by 10' long), and if that is not enough, perhaps two adjacent plots will do (thus doubling the cost). Larger graves mean larger crypts and that too adds to the costs. Lowering an obese body and outsized coffin into the grave may involve special lifting equipment or, sometimes, as many as ten or twelve strong men. A recently noticed problem is when the deceased has made all the required "pre-need" arrangements but then is unable to fit into the chosen casket and grave (Marsden, 2013).

Ah, but the real fireworks (I choose the word advisedly) for fat people's carcass disposal come with cremation and with it the risk of what one funeral director calls an uncontrolled "grease fire." According to the standard sources, obesity begins when body fat reaches 30% of overall body weight. Morbidly obese people have body fat percentages of 40% and up. A 400-pound woman could well consist of close to 200 pounds of pure inflammable lard. As this lard boils out of the obese corpse, it can ignite explosively. There are several recorded cases of the resulting fire burning the crematorium to the ground. These "grease fires" have happened in Austria, Switzerland, Germany, and America. Some facilities now simply refuse to accept morbidly obese corpses; others have installed larger retorts; still others ship outsized corpses to crematoria that are equipped to handle them safely. In one case, the funeral director hacked the corpse of an 800-pound woman into smaller pieces to make the body fit and lower the odds of conflagration.

Everything about disposing of the remains of an obese person adds to the funeral costs by thousands of dollars (Godfrey, 2004). "Burying an obese person…can be comparable to putting a down payment on a house."

Alcohol and Drugs

If we consider the term "drug" in its widest possible meaning, it includes a vast array of substances from aspirin to alcohol to crack cocaine and it becomes immediately obvious that drugs are used casually, therapeutically, or recreationally by the vast majority of the American population. In fact, the use of mood-altering substances is for all practical purposes a universal human behavior embraced by practically all known cultures around the world (Weil, 1972). Nearly all of us are "drug users" for one or another purpose at one or another time.

The use of various mood-altering substances is rooted deep in the history of our species on the planet. Opium is a natural exudate of the poppy plant from which heroin is manufactured and has been recognized as a potent analgesic and as a euphoria-inducer for several thousand years (that is, throughout the whole of recorded history). Beer was brewed in ancient Egypt, and likewise ancient China, and every known civilization has had some sort of alcoholic beverage in common consumption. References to marijuana use appear in early Greek, Hindu, Persian, Arab, and Chinese writings (Inciardi, 1986). When the Spanish *conquistador* Francisco Pizarro began his pillage and plunder of the Incan civilization in 1513, he discovered that chewing coca leaves (from which cocaine is derived) had been part of the Inca's custom and mythology for several centuries.

The early history of *Homo sapiens* can be written as a history of beer (just as the history of later periods can be written as a history of wine, distilled spirits, and, ultimately, Coca-Cola). Just such a history is found in Tom Standage's marvelous book, *A History of the World in Six Glasses* (2006). Standage points out that beer cannot be older than agriculture so the bubbly intoxicant had to have been invented sometime after about 10,000 years ago. However, beer consumption was widespread throughout the Near East (Egypt, Mesopotamia) by 4,000 years ago. Egyptian records mention at least seventeen different kinds of beer, all with names such as "the joy-bringer," "the heavenly," "the beautiful and good." The singular attraction of beer, aside from its delightful intoxicating qualities, is that it was the most effective means known to preserve grain from one growing season to the next. Beer, Standage reminds us, is essentially rot-proof liquid bread.

One of the oldest surviving examples of written language is an inscribed clay tablet from Sumeria dating to about 4,000 years ago. It is a recipe for making beer. In short, once humans figured out the value of writing things down, and how to do so, one of the first things we bothered to write down was our favorite beer recipe! (The instructions on the tablet are sufficiently precise that Sumerian beer can be made today. It comes in at about 3.5% alcohol concentration, about the same as a can of Miller's Lite, and is said to have a flavor similar to hard apple cider.)

The ancient habits of alcohol consumption were replicated in Colonial America, of course (Crews, 2007). A 1790 government report on alcohol consumption said that among persons over the age of 15, annual alcohol consumption amounted to thirty four gallons of beer, five gallons of distilled spirits, and a gallon of wine. "Americans thought alcohol was healthful. To their minds, drink kept people warm, aided digestion, and increased strength." On the other hand, the water could kill you – it swarmed with disease-causing infectious agents. Beer was a much better choice.

In addition to beer and hard cider, Colonial-era Americans were also fond of rum (made from sugar) and whiskey (usually made from grain). The Father of the Country, George Washington, after defeating the British and serving two terms as the first President of the United States, saw that his personal fortune had dwindled and that he needed some way to pump up his income, so he opened a whiskey distillery on the Mt. Vernon estate. By the time of his death in 1799, his distillery was pumping out 11,000 gallons of whiskey a year, making it one of the largest distilleries in the new nation.

The use of drugs other than alcohol was also commonplace throughout American history, from Colonial times up through the early 20th century. At least one observer has characterized 19th century America as a "dope fiend's paradise" (Brecher, 1972: 3) where opium, heroin, morphine, and their numerous pharmaceutical derivatives were as freely accessible as aspirin is today. Opium "dens" were common in American, European, and many Asian cities throughout the 19th century; many nostrums and palliatives available in the late 19th century contained doses of opiates that would be shocking and dangerous by today's standards. The very term chosen to name a popular beverage, *Coca*-Cola, leaves no doubt about its original narcotic content.

How, then, do we stack up today in our consumption of alcohol and drugs? Is our consumption gluttonous? Contrary to a popular indictment, not so much. As of 2014, 88% of the US adult population had used alcohol at some point in their lives; 71% did so in the past year; 57% in the last month (National Institute on Alcohol Abuse and Alcoholism, 2016). A Gallup survey is somewhat more revealing (Blizzard, 2004). A sample of US adults was asked, "Do you have occasion to drink liquor, beer or wine, or are you a total abstainer?" 63% admitted to the occasional drink (about the same as the 57% who drank in the last month); 37% were teetotalers. Men were more likely to be drinkers than women; persons under 50 more likely to drink than seniors. Men who drink at all average 6.6 drinks per week, or about one drink a day; the corresponding average for female drinkers is 2.9 drinks per week. On the other hand, about a tenth of male drinkers have 20 or more drinks a week – something perhaps bordering on excessive.

Gluttonous consumption of alcohol, of course, means not just drinking, but drinking too much. A follow-up question asked only of drinkers was, "Do you sometimes drink more alcoholic beverages that you think you should?"

29% of male drinkers and 18% of female drinkers said yes. Younger drinkers were sharply more likely than older drinkers to say yes to this question. Another question showed that one in three of all respondents (whether drinkers themselves or not) thought that drinking had been "a cause of trouble in your family" at some time.

Let's see now: About two-fifths of the US population never drinks, and of the 63% who do, about three-quarters say they don't overdo it, so that adds up to about 85% who either don't drink at all or do so responsibly. Of the 15% who overdo it, fewer than half (6.8% according to the latest figures from the Federal government) have an "alcohol use disorder" (or AUD, the politically correct term for what we used to call alcoholism).[6] That doesn't sound too bad – what's the big deal? One (correctly) senses another moral panic here, one that began before Prohibition and has continued ever since, albeit at variable levels of intensity over the years.

Alcohol, despite its positive qualities, has always been accused of promoting everything from crime to loose morals to gambling to cardiovascular and liver disease, even in Colonial America, when more people drank more alcohol than they do today. Benjamin Rush, a Philadelphia physician and one of the signers of the Declaration of Independence, published his *Inquiry into the Effects of Ardent Spirits Upon the Human Body and Mind* in 1785. He was among the first to discuss excess drinking as an addiction or a disease (as opposed to a failure of moral will) and, anticipating a great deal of later thinking, advised that abstinence was the only "cure." He advised his alcoholic patients, "Taste not, handle not."

In the run-up to Prohibition (enacted via the 18th Amendment in 1920, repealed by the 21st Amendment in 1933), the nation was awash in Irish and Italian immigrants (and in the South, recently emancipated slaves) who were widely assumed to be the cause of the rising rate of crime (much as Mexican immigrants are depicted today) and that was said to be a direct result of their intemperate consumption of alcohol. Get rid of alcohol, the Temperance Movement believed, and you would simultaneously rid the nation of crime, alcoholism, gambling, addiction, prostitution, unemployment, vagrancy, and a wide variety of other social ills. Prohibition was touted by the "dry" crusaders everywhere as an anti-crime measure.

Every parent learns sooner or later that the best way to pique children's interest in something is to tell them, "You can't have it!" And so too, it seems, with adults. The Roaring Twenties, not widespread temperance, were the immediate offspring of Prohibition. Crime rates didn't go down, they soared. Enforcement was nearly impossible and a great many opportunities for official corruption were created (and taken). And while it is probably true that average consumption declined during Prohibition, enough interest in illegal alcohol remained to feed the rapacious Gangster Era and spawn a vast, organized criminal network to produce, transport, and deliver drink to the thirsty American population. Many present-day fortunes were made bootlegging liquor during Prohibition.

Prohibition had a few other counter-intuitive effects that are worth mentioning. First, it sparked interest in hard liquor and shifted tastes away from beer and wine. Why? Liquor packed more alcohol into a smaller quantity of liquid and was therefore easier to hide from authorities. Prohibition probably also spurred an interest in marijuana, which remained legal until 1937. Men (and women) who might have formerly popped into a bar for a couple of beers after work now frequented the local "teahouse" and smoked marijuana instead.

Prohibition ended a few years after the Great Depression had begun, and these events are probably causally related. By 1929, it was entirely obvious that Prohibition had failed to achieve any of the hoped-for goals, but it certainly had ravaged Federal tax revenues. Prior to the national income tax, enacted in 1913, about a third of the Federal revenue came from taxes on alcohol. (Most of the rest came from duty on imported goods.) Income tax generated comparatively vast revenues for the government – until the economy fell apart in 1929, after which, income tax revenues plummeted. (Income tax collections in 1933 were 60% lower than they had been in 1930.) Desperate for a substitute source of revenue, the idea of repealing Prohibition and taxing legal alcohol became very popular. Thus was the hated 18th Amendment repealed in 1933. (The preceding is taken from Boudreaux, 2007.)

Today, the moral crusade against alcohol is based mostly on its allegedly deadly consequences and the costs of alcohol abuse to the nation. A flyer on "Alcohol Facts and Statistics" from the National Institute on Alcohol Abuse and Alcoholism warns that "nearly 88,000 people die from alcohol-related causes annually, making it the fourth leading preventable cause of death in the United States." Moreover, "in 2010, alcohol misuse problems cost the United States $249.0 billion," three quarters of which is "related to binge drinking" (i.e. to the AUDs).

Some years ago, I had occasion to review the methodology behind such estimates (Wright and Devine, 1994). The conclusion was expressed as a warning: "*The Statistics-General has determined that uncritical consumption of information about the high costs of the drug [and alcohol] problem is dangerous to your intellectual well-being.*" In no other area of the debate over alcohol and drugs does one encounter as much statistical shenanigans.

To begin, as one would anticipate, there are huge uncertainties in estimating all of the various cost components; the methods available for estimating the health care costs of alcohol and drug use are all inferential and indirect. For example, measuring the direct treatment costs (or "direct core costs") of, say, alcohol abuse requires that we know which specific health problems result from alcohol abuse rather than from other factors. In some cases, this is very straight-forward, for example, in cases of drug overdose, alcohol poisoning, acute drug toxicity, or babies born with FAS. In other cases, the attribution of a disorder to substance abuse is less clear. Most *but not all* cases of cirrhosis of the liver result from alcohol abuse; most *but not all* cases of lung cancer result from cigarette smoking, etc. In practice, all cases of various disorders (e.g. cirrhosis, lung cancer, etc.) are treated as resulting from substance abuse in making health care cost estimations. The total costs of treating the diseases that fall within these categories are then included in the overall estimate. Whether the result of these procedures is a net upward or downward bias in the overall estimate is unknown, but they surely increase the uncertainty.

My father was a hardcore alcoholic all his adult life. The cause of death listed on his death certificate is "acute digitalis toxicity." Translated, this means that his cirrhotic liver was no longer capable of detoxifying the quantity of digitalis required to keep his compromised heart ticking. In reality, he drank himself to death, but nothing in his death records would lead one to believe that.

In the end, estimating the costs of alcohol and drug use and abuse has turned into a game, the object of which is to come up with the highest conceivable number that no one will laugh at. One man's meat, it is said, is another man's poison, and likewise, what qualifies as a cost from some points of view is a benefit from other points of view. The cost of a car to a buyer is a benefit to the seller; the cost of drugs to users is a benefit to dealers; the cost of alcohol abuse to the nation is offset by the profits it generates for the manufacturers, transporters, and sellers of alcohol. The truth is, we really do not know with any certainty how many "preventable" deaths alcohol causes each year nor do we know with any certainty the overall costs (or benefits) to the nation. Shrill assertion is no substitute for compelling evidence.

To restate, about two-fifths of the US population never drinks anything; another two-fifths drink but in acceptable moderation; yet another tenth drinks more than they should; and the final tenth does so often enough that they could be considered to have a drinking problem. Given that alcohol is legal everywhere, widely available, and relatively inexpensive, it is hard to see the overall pattern of consumption as gluttonous.

As well, the medical establishment has finally begun to realize what has been obvious to health researchers for decades, namely, that the moderate consumption of alcohol (a drink or two a day, about what the average American male drinker drinks) is *good* for your health. From the NIAAA flyer referenced in note 6,

> Moderate alcohol consumption may have beneficial effects on health. These include decreased risk for heart disease and mortality due to heart disease, decreased risk of ischemic stroke (in which the arteries to the brain become narrowed or blocked, resulting in reduced blood flow), and decreased risk of diabetes.

But the urge to nag runs deep. In the very next paragraph we are told: "Expanding our understanding of the relationship between moderate alcohol consumption and potential health benefits remains a challenge, and although there are positive effects, alcohol may not benefit everyone who drinks moderately."

What about drugs other than alcohol? The National Institute on Drug Abuse has a flyer, *Drug Facts,* that states the essentials as of 2013 (NIDA, 2015). In the month prior to the 2013 National Survey on Drug Use and Health (NSDUH), 9.4% of the population 12 or older had used an illicit drug (up from about 5.8% in 2007). The lion's share (about 80%) of illicit drug use was of marijuana, followed by misuse of prescription drugs. Things like cocaine, hallucinogens, and heroin were used only by very small percentages.

The uptick from 2007 was virtually all in marijuana use. Usage of everything else has been constant or declining. In the interim, of course, recreational use of marijuana was legalized in Colorado, Washington, Oregon, and Alaska and decriminalized in 13 other states, and medical use of marijuana was legalized in several more. Outright prohibition of marijuana for any purpose now pertains in only eleven states, although "pot" still seems to be illegal under federal law. Thus, an increasing share of marijuana consumption is not *illicit* but rather legal, at least insofar as the states are concerned. Then too, as of 2015, a majority of 58% believes that marijuana should be legalized. Without doubt, these trends are linked to the increased use of pot "in the last month."

Compared to the rest of the world, and based on survey data about *lifetime* use, Americans are more likely to try illegal drugs than pretty much everyone else (Degenhardt et al., 2008). About 42% of Americans say they have tried pot at least once. In comparison, only 20% of Netherlanders have done so despite that nation's world-renowned tolerance of such things. We also rate number one in the world in the percentage who have tried cocaine (16% vs about 2% everywhere else). Even in Colombia, only 4% have ever tried the stuff. More Americans have also smoked cigarettes at some point in their lives (75%) compared to about half in most of the European nations. Finally, we also come in first in prescription painkiller abuse, but lag behind the Middle East and Southwest Asia in opiate use.

A key point with respect to all abusable substances is that the rate of abuse or addiction is "quite low compared to the overall rate of use, which is an inconvenient truth for drug warriors" (Szalavitz, 2014). Cigarettes may be the exception here, but in all other cases, clinically significant abuse is rare relative to overall use. Three-fifths of the adult population drink at least occasionally but the ranks of AUD number fewer than a tenth. And while maybe a tenth of the US population uses illicit drugs of some sort monthly, the number in treatment for drug disorders is infinitesimally smaller. If the American fondness for drugs was truly *gluttonous*, diagnosable abusers would presumably be much more numerous than they are.

The Social Value of Gluttony

On the surface, gluttony would appear to be pure evil, and like pornography, devoid of social value (but see the next chapter). But even superficially, gluttony keeps the American food business booming and the production and sale of alcohol profitable. In the US alone, total retail sales of food amount to more than $5 trillion a year; grocery store sales alone, to about $600 billion. Alcohol sales, likewise, amount to more than $200 billion annually. How much these numbers might fall if all gluttony disappeared is anyone's guess, but my guess is that this would stimulate a pretty serious recession in the food and alcohol industries.[7]

Priscilla Parkhurst Ferguson (2004) has taken rather a longer view on the social value of gluttony. She references the novel *Gourmandise* by Eugene Sue (one of several novels in the series by Sue on the seven deadly sins). While all the deadly sins have social value, gluttony is accorded "the pivotal role." The *gourmandise* develops a "refined and disordered love of good food" (p. 90) and thus develops "experiments in sensuality." From this, or so Ferguson argues, comes the entire French gastronomic invention, the French cuisine so beloved around the world as the finest expression of the culinary arts. No gluttony, no *gourmandise,* no French culinary tradition, no Julia Child. One shudders at the thought.

Ferguson also revisits the "monumental dictionary-encyclopedia" of Pierre Larousse (published between 1866 and 1879). That work devotes two columns of discussion to *gourmand* and *gourmandise* and four columns to *gastronomie.* *Gastronomie* is a moral force, a model of discipline and control. The *gourmand,* Ferguson tells us, "has only a belly, whereas the *gastronome* has a brain" (p. 91) – a brain devoted to pursuit of the "useful and agreeable, the beautiful and the good...No one blushes to be a *gastronome* anymore." At the same time, no one would want to pass as a gourmand or a drunk. But the line between sensitive appreciation of the good things life has to offer and sheer debauchery is awfully thin.

What about Temperance?

The word temperance calls to mind the Temperance Movement, the 19th- and early 20th-century moral crusade against the consumption of alcohol. Temperance imagery includes most dramatically the flinty Carrie Nation attacking bars and taverns with a hatchet, thoroughly convinced of the evils of alcohol and of the righteousness of the temperance cause. Today's temperance enthusiasts no longer attack their prey with hatchets but they also give no quarter to Carrie Nation in their righteous indignation. Their weapons are moral disapproval and public opprobrium. They are most easily recognized by their fealty to the mantra of *zero tolerance,* a mantra that has wormed its way very deeply into modern American culture. In the process, they have turned "temperance" from a holy virtue to a counter-productive form of aggressive nagging about anything of which someone might disapprove.

The concept of "zero tolerance" was popularized in a 1994 report by George Kelling and collaborators to the New York Police Department concerning what the NYPD could do about "squeegeeing," the then-common habit of homeless men jumping out at stoplights, squeegeeing windshields and then asking to be paid for the service. The behavior had become widespread and annoying enough that then-candidate-for-Mayor Rudy Giuliani made the "squeegee men" a symbol for the deteriorating quality of life in the city. The subsequent no-holds-barred crackdown effectively ended the practice. As one of the squeegee guys put it,

> Now the police drop out of the sky, harass us from behind our backs and arrest us. They want us off welfare. They don't give us a job, and now a man can't hustle for a living no more. One way or another we've got to make a living.[8]

Giuliani, of course, promoted the squeegee man problem as symbolic of what had happened in liberal New York with its famous tolerance of practically all deviant behavior, regardless of its effect on the quality of life, and he also took Kelling's zero-tolerance recommendations, soon elevated to what became known as the "broken windows" theory of crime, as the all-purpose solution. Soon enough, the city came to have zero tolerance for graffiti "artists," zero tolerance for street walkers and hustlers, zero tolerance for drug dealers, vandals, loud noisy bars, drinking in public, and eventually even smoking, trans fats, and sugary soft drinks. Zero tolerance rapidly swept through American alcohol and drug policy-making circles and also found a comfortable reception in the nation's schools, which soon enough had zero-tolerance policies in place for school dress codes, alcohol and drugs, firearms, bullying, truancy, plagiarism, expressions of sexuality, and a host of other indiscretions, all of them evidently unforgivable.

Zero tolerance is based on the old saw, "Give 'em an inch and they'll take a mile." If moderately offensive behavior X is tolerated, miscreants will swiftly come up with slightly more offensive behavior X + 1, then X + 2 and X + 3 until someone finally screws up the courage to say this has got to stop. But by then, a great deal of offensive behavior has become normative and institutionalized. The most effective way to intervene is to nip it in the bud, that is, to tolerate nothing that might lead to an escalation of offensiveness.

The "broken windows" theory of crime is only an extension of this logic. Seriously run-down crime-generating neighborhoods often begin with a few broken windows. Next a few boarded up and abandoned houses appear, then dealers come onto the scene vending their wares openly on street corners, and on into the abyss of urban decay. Thus, general disorder, incivility, and community decay are causally linked to the occurrence of more and more serious crimes. The time to intervene is at the beginning, when the only signs of decay are a few broken windows. Giuliani and many others have credited this theory with turning New York from a festering behavioral sink into the livable city it is today.

Today, zero tolerance is often invoked in the face of *any* deviation from what is considered proper or acceptable behavior. Such deviations receive swift and automatic punishment, sometimes mild but often Draconian. No discretion is given in the act of enforcement, no allowances for extenuating circumstances are made, and no consideration of culpability is relevant. Deviations from what is considered proper are simply forbidden. Improper behavior, in turn, is anything felt to be offensive, risky, dangerous, or deviant. It is the preferred public morality of the extremely straight-laced, the Temperance Movement reincarnate.

Does "zero tolerance" work? Not very well, it seems. The question has been studied most extensively in schools (although, admittedly, even the school literature is pretty sparse and unpersuasive). In 2008, the American Psychological Association (APA) convened a task force to review the literature on the effects of zero tolerance in schools and concluded:

> there are surprisingly few data that could directly test the assumptions of a zero tolerance approach to school discipline, and the data that are available tend to contradict those assumptions. Moreover, zero tolerance policies may negatively affect the relationship of education with juvenile justice and appear to conflict to some degree with current best knowledge concerning adolescent development.
>
> *(APA, 2008)*

The APA report was devastating. Zero tolerance policies have *not* made schools any safer, punishments for offenses have *not* gotten more consistent, suspension of offending students does *not* create more favorable learning environments, overall student behavior has *not* improved, schoolyard bullying has *not* diminished, parents and students do *not* support the policy in overwhelming numbers, zero tolerance has fallen most heavily on the shoulders of black and Latino students, and many alternative and more effective punishment strategies are available. It is hard to imagine a firmer indictment of a policy that has, for example, had students expelled from school for throwing snowballs, farting in class, bringing epi pens or cough syrup to school, or planting an innocent little kiss on a classmate's cheek. There is also a huge and so far inconclusive debate within criminology whether Broken Windows works as a crime reduction strategy or not. Many employers have experienced employee backlash at zero tolerance policies in the workplace. And zero tolerance has been largely abandoned in alcohol and drug treatment circles, where more and more practitioners have come to accept that relapse is an inherent part of recovery. According to the American Bar Association, "many lawyers say zero tolerance-like policies have outlived their usefulness and may in fact be doing more harm than good."[9]

The lack of evidence for effectiveness has apparently not, however, begun to thin the ranks of the zero-tolerance moral entrepreneurs. The philosopher Frank Furedi (2011) writes, "…moral entrepreneurs advocate a policy of zero tolerance towards their targets." As examples, one might cite the fate of skeptics who question human responsibility for global warming, of carnivores who steadfastly refuse the admonitions of their vegan and vegetarian friends, of smokers even when they agreeably sneak out to the back yard to indulge their destructive habit.

> The language used to condemn the heretic typically appeals to a sacred authority that must not be questioned. According to this model, 'overwhelming evidence' serves as the equivalent of revealed religious truth. Those who dare question that [truth] are guilty of blasphemy.
>
> *(2011: 174)*

One cannot help but note the similarities between today's zero tolerance entrepreneurs and the original Temperance personality, Carrie Nation, who described herself as "a bulldog running along at the feet of Jesus, barking at what He doesn't like." Like many others before and since, Ms. Nation claimed a divine ordination to promote her chosen cause.

I spent more than 20 years teaching my children to be tolerant in all things, and just about the time I succeeded and they were ready to launch into adulthood, along comes "zero tolerance" and the absolute moral certainty that accompanies it. So let's get real: Zero tolerance is *intolerance,* and intolerance is never a good thing. Today's temperance, I fear, is no longer the wise recommendation to seek moderation in all things but rather a gluttony of moral disapproval dispensed indiscriminately to all who deviate from Puritanical norms.

Notes

1 Mariani's account apparently relies on a 1934 biography written by one Parker Morell (published 17 years after Brady died). Kamp (2008) has critically reviewed Morell's original account and concludes that it is seriously exaggerated. Still, then-contemporary accounts of Brady's meals leave no doubt that he was a seriously gluttonous trencherman.
2 Visual evidence of the gluttony of the condemned can be found at www.buzzfeed. com/alanwhite/12-pictures-of-death-row-prisoners-last-meals#.upv1BAyB.
3 5'8" = 1.72 meters, the square of which is 2.983. 200 pounds = 90.7 kilograms. 90.7/2.983 = 30.1.
4 See www.reddit.com/r/fatlogic/comments/23z5ce/embalming_the_obese/.
5 The Goliath Casket Company (Motto: Serving the needs of the oversized casket community for over 25 years) has a very informative website with step-by-step instructions on what to look out and prepare for when planning funeral services for the morbidly obese. See www.oversizecasket.com/funeralprofessional.html.
6 The figures for AUD come from an undated flyer, Alcohol Facts and Statistics, distributed by the National Institute on Alcohol Abuse and Alcoholism. See also Esser et al., 2014.
7 All numbers via *Statista: The Statistics Portal (www.statista.com).*
8 www.nytimes.com/1994/02/07/nyregion/study-suggests-it-is-easy-to-banish-squeegee-men.html.
9 www.abajournal.com/magazine/article/schools_start_to_rethink_zero_tolerance_policies/.

3
LUST

The Sexualization of Society

Lust comes in many forms. Ordinary language recognizes blood lust, wanderlust, lust for freedom, for liberty, for food and drink, for power, and even a lust to kill. The lust for money is greed; the lust for food and drink is gluttony; so we have already visited lust in these pages. Here in Chapter 3, we consider lust in the more limited sense of crushing libidinal urges, overwhelming sexual desire, and the lust for carnal knowledge. As Mary Eberstadt has observed,

> Say what you like about anger, sloth, envy and the rest of the low-tech capital vices: They're not really what most of us first reach for in that grab bag [of sin]. No, we all know who's the real preening diva among these serpents, just whose big topaz eyes paralyze us fastest. Let's face it: Lust is everyone's secret favorite Deadly Sin, the 'it' vice of the capital list.[1]

Journals of Christian commentary go on and on about lust – what it is, how to avoid it, how lust differs from love, from fornication, and from simple sexual desire. Often, lust is considered the equivalent of adultery. President Jimmy Carter, as strait-laced a man as the 20th century ever produced, confessed in a *Playboy* interview that he had "looked on a lot of women with lust" and had "committed adultery in my heart many times." Evidently, at least in the minds of many pious men, you can commit the "favorite deadly sin" without the benefit of intercourse or sexual gratification. Mere thoughts apparently suffice.

Or maybe not. Carter's comment derives from a passage in Matthew 5: 27–28, quoting Jesus: "You have heard that it was said, 'Do not commit adultery.' But I tell you that anyone who looks at a woman lustfully has already committed adultery with her in his heart" (from the New International Version). It has been pointed out that the Greek word usually translated as "lust" in this passage happens to be the same word used to translate the Hebrew word for "covet."[2]

Thus, the passage only restates the Tenth Commandment: "You shall not covet your neighbor's house; you shall not covet your neighbor's wife, nor his male servant, nor his female servant, nor his ox, nor his donkey, nor anything that is your neighbor's." The common interpretation, that lust is the equivalent of adultery, is therefore wrong. Contrary to Carter's implication, seeing a woman (or man) and finding yourself attracted to her (or him), which is generally OK, and in any case, unavoidable, is *not* the same as actively seeking an illicit liaison (which is true lust and therefore sinful).

Alas, actively seeking illicit liaisons is pretty common behavior for both men and women and not infrequently *the* reason why marriages break up. So if you agree that broken marriages are a bad thing (not everyone does), then they must be counted as one cost to society of unbridled lust. Thus, it is with infidelity and adultery that we begin.

Infidelity, Adultery, and Divorce

The stereotypical divorce scenario is that two initially loving couples find themselves "growing apart," developing separate interests, facing the loss of sexual attraction, and finding themselves bored with each other, until at some point in the process they mutually agree that the marriage is no longer working and decide to end it, citing "irreconcilable differences" in an agreed-upon no-fault divorce. And surely, this is how some marriages end. But a surprising percentage end in what Angus Campbell called "brusque terminations" – where one party actively seeks termination "with the other not feeling any strong dissatisfaction with the relationship until the news is broken" (1976: 101). In most of these cases, the "brusque terminators" are driven to their marriage-ending announcements because they have entered into "illicit liaisons" with another person.

To be sure, hard data on the point are scarce. But there is a website that actively archives divorce and infidelity statistics.[3] The site is bereft of citations or references but the numbers found there generally ring true. So taking this to be reliable information, we learn:

- The infidelity rate has shot up dramatically in the last 25 years. (Reason: More women are in the labor force where they can meet potential sex partners.)
- Cheating on the spouse spikes initially at the end of the first year of marriage.
- Birth of the first child generates another infidelity spike.
- The "seven year itch" is real. Infidelity spikes again between the fifth and seventh years of marriage.
- A final spike comes at the mid-life crisis, once the children are grown, the nest is empty, and middle-aged eyes begin to wander.

There are interesting gender differences in infidelity. Men cheat on their wives because they seek sexual variation and need to prove to themselves that they can still "do it." For men, infidelity is sexual adventure. Women cheat on their husbands to establish an emotional connection, to compensate for the lack of emotional satisfaction provided by their husbands. For women, infidelity is an emotional experiment.

Something in the vicinity of one in five divorces (and possibly an even higher percentage: Some studies put the number at more than one in four) occur primarily because of adulterous liaisons by the husband, wife, or both. Surveys show that about 22% of married men and 14% of married women have cheated on their spouses at least once. (Since these numbers come from direct questions to survey respondents, it can be assumed that they err on the low side.) Among all men and women, whether married, single, divorced, separated, or widowed, more than a third admit to having an affair at some point in their lives with a co-worker; an identical percentage admit to affairs while on business trips; about one in six admits to having an affair with their spouse's sibling (a sister-in-law or brother-in-law). Astonishingly, 2%–3% of all children (some studies have said as many as 10%) are conceived in adulterous acts and are unknowingly raised by men other than their biological fathers. And while majorities of 90% and up think that extramarital sex is wrong, far fewer (around 60%) say it should be punished as a crime.

As an aside, the US is by no means unique in the rate at which married people go around boinking folks other than their spouses. Betzig (1989) studied the "causes of conjugal dissolution" in 186 different cultures, nations, and societies. Results showed that dissolutions following adultery or infidelity had been reliably reported in at least 88, which "makes adultery a significantly more common cause than any other except sterility" (p. 658). Predictably, adulterous wives cause unions to dissolve more frequently than adulterous husbands. Globally, it seems to be more or less expected, and, therefore, tolerated, that men will cheat on their wives, but wives, almost universally, are expected to be faithful to their husbands.

After many years of continuous increase, the divorce rate has finally levelled off, but extramarital affairs remain the most common precipitating incident. According to a 2004 study, [4] as many as 27% of all divorces (in America) are the result of infidelity – well ahead of family stresses and strains (18%) and domestic abuse and violence (17%). In a related study (discussed in the same source), more than 25% of women cited their husbands' infidelity as a factor in their divorce, more than twice the rate for men. Indeed, men were more likely to blame their in-laws for their divorce (12%) than their spouse's extramarital dalliances (11%).

One might hope that these infidelities at least lead to happier and more stable remarriages, but no. Sexual adventurers rarely marry the lovers who caused the breakup, and when they do, the result is even more rarely a happy marriage. The grass may very well *look* greener on the other side of the fence, but it usually isn't. It's the same dull shade of brown.

Two related factors may be implicated in the (apparently) rising rates of infidelity: Internet hook-up sites, which make finding paramours easy; and Internet pornography, which may well stimulate interest in these sexual adventures in the first place. We come back to the issue of porn later in this chapter, but there is some evidence (from a survey of divorce attorneys) that porn-enthusiast partners are being mentioned more and more frequently as a reason for divorce. As one attorney put it, "If there's dissatisfaction in the existing relationship, the Internet is an easy way for people to scratch the itch."

Divorce rates vary sharply over the age of the marriage. The first five years seem to be most critical (e.g., Nock et al., 2008). And while financial troubles and emotional immaturity are the root causes of most early divorces, marital infidelity is also a common cause. The younger people are when they enter into a marriage, the more likely they are to leave it.

In sum, illicit sexual liaisons frequently cause marital dissolutions, along with other factors. Although specifically mentioned in the Ten Commandments as a big-time No-No, coveting "your neighbor's wife" or other wives (and husbands) in general is obviously pretty common and, we should add, pretty devastating to the wives (and husbands) who are left behind.

Lust vs. Love

One line of psychoanalytical reasoning attempts to explain extramarital infidelities as the result of the "love-lust" dilemma (e.g. Frommer, 2007; Resnick, 2012). In Resnick's version, the dilemma is this: "As the emotional attachment in an intimate relationship grows, the sexual desire often dwindles, yet without desire, the relationship is at risk of failing." This, Resnick argues, explains all sorts of modern problems – sexless marriages, low desire, infidelity, compulsive use of pornography, chronic marital conflict, and marital boredom. The dilemma manifests itself in the common marital break-up line, "Yes, I still love you, but I am no longer *in love* with you." Translation: You no longer give me the hots. Oh, and by the way, someone else does!

Psychoanalytic types have a field day with the internal struggles between lust and love. One such (Frommer, 2007) writes of the "psychic tensions and potential sources of breakdown present in combining lust with love." In the same article, Frommer proposes that

> erotic experience is predicated on an experience of otherness within the self.... The dampening or deadening of desire in long-term relationships may be understood, counterintuitively, not as a failure of the integration of lust with love but as a breakdown of the normative dissociative processes on which the emergence of lust depends.

> *(2008: 639)*

This seems to be saying (who can say for sure?) that as couples grow closer emotionally, "otherness" diminishes and lust disappears.

It is true that both sexual desire and sexual frequency decline with age, often precipitously (Karraker et al., 2011). And yet a recent survey of persons over age 50 done by the AARP found that 31% of over-50 couples have sex several times a week; 28% have sex a couple times a month; and 8% have sex about once a month (Northrup et al., 2013). That adds up to two-thirds of over-50 married couples who still "get it on." As for the one-third who don't, surprisingly large percentages report that they are happy nonetheless. Assuming love and not lust is what keeps marriages together for many decades, and that lust is adequately indexed by the frequency of intercourse, it seems that a fair number of oldsters manage their love-lust "psychic tensions" pretty adequately after all, in spite of psychoanalytic theory suggesting that this is not possible.

There are, of course, gender differences in these matters. In general, men of all ages say they want more sex than they get. Women, in contrast, say they get all the sex they want but not enough emotional support and connection. It was ever thus. It is also worth mentioning that sexual activity declines with age for reasons other than diminishing lust – various endocrinological and hormonal changes associated with aging, sexual and erectile dysfunctions, menopause, widowhood, and on through a dreary list.

The definitive statement on sexuality over the life course is Waite (2015). Recent studies reviewed by Waite suggest that about a third of adults ages 57–85 have been sexually inactive at least for the last year. Still, that leaves two-thirds whose sexuality, although perhaps diminished, has not yet been extinguished. Continued sexuality in old age depends critically on the physical ability to engage in sex, although in such matters, it is the ability of the husband that matters most. The onset of chronic physical disease certainly depresses sexual interest (and ability), and at some point in the progression of disease and disability, people come grudgingly to the conclusion that "their sexual relationships with their spouses are finished. For many of these individuals, this transition marks the end of their partnered sexual lives." At that point, "older adults in long-standing marriages may fall back on a lifetime of shared activities, shared children, and memories of an active sex life in the face of declining physical or cognitive function of one or both partners."

What all this says about the "love-lust" dilemma is not clear. What is clear is that many people who have been married to their spouses for decades still manage to find enough lust in their hearts to sustain a reasonably active sexual existence. Lust, that is, does not always fade even as a relationship emotionally matures. It is also clear that those who do sustain an active sex life have happier marriages and happier lives overall than those who do not. There are, it seems, many people in their seventies and even eighties who still get aroused watching their spouses undress, and are still capable of acting on their arousal, even if they have "been there, done that" a thousand, nay, many thousands of times before. As my father was fond of saying once he was in his seventies, whenever an attractive woman would turn his head, "Ain't no fire in the grate, son, but there's still a little steam in the boiler…"

Falling Birth Rates

If we were looking for evidence that the advanced societies could use a healthy infusion of lust, we'd need look no further than at present day birth rates, which have plummeted throughout the West. Have we come, collectively, to the point where there's no fire left in the grate *and* no steam in the boiler?

The declining birth rate is real enough, and pretty near universal (in the advanced societies). Demographers put the fertility "replacement value" at about 2.1–2.2 children per fecund woman. No advanced industrial society is currently reproducing at or above this replacement rate. At present, the US birth rate is about 1.87 children per fecund woman and most Western European rates are as low or lower. The birth rate in Hong Kong is 0.98; in Italy, 1.29; in Russia, 1.39; in Canada, 1.61, to cite just a few examples. More and more nations are therefore enacting pronatalist policies to encourage women to bear more kids:

- In Singapore, whose birth rate is among the lowest in the world (currently 1.07), the official motto is now "Three or More!" (This has replaced "Stop at Two," which was the policy from WW II up until recently.) Singapore even has a government matchmaking agency, the Social Development Unit, to encourage Singaporeans to hook up and get it on. (Hip locals say that SDU stands for Single, Desperate, Ugly.)
- In Russia, women who give birth to a second child receive a lump sum payment amounting to US $9,200. Polish women are also paid for having additional children, although not as handsomely.
- In much of Western Europe, there are pronatalist incentives that are coupled with special welfare state provisions. Family leave policies are generous almost everywhere, and government income subsidies increase when additional children are born.
- Australia (birth rate: 1.76) announced its new pronatalist policies with the slogan, "One for you. One for him. And one for the nation!" Each additional Aussie child brings its parents a payment of about US $3,000.
- According to one report, the Taiwanese government is pushing pornography as a possible antidote to the island nation's extremely low birth rate, apparently on the theory that more porn = more arousal = more copulation = more Taiwanese babies. Elsewhere (for example, in nearby Japan), increasing consumption of pornography is seen as partly responsible for the falling birth rate, on the theory that more porn = more masturbation = less copulation = fewer babies.

• Japan's birth rate is so low (1.3) and its life expectancy so long that soon enough, the entire nation will have the demographic profile of a large retirement community. According to one estimate (probably exaggerated, but it drives home the point), by 2040 Japan will have as many centenarians as newborns! To combat low fertility, the Japanese government has done large surveys of population attitudes toward sex. Among the findings: About a quarter of all Japanese women think that sex is "bothersome." Half the population has not had sex in the past month. One in five men said they were too tired to have sex after work. Almost half of young Japanese women (45% of those ages 16–24) are either "not interested in" or actually "despise" sexual contact of any sort. All this adds up to what has been called Japan's libido crisis. One local TV personality has proposed a "handsome tax" to penalize good looking men and make it easier for ugly men to find mates and get laid.

One explanation for falling birth rates throughout the West has been the advent of what is called the "porn generation," a generation of Internet-addicted young people whose sexual fantasies find release in freely available Internet porn sites and video games involving highly sexualized anime characters. In one rendition of the theory, "The limitless sexual license of the porn generation is not without consequence. It leads to spiritual desensitization, emotional removal, and lack of commitment" (Shapiro, 2005).

There are, of course, other more prosaic and probably more telling accounts of why birth rates are falling. Increased housing costs and the more general increase in the cost of living have come more and more to require two incomes, so around the world, two-earners households are on the increase. The liberation of women from the shackles of tradition has made careers more attractive and traditional mothering and housewifery less attractive. Delayed marriages, delayed fertility, smaller families, and increased voluntary childlessness have been the result. These days, women have many more ways to assert their identities than by giving birth. One hundred or even 50 years ago, this was not so true. So economic and social changes are probably more responsible for declining birth rates than the alleged "libido crisis."

On the other hand, perhaps there is more to the libido crisis than initially meets the eye. Drugs to treat erectile dysfunction (ED) have only been on the market since 1998 and these drugs now generate about $4 billion in sales annually through about 10 million annual prescriptions. (The market did take a hit in 2006 when many insurance companies stopped covering ED drugs.) Big Pharma is also actively seeking a drug to treat female sexual dysfunction ("female Viagra"). As many as 20 million American men suffer from ED and they consume ED drugs so they can have sex successfully. In some cases, this is the only way men can get an erection, but in other cases, ED drugs are used to get erections on demand. Maybe Viagra is best understood as lust in a bottle.

Pornography

There was a time when pornography mainly meant "dirty" magazines hidden away on high closet shelves or decks of cards with nude women on them, often coyly posed so as not to reveal "too much." Porn movies also existed at that time, of course, but required projectors for viewing, which therefore could not be done surreptitiously. And there were a few porn movie theaters around that only hard-core perverts ever visited. Pornography was very much an underground industry and pornographers and porn performers were the moral equivalent of drug dealers ("pushers") who sold heroin to elementary school children. The entire porn industry had a very high yuck factor.

Today, pornography is big business. One study discussed by Braswell (2016) estimated that the adult film industry accounted for $13 billion in revenue in 2014, compared to Hollywood's $8 billion, an astonishing comparison. Studies of porn consumption patterns show that somewhere between half and *all* adult men and somewhere between a third and 80% of all adult women consume porn at least occasionally. Porn stars such as Jenna Jameson, Sasha Gray, and Ron Jeremy have become cultural icons, personages that young people seek to emulate. (They have also become incredibly wealthy: Jenna Jameson's net worth is estimated at about $30 million.) Too, the line between porn and nonporn has nearly dissolved. Witness, for example, the popularity (and the reasons for the popularity) of personages such as Paris Hilton or the Kardashian sisters, omnipresent stars in what has been described as "jiggle TV."

Porn has become ubiquitous in Western culture. As an indicator of porn's pervasiveness, I recently googled "free porn" and got 237 million "hits" in 0.23 seconds. Two more clicks and I had a porn movie playing on my iPhone. So while it is an exaggeration to say that "these days" porn is everywhere, it is certainly anywhere you want it to be.

How did we get from then to now? How did porn become mainstream? Precise dating of major cultural transformations is often difficult, but in this case, we look to December, 1953, and the publication of the inaugural issue of *Playboy* magazine, whose first issue featured nude photos of Marilyn Monroe and sold about 50,000 copies. Many commentators including the US Postal Service decried *Playboy* and the more general erosion of traditional moral values that it seemed to represent, but none were successful in stemming the magazine's instant popularity. The post office's efforts to deny *Playboy* second-class mailing privileges were struck down by the courts in 1955 and from that point forward, the magazine and all it stood for, including living the good life and viewing glossy three-page foldouts of voluptuous naked women, entered the American mainstream. Coy poses that only titillate were replaced by full frontal nude shots with nothing hidden. Soon thereafter, young girls began to aspire to become *Playboy* centerfolds, and with that, porn established a beach head in the culture that has yet to be turned back.

An interesting footnote to the *Playboy* story is that in October, 2015, after 62 years of publication, the magazine announced that it would stop publishing nude photos. The company's CEO Scott Flanders explained, "The onslaught of Internet pornography has made the nude images in Playboy passé. That battle has been fought and won. You're now one click away from every sex act imaginable – for free."

Quite a bit of ink and billable attorney time have been spilt debating whether *Playboy* and its ilk are or are not "real" pornography, a debate that need not concern us here. All I want to establish is that the lasciviousness required for porn to flourish made *Playboy* a highly profitable venture and that pandering to that same lasciviousness with more and more sexually explicit material has been a nearly fail-safe route to fame and fortune ever since. Sure, the base urges that pornography satisfies, whether "soft" porn or "hard," have existed forever. What *Playboy* and its ilk accomplished was to make those urges and their gratification socially acceptable.

The best recent summary of research on pornography is Hald and Malamuth (2015).[5] As indicated above, among men, consumption of pornography may well be nearly universal; studies report percentages between 50% and 100%. For women, the range is 30%–86%. Although the gender difference (men more likely than women to consume porn) has been reported in nearly all studies, female interest in pornography is surprisingly widespread. Men also "use pornography more frequently, spend more time on pornography consumption, be exposed to pornography at a younger age, and use pornography more often during masturbation" (2015: 614). A final gender difference of note is that men tend to watch porn alone, whereas women tend to watch with their sexual or dating partners.

Poulsen et al. (2013) studied the effects of porn consumption on the sexual quality of husbands' and wives' sex lives. They found that husbands' porn consumption lowered sexual quality for both husbands and wives whereas female consumption increased female sexual quality (but had no effect on males). Cause and effect, however, are difficult to sort out. Do men turn to porn when their sex lives are deficient, or does male use of porn reduce the quality of conjugal sex? The authors also report (as have many others) that female porn use was relatively low compared to men, although given the positive effects of female porn use on sexual satisfaction, perhaps it should not be.

A similar conclusion has been reported by Perry (2016), who studied the long-term (six-year) effects of porn consumption on the reported marital quality of husbands and wives in a nationally representative sample. In general, higher frequencies of porn consumption in 2006 significantly predicted *lower* levels of marital quality in 2012. Further analysis revealed that the effect was concentrated among men and most notable among men who viewed pornography once a day or more. As for the women, "Wives who view pornography more frequently report higher marital quality than those who view it less frequently or not at all." The suggestion, ironically, is that porn makes men lose interest in their wives while it makes wives more interested in their husbands. As the Macedonian Goce Smilevski put it, "There is no justice in this world."

One study (Edelman, 2009) monitored Internet usage patterns and reported that 36% of all users (regardless of age, gender, etc.) visited at least one adult entertainment site per month. Among that 36%, the average number of visits (per month) was 7.7, with each visit lasting about 12 minutes (on average).

Most pornography is "primarily of a non-violent nature," although in porn, what's violent and what's not is highly ambiguous. A content analysis of 50 adult film videos (all on the best-seller list for 2004–2005) showed that a clear majority featured some sort of aggressive behavior (spanking and choking were most common) but true violence as that term is normally understood (threatening with a weapon, hitting with a closed fist, torture, mutilation) was very rare (Bridges et al., 2010). To be sure, there is plenty of violent porn available for anyone who seeks it out.

Much of the debate about pornography focuses on the effects of porn consumption on things such as attitudes about violence against women, more general sexist attitudes, sexual permissiveness, and sexual behavior. Evidence from many sources converges on the conclusion that porn consumers tend to embrace attitudes supporting violence against women, sexist attitudes more generally (although here the evidence is weaker), and sexually permissive attitudes. Porn consumption is also associated with frequency of masturbation, lower age at first intercourse, number of lifetime sex partners, engaging in oral, anal, and group sex, and contracting STDs. Porn consumers are also more sexually aggressive than non-consumers. On the other side of this coin, porn consumption has also been shown to improve sex life, increase knowledgeability about sex, expand sexual horizons, and promote sexual experimentation, along with other benefits.

Concerning potential benefits of porn, we must also consider the arguments of Sean Braswell in his engaging polemic, "How pornography saved civilization." Braswell's fundamental argument is that the demands of the pornography industry "have fundamentally transformed communications technology, giving rise to a connected world in which censoring, undemocratic regimes like China find it increasingly difficult to control the thoughts of their citizens." In sum, the "desire to consume pornography with more privacy and less effort has been a driving force behind communications technology" over the centuries and certainly here in the 21st century.

Erotica has always been a driving force behind creativity and commerce. The famous cave wall paintings of Lascaux (France) and elsewhere throughout Europe include fabulously detailed sketches of deer, bison, and human hunters but are also replete with equally detailed images of breasts, buttocks, and gargantuan penises. Many of the rooms in the houses of ancient Pompeii are also festooned with frescoes depicting every imaginable sexual act and a great deal of phallic architecture and adornment. In one dig, archaeologists discovered an 18" terra cotta phallus protruding from a wall with the inscription "*Hie habitat felicitas*" (here dwells happiness). Phallic symbols can also be seen on public fountains, tombstones – indeed, pretty much everywhere in Pompeii. And this sort of pornography was not found just in Rome (or Greece) but around the world – in Asia, Africa, and everywhere else.

Alas, as Braswell points out, this sort of porn requires "a personal visit from the would-be porn consumer." The quest for private, easily consumable porn drove the evolution of communications technology from cave art forward to the present day. Gutenberg's printing press

> may have produced more prayer books than pornographic engravings, but it proved that an industry devoted to porn creation could thrive and that technology in turn could influence porn by lowering the costs of entry to both consumers and creators.

The biggest step forward (for porn) was the invention of photography, the pornographic potential of which was "immediately recognized" by both producers and consumers. By the mid-1980s, "adult" magazines had cornered 20% of the overall magazine market and porn films such as *Deep Throat* were grossing profits in the tens of millions.

Murray Webster has noted other indicators of the technology-porn linkage: Video cameras that could record images in near-dark conditions, making them ideal for folks who wanted to make home pornography, and Polaroid still cameras that made embarrassing trips to pick up photos at the drugstore unnecessary.

But the real influence of porn on communications technology came with the advent of video cassette recordings in the 1970s and thereafter. Early VCRs were expensive and clunky but offered hitherto unknown privacy, convenience and graphic sexuality to the porn consumer. By the late 70s, porn tapes made up *half* the total VCR market.

> Pay-per-view cable and satellite TV channels became widely available after pornographers introduced subscription services in hotels and digital networks. Similarly, pornographers were the pioneers behind Internet-streaming technology, peer-to-peer sharing and e-commerce functions like credit card verification and billing systems. Most important for the general public and all the film and television we now stream onto our computers, porn is responsible for growing bandwidth on the Internet. Even for those unfamiliar with the world of porn, according to Barss (2010), 'it is now easy to go online and be blissfully unaware that… the infrastructure that makes it possible to watch television… [and] all the other bandwidth-hogging… activities of the modern Internet, were created to serve the needs of the pornography industry.'

Modern communications technology, we are told, has given us instantaneous global information sharing, brought down authoritarian governments, thwarted censorship, promoted grassroots agitation, undermined tyranny and injustice, and created a truly global human community. Ironic as it may be,

> it is no exaggeration to say that pornography has played a key role in expanding democracy, free thought and everything that goes with the unfettered flow of information. If you want to change the world, it appears, you may want to consider holding off on the soldiers and lawmakers and send in the perverts and pornographers instead.

Porn and Religion

In 2014, a religious outfit called Proven Men Ministries undertook a nationwide study to examine porn consumption and addiction among Christian men.[6] Total sample size was a thousand, but the focus was on the 388 respondents who self-identified as "Christian men" in the survey. How do the porn behaviors of Christian men differ from those of men in general?

Answer: Not much. Nearly all Christian men (97%), like men in general, have viewed porn, most of them (78%) before they were 16 years old. Three-quarters view porn at least monthly; among those who claim to be "born again," the figure is still 65%. About two in five are on the porn sites "several times a week." Among young Christian men, more than one in three view porn daily and a like number confess that they have "an addiction" to porn. Many of these Christian porn consumers think that "perhaps you should view less pornography" but they watch it anyway. Also like men in general, Christian men prefer to watch porn on the Internet (60%), with television a distant second (12%) and magazines third (8%).

The Religious News Service (RNS)[7] commented on this study, somewhat sheepishly, that "the number of Christians viewing pornography virtually mirrors the national average," this even though the official position of conservative Christians is that "Porn is probably the greatest threat to the Church in its existence." Indeed, conservative Christian news outlets and journals of opinion quite regularly rail against pornography and sexuality and urge abstinence upon believers – so much so that one wonders if conservative Christians have not become obsessed with sex. The RNS concludes, rather sensibly, that while "American churches cannot bury their heads" in the face of the porn epidemic, "neither should they lose them."

There is also a large scholarly literature on religion and pornography. Despite the findings of the Proven Men Ministries survey, the general scholarly opinion is that religious people consume less porn than non-religious people (Poulson et al., 2013; Stack et al., 2004) and if the religious do consume porn, they feel guiltier about it…but do it anyway. Grubbs et al. (2015) report that religiosity is negatively related to admitted porn use in the prior six months (more religiosity = less porn) but among those who acknowledged porn use in the past six months, religiosity was unrelated to the number of hours porn was consumed. More religious porn users were also more likely to say that they had an "addiction to porn" even though they did not watch more (or less) hours of porn than the non-religious users. Moral disapproval of porn also depressed actual porn use and mediated the relationship between religiosity and porn consumption. In other words, religious men consume less porn largely because they morally disapprove of porn. But of course, even among very religious people who strongly disapprove of porn on moral grounds, a measurable percentage nonetheless visit the porn sites with some frequency.

Sexual Behavior

Just how lusty are the populations of the advanced Western democracies? How much sex of what sort do most people get? The sixties and seventies, we are told, brought forth a sexual revolution. Here a half-century or so later, has the revolution continued? Was it successful? For whom?

Our best summary of research on these issues is Iveniuk and Laumann (2015). As with the literature on porn use, the evidence on sexual practice is almost exclusively based on self-reports in surveys and as such, is prone to responses biases and various reporting errors. The situation today is far superior to that confronted in the 40s and 50s by Alfred Kinsey in the classic studies of sexual behavior, but is still far short of perfect.

A key point in the Iveniuk-Laumann review is that sexual scripts in the US are characterized by short periods of partner-seeking and partner turnover, "followed by longer periods of stable sexual partnerships." Most of an American's life, in short, is spent "off the market" in stable, monogamous relationships. Illicit dalliances, as we have seen, are not infrequent, but for most Americans most of the time, sex means sex with a spouse (or spouse equivalent) – not the sexual free-for-all that you might expect if you read *Playboy* more regularly than the *Archives of Sexual Behavior*.

The point is illustrated by data on the number of lifetime sexual partners. Over several surveys, on average, American women report having had *three* lifetime sexual partners, while American men report *six* (medians in both cases). Considered against the expectations of the so-called sexual revolution (which our authors admit has "slowed"), these numbers seem awfully small. But they are (about) the numbers reported in multiple surveys.

In general, one would expect the number of lifetime partners to be about the same for both men and women, and yet men report twice as many lifetime partners as women. Several possible explanations for the disparity come to mind. Gay male sexual encounters might be more numerous than lesbian encounters; the partner pool for men may be larger because of their greater geographical mobility; or men and women may have different definitions of what constitutes "having sex." (Men, for example, are more likely to consider manual stimulation to be "having sex" than women do.)[8]

As Iveniuk and Laumann summarize these findings, "Neither estimate confirms the stereotype that Americans are promiscuous, nor does it suggest that America, following the sexual revolution, completely eliminated scripted constraints on sexual expression." At one time, the "script" was that women would remain virgins until marriage and then be faithful in their marriages, which would yield a lifetime partnership count of just one. This ideal was (one assumes) only rarely attained, but it was the ideal notwithstanding. Today, after a half-century of sexual liberation, lifetime partnerships for women have jumped up – to three.

The basketballer Wilt Chamberlain once claimed to have slept with 20,000 women in his life. Assuming he started at age 15 (and was 55 when he made this claim), the math works out to 500 different women a year, or well more than one a day. The percentage of American men who claim twenty or more lifetime partners (one-thousandth of Wilt's alleged total) is on the order of one in six (among women, a mere 3%).

The preceding figures are for *lifetime* sexual partners. In the average year, the vast majority of the American population reports but one sex partner – the spouse (or committed partner). On average, "the modal frequency for sex for both men and women is only a few times a month, and sexual duration is only usually about 15–60 minutes per event." (10% of men and 14% of women said they had no sex at all in the past year.) Of course, there are lots of people on the promiscuous extremes of these distributions, but for the vast majority of us in the middle (plus or minus a standard deviation or two of the mean scores), the sexual revolution has passed us by. Thus,

> Thus the role of partnered sex in American respondents' lives is actually relatively small, as measured by time spent. Sexual partnership, of course, plays a much larger role in other respects, but sex is so heavily organized by sexual scripts that the real probability of a 'free-for-all' of sexual expression is surely very small.

Despite the "relatively small" role of sex in people's lives, most (58%) pronounce themselves "extremely" or at least "very happy" with their sex lives, another 29% are "generally satisfied," and only 13% are "unhappy." The most satisfied are those who report just a single partner (64% extremely or very happy with their sex life). Among those reporting five or more partners in the last year, only 47% are extremely or very happy – not much more sexual satisfaction than reported by those who have not had any sex at all in the past year – 41%. On the other hand, regardless of the number of partners, the proportion extremely or very happy increases the more sex they have, peaking at 69% among those who have sex two or three times a week.

In the majority, sex is vaginal intercourse – that was the case for about 95% of the most recent sexual episodes. But 79% of men and 73% of women have also received oral sex at some time in their lives, and equal numbers have given it. (Men find oral sex more appealing than women, 45%–29%. Men are also more turned on than women by watching their partners undress, 48%–29%.) Approximately 26% of men and 20% of women also report at least one life-time episode of anal sex. And 23% of women also report at least one lifetime experience of being forced to have sex.

There are also fairly large national differences in the level of sexual satisfaction. In general, sexual satisfaction is highest in the advanced Western democracies, middling in the Islamic and selected Asian countries, and low in East Asia (China, Japan, Thailand, Indonesia, and Taiwan).

Sexual behavior in the UK serves as a useful point of comparison with the US experience and very high quality data are available, specifically, the third National Survey of Sexual Attitudes and Lifestyles (NATSAL), main results of which were reported in six articles in *The Lancet* in November, 2013. These are large surveys done about every 10 years and, thus, give good indications of trends in sexual expression in the UK. Sample size for the most recent admin-istration was 15,162 people between the ages of 16 and 74.

Although sexual behavior in the two nations differ in small details, the broad outlines are very similar. Average age at first intercourse is about 16, roughly the same as in the previous survey but down from the initial NATSAL in 1990–1991. And Brits remain sexually active into their 70s, although (again, as in the US), the frequency of sex diminishes as people grow older. On average, people in the UK have sex just less than five times a month, or roughly once a week, about the same as (or a little more often than) in the US. Oddly, frequency declined from the 1999–2001 survey, even among those living with a partner.

Average lifetime sex partners for women ages 16–44 have more than dou-bled since the first survey, from a mean of 3.7 in 1990–1991 to a current average of 7.7. Among men in the same age group, the increase has been from 8.6 to 11.7, so the gender difference here has narrowed. Precise comparison is not possible, but these numbers seem higher than the numbers for the US. On the other hand, lifetime experience of oral sex is about the same (77% for men, 75% for women) but the numbers for anal sex in the last year are lower (17% for men, 15% for women). As in the US, the UK data also show increasing favorability toward same-sex unions but less tolerant attitudes about extramarital affairs.

One of the study's investigators commented thus:

> We tend to think that these days we live in an increasingly sexually liberal society, but the truth is far more complex. The context in which we have sex, and the variability of sexual lifestyles we have, continues to

change and, while we think of sex as being more widely available, with more explicit TV programmes and films and extended social networks, in fact, as a nation, we are having no more sex nowadays than we did a decade ago.

One important change in sexual behavior noted by Ivenuik and Laumann, at least in the US, is the emergence and institutionalization of so-called "hook-up culture," and here the definitive source is England and Ronen (2015). "'Hookups refer to casual sexual encounters that do not necessarily involve intercourse. While premarital sex has been common for decades, the hookup culture is distinctive in that sexual behavior is accepted in casual liaisons." Hook-up culture is mainly confined to college campuses.

Hooking up is a natural evolution in the long-term trend toward casual, premarital sex. Once considered taboo, about 90% of Americans born after 1960 had sex prior to marriage, even people whose religious beliefs are that premarital sex is morally wrong (Finer, 2007; Regnerus, 2007). But in the past, most premarital sexual encounters were between romantically involved persons. Not so hooking up, which often occurs "outside even the modicum of commitment entailed in a boyfriend-girlfriend romantic relationship." Casual sex, to be sure, is nothing new. One-night stands have existed forever. But this relatively new hookup culture "implies that casual sexual encounters are normatively accepted, at least within parts of the youth culture."

Hookups are sexual but do not necessarily entail intercourse. One study found that 76% of college seniors had "hooked up" while in college, with an average (median) frequency of occurrence of 5. Of these encounters, 31% involved just "making out," 16% involved genital manipulation, 15% involved oral sex, and the remainder involved intercourse.

Inevitably, there are gender inequalities in hooking up, which is considered OK for men but trashy for women. Men who are adept at hooking up are known among their peers as "players" or "studs," while women bear labels such as slut, tramp, or whore. Another gendered difference is that men are generally more interested in casual sex with large numbers of partners, whereas women prefer sex that occurs within romantic committed relationships. But these are general tendencies, not categorical differences.

England and Ronen conclude:

> Contemporary debates about hooking up suggest a divide between those who think casual sex can be pleasurable and those who see danger in hookup culture. Like the Sex Wars before them, contemporary debate is mired in an irresolvable quandary, which suggests that hookup culture offers some combination of both liberated access to pleasure and increased risk of danger.

Sexuality and Marketing: Sex Sells...Or Does It?

It sometimes seems that the entire advertising industry is based on the theory that sufficiently attractive men and women in appropriate stages of undress can sell anyone anything. But as it happens, marketers are of two minds about the use of sexuality in advertising. One camp, which seems to be in the majority, believes, indeed, that sex sells. The other camp is dubious. Who's to say who's right?

On the "sex sells" side of the equation are market research firms such as Gallup and Robinson, who say, based on some half-century of testing marketing effectiveness, that erotica is of above average value in communicating with the marketplace, although admittedly a relatively risky one.[9] After all, the point of advertising is mainly product recognition (not sales specifically) and the association of erotic imagery with a product evidently helps consumers recognize the product. Basically, sexuality is used to grab the consumer's attention, which has some benefit even if the attention is short-lived.

On the other hand, overly sexualized imagery can also repel some consumers. Calvin Klein's advertising campaign, which used highly sexualized imagery of very young-looking people, seemed in the minds of many to border on child porn and the consequent consumer backlash was swift and damaging. Then too, sexualized advertising appeals more to men; female consumers often have negative reactions. Breast cancer awareness campaigns using slogans such as "I love boobies!" or "Save the ta-tas" were apparently effective in reaching younger women (who are at low risk for breast cancer) but offensive to older women and to breast cancer survivors.

There is a small but intriguing research literature on the question whether "sex sells," and it is mostly negative. Bushman (2005) showed 336 adults TV programs in one of four categories: a violent program, a sexualized program, still another program with both violence and sex, and a program containing neither. The same twelve ads were embedded in all four programs. Immediately after viewing, participants were asked to rate how boring, exciting, humorous, violent, and sexy the program was, were asked to recall as many of the advertisers as they could, and were given a list of products and asked which they would be most likely to buy. They could also choose coupons for their preferred brands, an indicator of consumer behavior.

Results indicated that sex and violence impaired memory of advertised products. "Televised violence and sex also decreased intentions to buy advertised brands and reduced the number of advertised brands whose coupons participants chose" (p. 706). "Embedding an ad in a program containing sex or violence [or both] *reduced* (a) viewers' likelihood of remembering the advertised brand, (b) their interest in buying that brand, and (c) their likelihood of selecting a coupon for that brand" (p. 702). These effects were equally evident for both men and women and for persons of all ages. As the paper's title intimates, "violence and sex ...do not sell products." Similar results have been reported by Leka et al. (2013) and numerous other studies, both in the US and in Europe. Bushman summarizes this line of research as follows:

> Sex and violence do not sell, and in fact they may even backfire by impairing memory, attitudes and buying intentions for advertised products. Advertisers should think twice about sponsoring violent and sexual programs, and about using these themes in their ads.

So, does "sex sell," as many assume? Yes and no. If you are trying to market sexy lingerie to women, using attractive women clad in sexy lingerie is an effective marketing tool. And likewise, if you are trying to sell personal care products to men, using attractive hunky male models to promote the product makes sense. Products that are marketed as increasing sex appeal (beer, cars, designer jeans, etc.) will inevitably be promoted with highly sexualized advertising, and that advertising will be reasonably effective. But half-nude women will not sell diapers or baby food and hunky men will not sell Mucinex or new sofas. Sex indeed sells, but only some products, only to some consumers, and only under some conditions. As one marketing firm advises, "Sex, used sparingly and judicially, is a strong selling tool. But abuse it, and you will ultimately lose out."

With respect to the "larger issues" of this chapter, it cannot be said that the modern consumer society depends on highly sexualized or lustful marketing to sustain the level of consumer frenzy required for economic growth. The marketing of some products is indeed highly sexualized, but perhaps overly so or even counter-productively so. Marketing, we must remember, is only partially a science, and marketers are generally trial-and-error experimentalists, not evil geniuses who know how to convert a well-turned leg or a naughty bit of cleavage into ravenous consumer demand.

What about Chastity?

With the growing acceptance of premarital sex and with the average age at first intercourse around 15 or 16, there would not seem to be much cultural "space" left over for chastity, but this, of course, is wrong. Led by public figures such as the former pro quarterback Tim Tebow, "virginity vows" or "chastity pledges" seem to be something of a rage these days. And "abstinence only" sex education has staged a comeback too.

There was a time (I am told) when young men and women were expected to be chaste until marriage. That idea was pretty passé when I was a high school student in the 1960s and probably long before. But since the late 1990s, there has been a growing trend of young people, male and female alike, vowing to remain virginal until marriage, almost always for religious reasons. Often, these intentions are announced *en masse* at "purity balls," where young people vow before God, their boyfriends and girlfriends, and their parents that sex would just have to wait until they were married.

Virginity pledges raise all sorts of questions, many of which we have only begun to research. For those making such pledges, the initial and often burning question is, How far can you go before you violate your pledge? Is kissing acceptable? Fondling of breasts? Mutual masturbation? Oral or anal sex? Is it basically "anything goes" short of vaginal penetration? Or what?

Samantha Pugsley took a vow of virginity at the age of 10 and wrote about the experience in an essay entitled, "My Christian virginity pledge nearly destroyed me."[10]

> The church taught me that sex was for married people. Extramarital sex was sinful and dirty and I would go to Hell if I did it. I learned that as a girl, I had a responsibility to my future husband to remain pure for him.

Virginity, she notes, became "my entire identity by the time I hit my teen years." Once she met the man she would eventually marry,

> any time we did anything remotely sexual, guilt overwhelmed me. I wondered where the line was because I was terrified to cross it. Was he allowed to touch my breasts? Could we look at each other naked? I didn't know what was considered sexual enough to condemn my future marriage and send me straight to Hell.

Samantha and her husband were together for six years before they married and remained virginal throughout their premarital years. Her virginity was lost on her marriage night. Lacking all sexual experience:

> Sex hurt. I knew it would. Everyone told me it would be uncomfortable the first time. What they didn't tell me is that I would be back in the bathroom afterward, crying quietly for reasons I didn't yet comprehend. They didn't tell me that I'd be on my honeymoon, crying again, because sex felt dirty and wrong and sinful even though I was married and it was supposed to be okay now. When we got home, I couldn't look anyone in the eye. Everyone knew my virginity was gone. My parents, my church, my friends, my co-workers. They all knew I was soiled and tarnished. I wasn't special anymore. My virginity had become such an essential part of my personality that I didn't know who I was without it.

This state of sexual misery persisted for two years, at which point the couple sought counseling. The outcome of counseling: "I don't go to church anymore, nor am I religious. As I started to heal, I realized that I couldn't figure out how to be both religious and sexual at the same time. I chose sex." Coming late to a conclusion she shares with many modern-day feminists, "I'm now thoroughly convinced that the entire concept of virginity is used to control female sexuality."

Is Samantha's story typical of virginity pledgers? Are her experiences commonplace or rare? How often are pledges broken? Who vows to remain virginal in the first place? Alas, there is not a great deal of research to go on here, and vested interests are always trying to spin research results to favor their pet theories, but what little research there is has been capably summarized by Kunz (2015) and I rely heavily here on her account.

To begin, according to the Add Health survey, a very well-known longitudinal study of America's teenagers, about 13% of American teens have taken a virginity pledge. Whether this is a smaller or larger than expected number, I leave to readers to decide. In the same survey wave, 40% had already had their first sexual encounter, so that leaves 47% who were still virgins at the time of the survey but evidently did not intend to remain so until marriage (or at least, had not yet publicly vowed to do so).

Figures on how often these pledges are broken are all over the place. An unreferenced and unsubstantiated story in *Time Magazine* reported that 88% of virginity pledgers had premarital sex after pledging. But a survey of students at Northern Kentucky University put the failure rate at only 60%. So we are left with the rather unsatisfying conclusion that more than half but evidently fewer than all of these virginity pledges are subsequently broken.

That said, it is also clearly the case that virginity pledgers are much less likely to have premarital sex than non-pledgers. "The delay effect is substantial and almost impossible to erase. Taking a pledge delays intercourse for a long time" (Bearman and Bruckner, 2001).

Who takes these pledges? Teens from two parent households are more likely to do so than children from single-parent households; whites are more likely to do so than racial and ethnic minorities; younger teens more likely than older teens; and more religious teens more likely than less religious teens.

From what do virginity pledgers abstain? Many, like Samantha Pugsley, were uncertain what the pledge ruled out. Studies have indicated that

> while adolescents may be avoiding sexual intercourse, many are participating in oral sex. Some adolescents appear to be confused about what sexual 'abstinence' is. For example, many adolescents think that 'sex' is sexual intercourse while simultaneously not even considering any oral contact to be 'sex.' Several studies indicate that adolescents who describe themselves as 'virgins' had participated in oral sex along with other sexual behaviors that stop short of vaginal penetration.

The social policy side of virginity vows is abstinence-only sex education, which became very popular in the George W. Bush administration but is less so today.

As defined in federal law, abstinence-only sex education embraces eight related pedagogical goals:

1. To teach the benefits of abstaining from sex.
2. To teach that abstinence from sex is the expected standard for all school-age children.
3. To teach that abstinence is the only certain way to avoid pregnancy.
4. To teach that a mutually faithful monogamous marriage is the only acceptable place for sex.
5. To teach that sex outside of marriage has harmful psychological effects.
6. To teach that bearing children out of wedlock has harmful consequences for the child, parents and society as a whole.
7. To teach young people how to fend off sexual advances.
8. To teach the importance of attaining self-sufficiency prior to having sex.

These, moreover, are the *only* principles to be taught in sex-education classes (thus, abstinence-*only*). No mention is to be made of contraception, birth control, or anything else that would only be useful if you were already sexually active or soon intended to be.

Also studiously avoided is any indication of possible same-sex love, so abstinence-only sex education typically excludes and demeans LGBT youth, who have enough identity issues to confront without being told that their sexual identities are fundamentally immoral and not worth consideration in sex-education classes.

Many people – educators, parents and teens alike – felt that abstinence-only sex education was unrealistic, almost punitive, and would not work to delay the onset of intercourse or reduce the number of unwed births. Just as "virginity" can be seen an ideological frame to control female sexuality, abstinence-only could be seen as an ideological frame to control adolescent sexuality. Many people assumed that in the great battle between moral reasoning and hormonal urges, the hormones were bound to win.

There ensued a (roughly) 10-year period of research on the effectiveness of abstinence-only sex education. Research results are seldom unequivocal and so lend themselves to interpretations favoring pretty much any point of view. Here, for example is what the web page of the National Abstinence Education Association says about what the research shows:

> Despite what you may read in the newspapers, there is a growing body of research that confirms that abstinence-centered education decreases sexual initiation, increases abstinent behavior among sexually experienced teens, and/or decreases the number of partners among sexually experienced teens. And if individuals do initiate sex after being in an abstinence-centered program, they are no less likely to use condoms

than anyone else. Researchers acknowledge that it takes about a decade before a new program or strategy begins having positive published research. Abstinence-centered education has received widespread federal funding for little more than a decade, but there is already promising research to show what most people intuitively know – abstinence works![11]

And here is what the website of Planned Parenthood says about the same body of research:

Abstinence-only programs deny young people life-saving information by, instead, providing *mis*information and withholding accurate information that young people need in order to make informed choices. Abstinence-only programs do not delay sexual initiation or lower rates of pregnancy or sexually transmitted infections (STIs), according to a 10-year government study. It's no wonder the Institute of Medicine called for the termination of abstinence-only programs because they represent "poor fiscal and public health policy." The United States wasted more than $1.5 billion in federal and state funding on abstinence-only programs from 1996 to 2008—programs that fail to teach teens how to prevent pregnancy or STIs.[12]

It is true that studies can be found on both sides of the issue. Denny and Young (2006), for example, do report that abstinence-only sex education programs "did have some positive benefits that should be considered by those interested in abstinence education programming" (p. 414) and numerous other studies with similar conclusions can be found. But larger and more sophisticated studies have usually come to the opposite conclusion.

One of the best of these evaluations is that undertaken by Mathematica Policy Research, a very well-known and trustworthy research firm in Princeton, New Jersey (Trenholm et al., 2007). This research group studied four different abstinence-only programs, one each in Virginia, Florida, Wisconsin, and Mississippi. "The four selected programs offered a range of implementation settings and program strategies," reflecting the diversity of these programs nationwide. Results are based on follow-up data collected four to six years after students had completed the curriculum. (In contrast, most previous studies have follow-up windows of 6–18 months, so long-term effects were generally unknown.) Also, in each site, eligible students were *randomly* chosen either to receive Title 510 abstinence only sex education (the treatment group) or not (the controls). So the study also has the singular advantage of being a true experiment. "As a result, differences in outcomes between the program and control groups could be attributed to the abstinence education program and not to any pre-existing unobserved differences between the program and control groups" (p. xvi).

Findings indicate that youth in the program group were no more likely than control group youth to have abstained from sex and, among those who reported having had sex, they had similar numbers of sexual partners and had initiated sex at the same mean age. Contrary to concerns raised by some critics of the Title V, Section 510 abstinence funding, however, program group youth were no more likely to have engaged in unprotected sex than control group youth.

In short, participating in an abstinence-only sex education curriculum had no discernible subsequent effect on students' sexual behavior. This was true for the overall sample and in each of the four study sites. In no site and in no subgroup of students did abstinence-only sex education increase the rate of sexual abstinence. As others have also concluded, "Although abstinence is a healthy behavioral option for teens, abstinence as a sole option for adolescents is scientifically and ethically problematic" (Santelli et al., 2006; see also Kohler et al., 2008).

The most recent study I have found of the topic is Jemmott et al. (2010), which used 24-month follow-up data to evaluate several sex-education alternatives, including an abstinence-only program. The program, however, differed significantly from the usual eight-point abstinence programs we have been discussing. Among other things, the program did not promote abstinence-only-until marriage, only abstaining from sex until "a time later in life" when adolescents would be better prepared to handle the emotional and physical consequences. The program was also infused with medically accurate information, was not moralistic, and explicitly did not avoid discussion or systematically disparage the value of contraception. Results showed that participants in the program deferred intercourse compared to the control groups. Thus, in the words of the Alan Guttmacher Institute, this new study "adds to, but does not contradict, the body of evidence about 'what works' in sex education."

What can be concluded with certainty about chastity as a lust-management strategy among young people? First, it is obvious that many adolescents will have sex at their very first opportunity to do so, whether or not they have pledged their virginity until marriage or have been told that abstinence is the only safe, moral, healthful choice. Second, for all their publicity, virginity vows are broken more than half the time (and maybe as often as 90% of the time). Third, moralizing, religiously motivated exhortations to abstain from sex until marriage have no discernibly useful effects on teen sexuality, although there is now some evidence that sober, well-considered and information-laden advice to defer sexuality may cause some young people to do so.

Finally we must ask, What does it mean to say that a sex education program "works?" Works to achieve what end? The abstinence-only programs seek to postpone all sexuality until marriage and even the so-called comprehensive programs begin with the grudging recognition that since having sex is inevitable, we should at least make it "safe." Where is the recognition that sexuality is an essential, unavoidable, and pleasurable element of humanness, programmed into our genes and hormones by millions of years of biological evolution? Where's the effort to teach young people how to enjoy their sexuality – safely, yes, but fully and joyfully as well? As Paul Ward of the Terrence Higgins Trust once said:

> With more opportunities to have sex than ever before, and more types of sex in our repertoires, we need to make certain that young people have the facts they need to have safe, fulfilling sex lives. Sex education in this country is a relic of the last century. Teaching a teenager to put a condom on a banana is no bad thing, but it won't tell them how to deal with being pressured into sex before they're ready, the do's and don'ts of online friendships, or that what they see in porn is not necessarily what a partner wants in the bedroom. A decent program of sex and relationships education, embedded in the curriculum and fit for the 21st century, can help young people have the best, safest sex at the time that's right for them.[13]

Conclusions: Lust and the Sexed-Up Society

Although devout Christians and social conservatives are often apoplectic about the sexualization of modern society and what they see as the ever-present sexual imagery that seemingly pervades all aspects of contemporary existence, the sex lives of the vast majority seem rather ho-hum. The sort of sexual experimentation and rampant promiscuity that was promised by the "sexual revolution" seem at best to characterize a comparatively few years of adolescence and maybe once or twice thereafter – say, during the occasional fling or in the aftermath of divorce, but for most Americans most of the time, sex happens a few times a month, is pretty conventional, and involves a spouse or committed partner. Throw in an occasional visit to the porn sites and a brief bit of auto-eroticism, and that's about as close to real lust as most people ever get. Compared, say, to greed or gluttony, lust just does not seem to rise very high on the agenda of national concerns.

The popular media and journals of opinion are full of anxious alarms about the pernicious effects of sexualization on American culture. The *Huffington Post* warns that "Sexualized Culture Is Creating Mental Health Issues in Our Youth."[14] The *Jerusalem Post* alerts us that "The Sexualization of our Teens is Becoming Endemic."[15] Even the American Psychological Association has published a Task Force Report on the Sexualization of Girls (2007), warning sternly about the dire cognitive and emotional consequences and the disruptions sexualization can cause in the development of a mature, healthy sexuality. These problems, and the larger social trend, are real enough. Popular culture (music, magazines, billboards, blog posts – you name it) is full of imagery that degrades and objectifies women. Women are encouraged to present themselves in a highly sexualized manner. Men, it is said, come to expect it. Even young children are portrayed in the popular culture as sexual objects that stimulate desire. All true, and all to be condemned, of course.

At the same time, popular culture is also full of imagery promoting the use of alcohol, and still the large majority of the population either does not drink at all or does so responsibly. So it is not necessarily the case that the sexing up of the culture has turned the nation into a band of slobbering rapists or masturbating voyeurs. One hopes, desperately at times, for alternative role models of sexuality for both young men and young women. But clearly, once the passions of youth have subsided, most people settle into extremely conventional, even boring sex lives.

Notes

1 www.osv.com/MyFaith/MarriageFamilyandSexuality/Article/TabId/682/ ArtMID/13726/ArticleID/5923/ Lust--why-its-the-it-vice-among-the-Seven-Deadlies.aspx.
2 www.jasonstaples.com/bible/most-misinterpreted-bible-passages-1-matthew-527-28/.
3 www.divorcestatistics.info.
4 Discussed at www.futurescopes.com/affairs-and-infidelity/8948/marriages-end-divorce-after-affair-statistics.
5 Most of the available research on porn relies more or less exclusively on individual self-reports of consumption patterns, outlooks, and behaviors. As these are potentially sensitive or embarrassing questions, presentation-of-self issues and other reporting biases must be considered in evaluating the results. For example, it is almost certain that true porn consumption is higher than self-reports would suggest.
6 www.provenmen.org/2014pornsurvey/christian-porn-stats/.
7 www.religionnews.com/2016/01/21/pornography-christian-crisis-exaggerated-issue-commentary/.
8 In a large survey of imprisoned felons (Wright and Rossi, 1986), one series of questions asked how old men were when they first did various things: fired a gun, smoked marijuana, committed a serious crime, or "had sex with a woman." More questions were raised about the latter question than about any other question in the survey: Did "having sex" include oral sex? Mutual masturbation? "Dry humping?" Did it have to be vaginal penetration? Did it have to be sex with a *woman*?
9 Alas, my only reference for this claim is the Wikipedia entry on Sex in Advertising https://en.wikipedia.org/ wiki/Sex_in_advertising.
10 http://www.salon.com/2014/08/10/my_christian_virginity_pledge_as_a_child_nearly_destroyed_my life_partner/.
11 http://www.abstinenceassociation.org/faqs/.
12 https://plannedparenthoodaction.org/issues/sex-education/abstinence-only-programs/.

13 http://www.huffingtonpost.co.uk/2013/11/26/sex-brits-teenage-years-to-later-life_n_4341983.html.
14 http://www.huffingtonpost.com/darryl-roberts/sexualized-culture-is-creating-mental-health-issues-in-our-youth_b_5994148.html.
15 http://www.jpost.com/Opinion/Columnists/The-sexualization-of-our-teens-is-becoming-endemic-309123.

4

SLOTH

The Besetting Sin of the Age?

In his review of J. F. Powers's *Prince of Darkness and Other Stories,* Evelyn Waugh noted that the book was "a magnificent study of sloth – a sin which has not attracted much attention of late and which, perhaps, is the besetting sin of the age." A besetting sin is a weakness to which one is particularly prone, one that leads to other weaknesses. To beset is "to surround with hostile intent" or to "besiege." The image of a besetting sin is thus one of being surrounded by the forces of sin, so much so that the ability to resist is regularly overpowered. What Waugh is claiming, in short, is that the moral, political, and spiritual conditions of modernity make us particularly prone to slothfulness.[1]

That sloth (or idleness) is a deadly sin derives from the Christian doctrine that all living things should earn their daily keep with the sweat of their brows and that no one should be content to sit back and live through the efforts of others. Synonyms of sloth include an aversion to work, indolence, laziness, negligence, idleness, apathy, languor, and lethargy, along with many others. In nature, of course, a sloth is a medium-sized, slow-moving mammal that spends its day eating and lazing around. Sloths move only when absolutely necessary, and then very, very slowly. In the Disney film *Zootopia,* all the sloths worked at the Department of Motor Vehicles, a searing social commentary if ever there were one.

At about the same time that Waugh was waxing philosophical about sloth as the besetting sin of the age, the American longshoreman–cum–philosopher and social critic Eric Hoffer was writing (in *The True Believer,* first published in 1951) that

> ... the mad rush of the last 100 years has left us out of breath. We have had no time to swallow our spittle. We know that the automated machine is here to liberate us and show us the way back to Eden; that it will do for

us what no revolution, no doctrine, no prayer, and no promise could do. But we do not know that we have arrived. We stand there panting, caked with sweat and dust, afraid to realize that the seventh day of the second creation is here, and the ultimate Sabbath is spread out before us.

So, which, we must ask, poses the greater threat to the overall well-being of the present-day population: The "dizzying pace" and workaholism of the age, or the "besetting sin" of slothfulness? Do we work too hard, or not hard enough? Too much, or too little? Should we listen to the performer Eddie Cantor, whose advice was to "Slow down and enjoy life. It's not only the scenery you miss by going too fast – you also miss the sense of where you are going and why." Or do we heed instead the advice of the novelist Stephen King: "Talent is cheaper than table salt. What separates the talented individual from the successful one is a lot of hard work."

Work and Labor

In the United States, the "labor force participation rate" is the percentage of the over-16 population that has a job or is currently looking for work. Those without a job and not looking for one are not considered labor force participants. Over the years, the labor force participation rate has varied from an all-time low of 58.1% in 1954 to an all-time high of 67.3% in January 2000. As of January 2016, the rate was 62.7%, very near the long-term average of 63.0%. So, while the rate goes up and down, there has not been any *long-term* trend toward decreasing labor force participation, which is to say, we are evidently no more slothful (work-averse) today than at any previous time in our post-World War II history.

From the onset of the Great Recession in 2007 up to the current year (2016), there was a general downward drift in the rate of labor force participation, but the downward drift was in a fairly narrow range. In January, 2007, the rate was 66.4%; in November, 2015, the rate bottomed out at 62.5%, and has begun climbing back up since. It is universally conceded that this drop in labor force participation since 2007 was the result of a lousy economy, not some sudden surge of laziness on the part of the American people.

What about the one-third to two-fifths of US adults who are not in the labor force? As of October, 2015, they numbered about 92 million persons. What do these people do to fill up their time? Are they, like the slow-moving mammals, just lazing about all day? Hardly. There are a few obvious points to the contrary according to a 2015 study conducted by the Federal Reserve Bank of Atlanta and republished in the Wall Street Journal (October 21, 2015).

First, labor force participation varies sharply by age: It is relatively low among those aged 16–20, higher among middle-aged adults (21–55), with sharp fall-offs after age 55 (and especially after age 65). Young people are not in the labor force mainly because they are still in school; seniors are not in the labor force mainly because they are already retired (or in some cases disabled). There are also some so-called "discouraged workers," people who want a job but have left the labor force because of a series of failed efforts to find one. Then there are those who are not in the labor force because they are taking care of family.

In short, almost everyone in modern American society who is not in the labor force (i.e. does not work for pay in the regular economy) has a good reason why: They are disabled, already retired, going to school, caring for family. Whither the lazy, shiftless bums – the true sloths of the modern economy? They have to be concentrated in two categories: Those who "want a job, but are not in labor force" (the discouraged workers, who might well be as lazy as they are discouraged) and a miscellaneous category of "others." At best, the two categories combined add up to a few million potential workers.

In short, almost everyone in American society who is in a position to work does so. If the true measure of sloth is an aversion to work, then the sloths cannot amount to much more than a few percent of the total population – the first of several points of evidence that render doubtful Waugh's claim that sloth is the "besetting sin of the age."

How about hours worked among those in the labor force? A full-time year-round job (40 hours per week, 52 weeks per year) would amount to 2,080 hours of labor per year. Taking off a couple weeks of vacation leaves the annual possible total at about 2,000 hours. According to the Organization for Economic Co-operation and Development, in 2014, the average annual hours actually worked per American worker was 1,789, or nearly 90% of the theoretically available 2,000 hours – well ahead of workers in, say, Germany (who only average 1,371 hours per year), France (1,473), and even the industrious Japanese (1,729).[2]

Since American workers average about 90% of the maximum hours worked per year, it follows that many workers only work part-time. In 2015, about 25% of all employed persons were employed part-time (35 hours per week or fewer). Of the part-timers, about 20% are "involuntary part-time workers," meaning that they would work more hours if their employees gave them more hours to work.[3]

Offsetting the part-time workers are workers who hold multiple jobs. Moonlighting is not something the Bureau of Labor Statistics (BLS) keeps careful track of, so a precise percentage or number is not available, but the consensus opinion seems to be that something on the order of a million workers have two or more jobs. USA Today puts the figure at about 5% of the labor force, or considerably more than a million.[4]

The time commitment to work extends somewhat beyond the hours on the time clock. It also includes the unpaid time spent getting to and from work. The Bureau of Labor Statistics estimates that the average American worker now spends 42 hours a year commuting to and from the workplace, and that number is increasing. So, commuting effectively adds a week to the average American's work-year (Schrank et al., 2015).

Recently, the Census and some analysts have remarked on the emergence of a new class of commuters, which is termed "extreme," "super," or "mega" commuting – commutes of 90 minutes or more each way or 50 or more miles each way, or both. About 5% of all commuters struggle daily with a "long" commute (50 or more miles each way), 2.5% of all workers now face an "extreme" commute (90+ minutes each way), and just under 1% face both. By either measure, workers in the San Francisco-Oakland-Fremont Metropolitan Statistical area face the worst commutes, with two other California metro areas occupying the second and third slots.

So, most Americans have full-time jobs, some have more than one job, some work part-time but would prefer more hours, some work part-time and are happy with the arrangement, many add a week a year to their working time just getting to and from work, and most of the rest have good reasons why they don't work (that is, don't work for pay in the regular labor force). There may be a bit of sloth tucked in and around these various categories. And surely, many who work don't work as hard as they *could*. But on the whole, the portrait that emerges from the labor force data is one of a pretty industrious population, not one riddled by indolence or laziness.

Welfare, Work, and Poverty

Looking for sloths in the employed middle class is clearly unproductive, so let's look instead at welfare recipients and at the poor more generally. After all, as George W. Bush is alleged to have remarked in a macroeconomics course at the Harvard Business School, "Look, people are poor because they are lazy."[5] How many lazy, slothful *poor* people do we have in the country?

According to official federal definitions and data, there are currently 46.7 million people below the federal poverty line, 14.8% of the total US population. In the hunt for true sloths, we can begin by peeling out the 16.7 million of the poor who are children under age 18 and also the 4.6 million who are over age 65. That leaves 25.4 million in their prime labor force participation years, slightly more than half the total. Of those, 14.9 million are adult women, most of them the mothers of the 16.7 million poor children. That leaves us with just 10.5 million poor adult men, of whom about nine million had earned income (i.e. worked at least part of) the previous year (two million worked full-time, year-round). So, what are we left with – a million, maybe two million, poor people who are not children, not elderly, not women with children, and didn't work at all last year? A couple of millions from a population of more than 300 million – well less than 1%. So, unless we are prepared to tell poor children, poor seniors, or poor women to "sober up, take a shower, and get a job," it seems that we are not going to find a great deal of sloth among the poverty population either.

And even that exaggerates. In 2012, there were about 15.8 million people below the poverty line that did not work *at all* in the previous year. Of those, about 4.9 million were ill or disabled, 1.3 million were already retired, 4.1 million had home or family obligations that prevented them from working, 3.4 million were in school, and 2.1 million "could not find work." By any reasonable jiggling of these numbers, the true sloths cannot number much more than one or two million, just as we concluded above.

There is a large research literature on the question whether the poor want to work, stretching back to the seminal study of the topic by Leonard Goodwin, *Do the Poor Want to Work?* (1973). Goodwin found that social psychological attitudes about work were about the same among the poor as among the middle class population. It would be an exaggeration to say that every subsequent study of work orientations shows the same thing, but not much of one. There are dozens of websites that debunk the "myth" that the poor are lazy, most of them making the same points that we have just made.

There is also a large literature on the working poor, that is, on people who are poor even though they are labor force participants (e.g., Bureau of Labor Statistics, 2013; Shipler, 2005). Some people are apparently surprised to learn that a working person can still be poor, but enough has been said and written about the working poor over the last decade that anyone who is surprised that this group exists has just not been paying attention. The BLS defines working poor as anyone who spends at least 27 weeks per year in the labor force but whose annual income remains below the federal poverty line. In recent years, they number somewhere in the 10–12 million range, or about a quarter of the poverty population.

Need it be added that continuing to work even though your wages do not get or keep you out of poverty is hardly indicative of slothfulness. These may well be the least slothful of any identifiable group in the American population.

It should be clear by now that while poor people can be and are poor for many reasons, being lazy is not prominent among them. Without doubt, *some* poor people are lazy. So are many affluent people. More and more, it seems, we come to the realization that many poor people are poor mostly because they are unlucky (and that good luck is what makes many rich people rich).

So, we arrive at last at what constitutes the "bottom of the barrel" in contemporary political discourse, the welfare population – often presented, in the words of Luic Wacquant (2008) as

> a formless aggregate of pathological cases,… as the creatures of a noxious ethnic culture, or yet as the beneficiaries of a profligate welfare state that perpetuates the very misery it is supposed to combat by rewarding sloth and vice.

Assertions that welfare creates and promotes sloth can be found almost anywhere. Current Speaker of the House Paul Ryan puts it this way: "We don't want to turn the safety net into a hammock that lulls able-bodied people to lives of dependency and complacency, that drains them of their will and their incentive to make the most of their lives." The most potent imagery of Ryan's "dependency and complacency" is the overweight welfare queen, sitting on the front porch of her public housing unit, eating junk food purchased with her food stamps, watching the world roll by (through eyeglasses paid for by Medicaid). Why work when you can live high on the hog with government subsidies?

Demonization of welfare recipients has become standard fare in the conservative political narrative. Republicans in several states have introduced legislation to require drug testing of welfare recipients, just to make sure they are not getting stoned with "our" money. Former Speaker of the House Newt Gingrich generated a national sound bite by claiming that "more people have been put on food stamps by Barack Obama than any president in American history." (In fact, George W. Bush and Obama are about tied for this dubious distinction.) An infamous Internet posting known as "Steak is for Fucking Taxpayers!"[6] is a diatribe against "welfare cheats" that evidently compelled Missouri Republicans to introduce a bill prohibiting Supplemental Nutrition Assistance Program (SNAP) recipients from buying steak, other cuts of beef, lobster, cookies, chips, energy drinks – even fish sticks and canned tuna – with their food stamps. Kansas's guardians of the public trust passed a bill in 2015 that would prohibit welfare recipients from withdrawing more than $25 in benefits per day and would also make it illegal to spend public aid on jewelry, tattoos, massages, spa treatments, lingerie, tobacco, movies, bail bonds, arcade games, visits to swimming pools, fortunetellers, amusement parks, or ocean cruises. Rush Limbaugh is so incensed by what he sees as the rampant fraud and abuse in SNAP that he has proposed eliminating the SNAP program entirely. His advice to those truly in need: Try dumpster diving.

To counter this sort of political invective, it is useful to stress that 93% of SNAP households are supporting children, seniors, or disabled people (Wright et al., 2018), so the rate of outright fraud cannot be very high. Too, in 2013, something like a hundred million dollars' worth of SNAP benefits were redeemed at military commissaries and about a million US veterans were SNAP recipients. Any volunteers for the job of telling these vets to dumpster dive if they need to supplement their food supply?

Much of the hostility to SNAP (and to welfare more generally) is due to misconceptions about who receives benefits (Kasperkevic, 2014). At the top of this list are the ABAWDs – Able-bodied Adults without Dependents, who at the very outside cannot be more than 7% of all SNAP recipients (and an even smaller percentage of the beneficiaries of other welfare programs). What people fail to acknowledge is that even SNAP, the easiest sort of welfare to obtain, restricts ABAWDs to three months of benefits every three years, and even then, only if they work at least part-time or participate in a job training program.

To be sure, large numbers of people receive one or another welfare benefit (are "on welfare"). SNAP enrollees numbered 46 million persons in 2015. About 59 million received Medicaid (designed for low-income and disabled populations); another 44 million receive Medicare (designed mainly for seniors). Temporary Assistance to Needy Families (TANF), what most people think of when they hear the word "welfare," is, by contrast, a very small program with only about 1.6 million currently enrolled. There is, of course, considerable overlap among all these categories. TANF women, for example, are automatically eligible for SNAP and Medicaid. Still, beneficiaries of federal means-tested welfare programs, including Medicaid, add up to more than a hundred million people, about a third of the entire population. Add in Social Security and Medicare benefits and various veteran's programs and you can get pretty quickly to the Mitt Romney meme that 47% of the American population "are dependent upon government, who believe that they are victims, who believe that government has a responsibility to care for them, who believe that they are entitled to health care, to food, to housing, to you name it."

But again, large numbers of "welfare recipients" are seniors beyond their working years (and more on them later) or youth who have yet to enter the labor force; many who are not too young or too old to work have various disabilities or family responsibilities that make work difficult if not impossible. And, of course, many of those who remain are in fact working (remarkably, at wage rates so low that they still qualify for welfare benefits – why is this legal?) Nationwide, the Census Bureau estimates that nearly one household in four that contained a working adult in 2012 also received means-tested benefits. Among Medicaid recipients, 28% of those ages 18–64 worked full time and another 15% worked part-time. Among SNAP recipients, about 60% of those of working age without disabilities were employed while receiving benefits. And so on.

Still, the idea that welfare *per se* makes people lazy is hard to shake. It is, of course, true that someone receiving, say, $500 a month in food stamps, housing subsidies, and cash transfers is not going to be as desperate to go out and find a job as someone who receives nothing. Still, as John Aziz[7] has argued:

> The best way to measure whether the unemployed are behaving lazily is by examining the ratio of job seekers to job openings. If the problem is that unemployed people are slacking off work to enjoy the fruits of government welfare, we would expect to see a shortage of labor in the economy. Employers trying to recruit workers to expand their businesses would come up against the fact that job seekers are in short supply. Job vacancies would go unfilled and wages would be bid upward as businesses

fight to recruit scarce labor away from the easy option of free welfare money. In such a scenario, cutting welfare would incentivize work, and help businesses fill vacancies.

But here, Aziz argues, is exactly where the evidence strongly undercuts the anti-welfare meme. As of 2014, there were approximately three people seeking jobs for each job opening. At the depths of the Great Recession, this ratio jumped to as high as seven to one. "The data shows decisively that the problem is not laziness at all, but a lack of job openings."

Direct evidence that cash transfers do not discourage work comes from a study by Banerjee et al. (2015). Noting that cash transfer programs to assist disadvantaged citizens have become commonplace around the globe and that policy-makers "are often concerned whether transfer programs of this type discourage work," these investigators reanalyzed data from seven randomized controlled trials of government-sponsored transfer payment programs in six developing countries, looking for negative effects on labor supply. They found none. "We...find no systematic evidence that cash transfer programs discourage work... the available evidence implies that cash transfer programs do not induce the 'bad' behaviors that are often attributed to them in the policy space."

There is plenty of US evidence that supports the same conclusion. Back in the late 1960s and early 1970s, a number of so-called "negative income tax (NIT)" experiments were undertaken in a variety of North American cities, all of them designed to test the viability of an NIT scheme as an alternative to the then-existent welfare system. The concept is simple: Below a certain level of income, income taxes become negative – rather than you give money to the government, the government gives money to you. Effectively, NIT schemes are guaranteed annual income strategies, and as always, the major concern was that an income guarantee would cause labor force participation to decline.

Rossi and Lyall (1976) reviewed the results of the largest of these experiments, the New Jersey-Pennsylvania Negative Income Tax experiment. Contrary to economic prediction and again undercutting the idea that welfare makes people lazy, "experimental treatments had little detectable effect on male heads' labor force participation or employment rates and only a small overall effect on hours actually worked" (p. 117). Wives had a somewhat different response and showed roughly a 15% decline in labor supply. This was not the result, however, of reducing hours worked but rather of exits from the labor force altogether. Further analysis revealed that the reduced labor was concentrated among white women and, in most cases, resulted from women leaving the labor force to go back to school or receive additional job training. In short, they took advantage of the income guarantee to enhance their human capital.

My first wife was Guatemalan and her brother was a well-to-do industrialist and investor. The brother and I had numerous conversations about the generally miserable state of Guatemala's society and economy and, of course, he insisted that all those poor Guatemalans were poor mainly because they were lazy. One day, following a particularly heated conversation about this point, my then-wife and I were driving through Chichicastenango, a small village in the Guatemalan highlands, where I saw many dozens of men, women, and children on the hillsides gathering firewood for home hearths (locally known as *leñadoras*, "wood gatherers"). All of them were bent over at the waist toting improbably large bundles of sticks on their backs up the sides of the mountains so that the village would have the fuel necessary to warm beans and tortillas for the evening meal. Say what you will about these miserable wretches and the causes of their miseries, but please, do not call them *lazy*.

Retirement

Ah, the Golden Years, a time in life when you can kick back, relax, and be as slothful as you want. Is this where we will find our concentration of the "besetting sin of the age?" The Christian ethic is that every living human needs to earn his or her keep. Retirement would seem to be inconsistent with that ethic, or at least comprise a major exception to the rule. So just where did the concept of "retirement" come from in the first place? And is retirement indeed the period of extended and enriched leisure that it is often made out to be?

For all practical purposes, the concept of retirement was invented in 1881 (along with many other elements of what we now call the welfare state) by the Prussian Otto von Bismarck. Bismarck's idea was a government-run program to provide financial support for society's older members – in short, retirement. Prior to 1881, people did not "retire." They worked right up to the point where they were no longer capable of working and died shortly thereafter. Bismarck's program kicked in at 70, an age which few people in the late 19th century could ever expect to attain.

In the US, agitation for some sort of social insurance for elderly persons started in the 1880s and by the 1920s, quite a number of American enterprises were offering older workers some sort of financial support. Most set the retirement age at 65 although many felt that by age 60, workers should move out and make room for the newer generation. When the Social Security Act (SSA) was passed in 1935, the age of eligibility was set to 65 and that has been the target "retirement age" ever since. In 1935, life expectancy for American men was 58 years, so the fraction living to 65 and beyond was small, if not entirely negligible.

The idea of retirement as an extended period of leisure did not arise until life expectancies rose into the 70s and beyond, i.e. once the average 65-year-old could reasonably expect to live several more years. In the US, life expectancy for men did not reach age 70 until 1979; for women, that happened in 1949. So at least for men, the modern concepts and expectations about retirement have only been around for 35 or 40 years – the idea that retirement means a half decade or more of leisure time, reading, golf, sleeping in, and watching lots of TV. Prior to that, "retirement" was a comparatively brief interlude between working and death.

Today, of course, many look on a 20- or 30-year period of retired leisure as an inalienable right, as payback for logging all those years in the paid labor force, indeed, as an *entitlement*. Many evidently feel this way even though they do not have the income or assets to sustain the life of leisure they expect.

For a brief period in the 1980s, many of the European welfare states began lowering the retirement age and, in some cases, making retirement mandatory, in order to clear older workers out of the labor force and make way for the young. The recent trend has, of course, been in the opposite direction as the massive Baby Boom generations move into retirement age and wreak havoc on the Social Security Trust Fund. For most Boomers, the full retirement age is now 66, not 65, and there is talk of raising the retirement age even further.[8]

The contemporary image of "retirement," at least in the many retirement communities of Florida, is to sleep in, enjoy a leisurely breakfast, head off for a round of golf, get a bite of lunch at the country club, enjoy an afternoon of pickle-ball, pop in to the all-you-can-eat early bird buffet around four or five, then sip cocktails and play cards with friends until bedtime. The realities are, of course, quite different.

To begin, the very decision to retire is a function of many diverse and, sometimes, competing factors, some positive, others not so much. The most common reason given for retiring is wanting to spend more time with one's family, mentioned by more than a third; "wanting to do other things" was cited by about a quarter (National Institute on Aging, 2016). But almost a third said that poor health was why they retired and only about a tenth mentioned a strong dislike of work as the reason.

The decline in health that comes with age limits how much enjoyment people can derive from their retirement. Among persons who retired before the Social Security "early retirement" age of 62, more than half the men and a third of the women cited inability to continue working as the reason. In short, many early retirees don't retire early so they can enjoy additional years of leisure; they do so because they are unable to continue. (Other common reasons for early retirement include involuntary job losses and family changes, particularly the retirement of a spouse.)

And it is not just physical health that declines with age. Cognitive abilities wane too. Beyond age 70, more than a tenth suffer moderate to severe cognitive impairment. Severe depression also increases with age. And then there are those unanticipated health events that turn leisure into impairment – strokes, heart attacks, falls, seizures, and on through the dreary list. With all these impairments comes greater and greater difficulty negotiating the simple acts of daily living: Bathing, toileting, preparing one's own meals, taking the daily stroll, getting dressed, and the like. People who have trouble feeding themselves are unlikely to enjoy the occasional round of golf.

The majority of workers still say they would like to retire at age 65 (or 66, depending on where they sit in the Social Security cycle), but only those making $100,000 a year or more actually expect to do so.[9] Despite preferences, relatively few workers are in a financial position to retire – ever, much less at age 65 or 66. We have been told hundreds of times that American workers do not save enough to cover their retirement and the majority of not-yet-retired workers look to Social Security to provide the lion's share, if not all, of their retirement income. For many, this will entail a drastic cut in the standard of living. (On the other hand, studies show that many retirees are pleasantly surprised by their retirement resources and live quite comfortably on their retirement incomes.)

One result is that many retired persons remain in the labor force, often on a part-time basis, even after "retirement." Recent surveys show that as many as three-quarters of the workforce intend to work as long as they are able – some because they like to work, others because they think they will need the money.[10] Social Security provisions allow persons receiving Social Security payments to have substantial earned income before their SSA benefits are taxed. At age 65, about 35%–40% of men and about 30% of women remain in the paid labor force. Most Baby Boomers, many of whom are just now approaching retirement age or will in the next decade, expect to work past age 65 in any case.

Despite the many financial, health-related, and other struggles that retirees must face, most retired people (more than 60%) say that retirement is "very satisfying," and most of the remainder report moderate satisfaction. Fewer than one in ten report that retirement is not satisfying at all. Some early studies found that retired people reported more loneliness and unhappiness than working people, but subsequent studies have confirmed that this is because lonely and unhappy people are more likely to retire in the first place (and not because retirement makes you lonely or unhappy).

As for what retired people do with the time they formerly spent at work, studies show that both volunteering and TV watching increase. More about the latter in the next section of this chapter.

Clearly, while the retired are beset with many challenges, sloth appears not to be one of them. For many, retirement remains that "comparatively brief interlude" between working and dying. For those whose retirement years stretch out further in time, money worries, health problems, continuing work commitments, and deteriorating mental abilities are apparently more common than golf games or late night martini-and-canasta parties. If retirement is "the Golden Years," the gold is at best a thin gilt, and rather a tarnished one at that. As the Roman poet Horace so eloquently said, "We rarely find anyone who can say he has lived a happy life, and who, content with his life, can retire from the world like a satisfied guest." Rarely indeed!

Sedentary Lifestyles

Perhaps in our quest for sloth we should not look so much at what people do at or for work as at what they do when they are not at work. There are, after all, 168 hours in a week, only 40 or so of which are spent working (on average). What do people do with the other 128?

Obviously, the largest bloc of non-work time is spent sleeping. So how much do Americans sleep? Apparently, no one knows for sure, but however much we sleep, it seems to be "not enough."

Nobody Knows. There are large discrepancies across surveys in the reported average hours that people sleep. A recent (2013) Gallup poll reported an average per night of 6.8 hours, but the most recent American Time Use Survey (ATUS) says that the average American sleeps eight hours and 42 minutes a night. Over the course of a week, that adds up to a discrepancy of about 13 hours. Some have suggested that the difference might be between the time spent in bed and the time actually asleep. One study (Lauderdale et al., 2006) monitored 669 middle-aged subjects and found that while they spent an average of 7.5 hours in bed per night, their sleep only averaged 6.1 hours.

But It's Not Enough. The Centers for Disease Control (CDC, 2015b) has concluded that "Insufficient sleep is a public health problem." The details:

> Sleep is increasingly recognized as important to public health, with sleep insufficiency linked to motor vehicle crashes, industrial disasters, and medical and other occupational errors. Unintentionally falling asleep, nodding off while driving, and having difficulty performing daily tasks because of sleepiness all may contribute to these hazardous outcomes. Persons experiencing sleep insufficiency are also more likely to suffer from chronic diseases such as hypertension, diabetes, depression, and obesity, as well as from cancer, increased mortality, and reduced quality of life and productivity. Sleep insufficiency may be caused by broad scale societal factors such as round-the-clock access to technology and work schedules, but sleep disorders such as insomnia or obstructive sleep apnea also play an important role. An estimated 50–70 million US adults have sleep or wakefulness disorder.

The CDC report also notes that how much sleep we need depends a great deal on age. Younger people need more, older people less. Adults need seven to eight hours nightly, close to the ATUS average but clearly more than the Gallup or Lauderdale averages. Even if the average is about where it should be, that means that half of us get less sleep than we need (and half more). A recent National Health Interview survey, for example, reported that about a third of all adults get six hours or less of sleep each night (Schoenborn and Adams, 2010).

So, if the measure (or at least a measure) of slothfulness is sleeping more than you should or lolling around in bed all day, then on first appearances it would seem that Americans need to be *more* slothful, not less.

We are now left with the time in the average day not spent working or sleeping. How do we spend those hours?

The best data for such matters are the ATUS, now done annually as a spin-off of the Current Population Survey. The 2014 results discussed here are based on approximately 11,600 individuals. In short, this is a high-quality and highly reliable data source (Figure 4.1).

As indicated, the chart shows average time use on an average working day for 25–54-year-old people with jobs and with children, perhaps the busiest group of people one would find anywhere. For these busy people, work and commutation take up the single largest chunk, 8.9 hours, followed by sleeping (7.7 hours). Preparing, serving and eating meals, caring for others, mainly the children, and a miscellany of other household chores collectively consume 3.2 hours, leaving 4.1 hours for "leisure, sports, and other." Sloth time would be somewhere within those 4.1 hours.

For the entire civilian adult population regardless of age, gender, employment status, or presence of children, the activities and time commitments of the average weekday and weekend day break downs as follows (BLS, 2015) (Table 4.1).

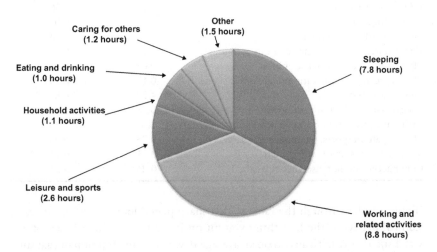

FIGURE 4.1 Time Use on an Average Work Day for Employed Persons Ages 25 to 54 with Children.

Note: Data include employed persons on days they worked, ages 25 to 54, who lived in households with children under 18. Data include non-holiday weekdays and are annual averages for 2015. Data include related travel for each activity.

Source: Bureau of Labor Statistics, American Time Use Survey.

TABLE 4.1 Time Spent in Various Primary Activities, Weekdays and Weekends: All Respondents (2014)

	Weekdays	Weekends and Holidays
Total	24.00	24.00
Personal care activities	9.33	10.16
Sleeping	8.54	9.40
Eating and drinking	1.13	1.29
Household activities	1.63	2.11
Housework	0.51	0.67
Food preparation and cleanup	0.57	0.62
Lawn and garden care	0.15	0.27
Household management	0.11	0.13
Purchasing goods and services	0.69	0.84
Consumer goods purchases	0.30	0.49
Professional and personal care services	0.11	0.04
Caring for and helping household members	0.56	0.49
Caring for and helping household children	0.42	0.39
Caring for and helping non-household members	0.17	0.21
Caring for and helping non-household adults	0.06	0.07
Working and work-related activities	4.54	1.38
Working	4.11	1.23
Educational activities	0.53	0.16
Attending class	0.33	0.02
Homework and research	0.16	0.13
Organizational, civic, and religious activities	0.24	0.52
Religious and spiritual activities	0.08	0.29
Volunteering (organizational, civic)	0.13	0.15
Leisure and sports	4.79	6.50
Socializing and communicating	0.58	1.02
Watching television	2.60	3.35
Participate in sports, exercise, recreation	0.28	0.33
Telephone calls, mail, and e-mail	0.15	0.14
Other activities, not elsewhere classified	0.24	0.21

If you wander through the table with a sharp pencil looking for instances of slothful behavior, the first thing you hit on is the two or three hours of TV watching that Americans do on an average day. Some tiny fraction of that time might be spent on the local PBS channel and, thus, potentially be educational, but the larger share must be couch-potato-style clicking through the mindless fare of commercial TV in the US – game shows, action series, reality TV, "jiggle TV," and all the other offerings of what critic Newton Minow once called "the vast wasteland" of American TV (in a speech given in 1961, no less).

Aha, true sloth at last! The term *couch potato* first appeared in print in the *LA Times* in 1979 but was first spoken aloud in July 1976 by one Tom Lacino on the phone to the wife of a friend. "Hey, is the couch potato there?" is said to be the first utterance.[11] The term has since come to refer to people who lie on the couch as much as possible, watch TV, and gorge on junk food. Whether two or three hours of TV and couch time a day qualifies as real couch-potato style leisure, I cannot say. But since the two-to-three-hour-a-day figure is an average, there are certainly a lot of people above that average, and for those well above it (and well above their ideal weight too), "couch potato" sounds like it might be the appropriate epithet.

Without doubt, those two or three hours of the day could be put to better use: Reading high-quality literature, say, or playing the piano, or taking a long stroll through the neighborhood, or any of dozens or hundreds of alternatives to yet another *Law and Order* rerun or another episode of *Keeping Up with the Kardashians*. At the same time, if, after a long day of work or grocery shopping or schlepping the kids to soccer practice and back, the average American wishes to soak his or her head in a couple of hours of warm TV, even nightly, who's to object? If our collective national sloth consists mainly of a couple hours of nightly relaxation in front of the boob tube, recharging one's batteries better to face the next day, this hardly seems to qualify as a besetting sin.

Alas, the TV hours are indicative of an even more serious and more subtle public health issue, namely, our so-called "sedentary lifestyles." And here the indictment is that we just spend way too much time sitting on our butts, much to our ultimate detriment. Sure, most Americans work, but more and more, work means sitting down, usually behind a desk or in front of a computer screen – doing brain work, perhaps, but not engaging in very much physical activity. We sit in our cars getting to and from work, sit on the school bus getting to and from school, sit while we work or study, sit while we eat, sit while we watch TV – sit, sit, sit throughout most of our daily activities. That is why sedentary lifestyles are often called the "sitting disease."

It is not as though Americans don't get *any* exercise. Sources ranging from the CDC to WebMD recommend 30 minutes a day of exercise as the minimum necessary for good health. Remarkably, based on the data from the ATUS (see the above table), that seems to be about what the US population averages. But one doubts that this is 30 minutes a day of vigorous cardiovascular exercise. More likely, we are talking about gardening or a leisurely walk at least as often as a 30-minute session on the treadmill. And what do 30 minutes a day of light exercise mean if we spend the other 23 and a half hours flat on our backs or just sitting?

The health risks of sedentary lifestyles have been summarized by Owen et al. (2010).

Compared with our parents or grandparents, we are spending increasing amounts of time in environments that not only limit physical activity but require prolonged sitting—at work, at home, and in our cars and communities. Work sites, schools, homes, and public spaces have been (and continue to be) re-engineered in ways that minimize human movement and muscular activity. These changes have a dual effect on human behavior: people move less and sit more.

Some of the trend data are stunning. In 1970, only about one American in five worked in a low-activity job; by 2000, that had jumped to two in five and has increased still further since. By early in the new century, six in ten working adults used a computer while at work; nine in ten children used a computer at school. In just 20 years, the number of homes with computers and Internet access leapt up from 15% (1989) to more than 75% today. "Other significant contributors to daily sitting time—watching television and driving personal vehicles—are at all-time highs, with estimates of nearly four hours and one hour, respectively."

Consequences of the sitting disease include increased cardiovascular risk, type 2 diabetes, obesity, and even some cancers. Some of these effects can, of course, be avoided by increased moderate-to-vigorous exercise. But more and more, exercise science reveals large differences between habitual sedentary behavior (too much sitting) and too little exercise, whether light or moderate. As indicated earlier, 30 or 40 minutes of vigorous exercise may not count for much if you spend the rest of your time sitting (or sleeping).

Accelerometers now make it possible to derive precise figures for how much time is spent in sedentary, light-intensity, and exercise behaviors. Sedentary means time sitting. Light activity means time spent standing, self-care activities, slow walking, perhaps pulling weeds in the garden, and the like. Exercise means serious aerobic exertion: A brisk walk, calisthenics, time on a treadmill, etc. Recent studies suggest that "the vast majority of daily non-sleeping time was spent in either sedentary behavior (58%) or light-intensity activity (39%), and only 3% in exercise time." There is further evidence that over time, there has been a shift from light activities to sedentary time so the situation is getting worse, not better. Finally, it is now clear that "all-cause mortality" (just what it says: Death from any and all causes) is associated with time spent watching television, overall daily sitting time, and time spent sitting in cars – i.e. time spent sitting.

The point here is that substantial health benefits can be derived from shifting sitting time to light-activity time, for example, by using standing desks rather than sitting desks, taking frequent breaks to walk around the halls, etc. (Alas, recent results do not suggest that standing desks confer any real health benefit; see Shrestha et al., 2016.) Vigorous physical exercise is probably even better, of course, but the problem is generally *not* that we get too little vigorous exercise.

The problem is that we spend way too much time sitting when we could be moving around. Even modest increases in light activity (vs. sitting) pay substantial health benefits. Whoever said "No Pain, No Gain!" was wrong.

Certainly we would be a healthier nation if people exercised more (and more vigorously) and watched TV less. But like anything, exercise can be overdone. A recent study in the journal *Circulation* (Armstrong et al., 2015) showed that strenuous exercise four to seven days a week *increased* the risk of cardiovascular disease, compared to two or three times a week. Media coverage of this news was widespread, much of it run under headlines such as "Couch Potatoes Rejoice: Strenuous Exercise May be Unhealthy" (the title of the item on the study that ran in the *Wall Street Journal*).

A final point is that to the extent prolonged sitting can be considered slothful, a great deal of present-day sloth is less a personal shortcoming and more an engineered feature of our environment. Cities are built to discourage walking and biking and to encourage the use of cars. Workplaces and schools are designed to be sitting environments, not places of active physical activity of any sort. Sure, almost all of us could sit less and move around more, and that would be beneficial, but doing so requires us to struggle against the design of the engineered world in which we live and not all of us have the energy or patience for that.

Do It Yourself

If the prevalence of the sitting disease can be taken as indicative of a high rate of sloth, then the American obsession with Do-It-Yourself (DIY) home projects is equally indicative of a high rate of industriousness. We seem almost habitually leery of contractors, repairmen, plumbers, carpenters and electricians and often insist on doing home fix-up and repair projects all by ourselves, even when (as is often the case) we possess neither the tools, knowledge or talent to do so.

Googling "do it yourself" turns up a rather astonishing range of DIY projects for which one can download advice, technical manuals, lists of do's and don'ts, and so on. A similar array of DIY material is available on YouTube. Among the obvious: How to repair a running toilet, fix a leaking faucet, rewire a three-way switch, or install a home irrigation system. But one can also find detailed how-to instructions on digging your own well, building your own home, installing solar energy systems, detailing your car, putting in a home security system, moving cross country, or installing a metal roof.

About a decade ago, the National Building Museum ran an exhibition entitled Do-It-Yourself: Home Improvement in 20th Century America. The brochure for the exhibition[12] is as close to a history of the American do-it-yourselfer as I have yet found. It points out, for example, that the arrival of the present-day DIY market was announced on the cover of *Time Magazine* for August 2, 1954.

as returning GIs and their counterparts on the home front encountered a host of new products and step-by-step instructions for how to use them. Members of this 'can-do' generation – primed by their fathers' basement workbenches and by Uncle Sam's Depression-era push to modernize the nation's housing stock – eagerly embraced the developing 'how-to' marketplace. Hobby enthusiasts and amateurs alike transformed themselves into handymen and handywomen as do-it-yourself grew from an acceptable, perhaps even desirable activity into an expected domestic leisure-time pursuit. The next generation pushed the do-it-yourself ethos further by focusing on older houses in need of care and repair.

There were earlier precursors, of course. The phrase "do it yourself" made its first appearance in 1912, in a magazine called *Suburban Life*, where men were encouraged to do their own interior painting rather than hiring painters. By 1930, Sears Roebuck featured a "building-materials catalog offering 'everything you need to build, remodel, modernize, or repair your house.'" By 1932, *Better Homes and Gardens* offered a "How We Rebuilt" contest, where readers were invited to send in "before" and "after" photos of their home renovations. *House Beautiful* followed suit the next year. And in 1952, *Business Week* noted that "In any suburb on any weekend, the master of the house is apt to turn into his own handyman. He's painting the porch, patching a pipe, or building an open-air fireplace so he can roast weenies in the garden."

Since the *Time* magazine article in 1954, power tools, building materials, paint, finishes, and a wide range of other products have been redesigned with the home DIY very much in mind. And do-it-yourself has evolved from a "dabbler's hobby" to an expected domestic pursuit and, by now, an integral part of American culture.

A century ago, few homeowners assumed they could make home improvements on their own – or even thought they should. Today, with resourcefulness and imagination, even homeowners on limited budgets can realize their aspirations. Once derided, then accepted, and eventually expected, taking tools in hand remains a leisure pursuit that provides a unique satisfaction: you can *do it yourself.*

Today, surveys show that about 70% of Americans prefer DIY over hiring professionals and that DIY has become a $40 billion a year industry.

A rather more scholarly treatment of the DIY movement can be found in the Proceedings of a conference held at the German Historical Institute, Washington, DC, April 25–26, 2014: *A Hands-on Approach: The Do-It-Yourself Culture and Economy in the 20th Century.*[13] The conference brought together historians, anthropologists, and other social scientists to consider DIY as the cultural link that ties together work, leisure, and consumption, "all three of which are important for defining individual as well as group identities."

A key theme in one of the sessions was the ongoing desire to demonstrate mastery over the environment by producing something independently of the industrialized consumer society. This, or so it was argued, "put DIY somewhere between opposition to and participation in the consumer society as well as the refusal and reinforcement of traditional values..." Yet another session contrasted handmade and homemade pornography with the more professionalized product.

> Arguing that mass-produced pornographic items did not necessarily reflect consumer wishes, [the presenter] emphasized how people articulated their individual sexuality, not least in places like prisons. Here, handmade pornography can be seen as a form of resistance to state attempts to control and organize sexuality.

(Handmade pornography? H-m-m-m.) A third session stressed the DIY movement as a "desire for a self-sufficient, egalitarian, community-based life that valued technical mastery and shared knowledge."

> The final discussion focused on general questions about the characteristics of DIY and its meaning in consumer societies. It was generally agreed that, both on a social and an individual level, DIY as a practice, a movement, and a market, offers deep insights into the social, cultural, and economic transformations of the twentieth century.

Who knew that a weekend of observation at the local Home Depot would yield "deep insights" into modern society? Evidently, it can.

Leisure Time Pursuits

We saw in an earlier table that the average American spends about 4 hours and 47 minutes on an average weekday and 6 hours and 30 minutes on an average weekend day engaged in leisure-time and sporting activities. Just what do people do in these times? What are the main leisure time pursuits of the American population?

ATUS gives us the following breakdown. The data are for all respondents regardless of gender, age, or labor force participation status and combine weekday and weekend activities. Clearly, the lion's share of our leisure time is spent in front of the television – TV watching eats up more than half our leisure time. "Socializing and communicating" come in second (38 minutes a day), followed by leisure time uses of the computer (27 minutes a day). "Sports, exercise, and recreation" get a meager 17 minutes a day, about the same amount of time that people spend "relaxing and thinking" (Figure 4.2).

A recent (2013) Gallup poll[14] asked people to name their two or three most preferred leisure time pursuits. As always, TV was the most commonly

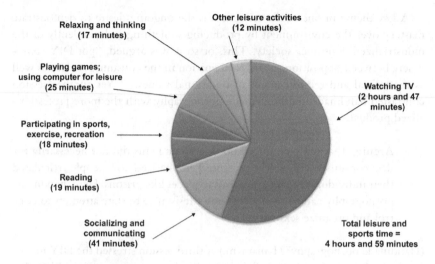

Relaxing and thinking (17 minutes)

Other leisure activities (12 minutes)

Playing games; using computer for leisure (25 minutes)

Watching TV (2 hours and 47 minutes)

Participating in sports, exercise, recreation (18 minutes)

Reading (19 minutes)

Socializing and communicating (41 minutes)

Total leisure and sports time = 4 hours and 59 minutes

FIGURE 4.2 Leisure Time on an Average Day.

Note: Data include all persons age 15 and over. Data include all days of the week and are annual averages for 2015.

Source: Bureau of Labor Statistics, American Time Use Survey.

mentioned (42%), followed somewhat surprisingly by reading (37%), then play-ing on the computer (29%) and "spending time with family and friends" (18%). The only other activities mentioned by 10% or more were going to the movies (11%) and working out (10%). Exercise, working out, walking, running, and jogging combined (in short, all the leisure activities that require physical ex-ertion) were only mentioned by 18%. So even our leisure time is dominated overwhelmingly by activities that require sitting.

Studies of leisure time activities in the United Kingdom show largely the same pattern: Watching TV is again Number One (the average Brit watches 25 hours of TV per week), followed by listening to the radio, then getting together with family and friends, going to the movies, and eating out. As for leisure activities outside the home, going to the local pub is the most popular.[15]

What do Americans watch when they watch TV? This was an easier ques-tion to answer back in the fifties and sixties when people only received three or four channels of programming on their home TV sets. Today, on average, Americans receive 189 separate cable channels (but only watch 17 of them). And what they watch most often on their 17 channels are sports (particularly foot-ball), dramas (the two most popular dramas in 2015 were Empire and Scandal), comedies (The Big Bang Theory and Modern Family were the two top rated comedies in 2015), and reality TV (here, The Voice led the list). News? Hardly. The top-rated TV news show, 60 Minutes, finished 2015 as the 79th most popular show on TV. Public television? The most successful PBS production of all time is probably Downton Abbey, and its market share for 2015 (3.5) would have put it 17th on the overall list, just behind Criminal Minds (a CBS reality offering that promises to take viewers inside the minds of selected heinous criminals). To call time spent in front of the TV "time wasted" is probably a bit harsh, but at the same time, there is very little on the list of most-watched shows that would be described as intellectually or spiritually uplifting.

What about Industriousness?

American workers put in more hours per working week than workers in any other industrialized nation except Korea, and are more productive (create more wealth per hour worked) than workers everywhere except Germany and France. There are many ways to measure worker productivity and not all of them give the same results, but American workers almost always finish somewhere in the top three or four in these rankings. US worker productivity has steadily increased each year since at least 1979 and at a much faster pace than wages have increased (in fact, despite the productivity gains, wages have barely increased at all). Sharply in contrast to the image of slothful or lazy workers, these facts regularly generate stories such as "Overworked America," "The US is the Most Overworked Nation in the World," "Americans Working Harder, Relaxing Less, than their Peers," and so on.

Concerns about what are called "compulsive workers" or "workaholics" have spawned a sizable research literature. The term workaholic was coined by a theologian, Wayne E. Oates, who published *Confessions of a Workaholic* in 1971 and used the concept to identify his own compulsive fixation on work. (The man wrote 57 books in his lifetime dealing with the relationship between theology and psychiatry, so "compulsive fixation" seems not to be an exaggeration.) Since then, psychologists, psychiatrists, sociologists, and organizational scientists have debated just what workaholism is, how it should be measured, whether it is always bad or can sometimes be good, the effects it has on marital stability and workplace aggression, how it might be prevented or treated, and how it is correlated with various social background variables and personality traits. All agree that the literature on workaholics has expanded exponentially in the last few decades.

As might be expected, there is no universally agreed upon definition of the concept and, therefore, no consensus on just what percentage of American workers actually display the compulsive worker syndrome. One common definition of workaholic is anyone who averages more than 50 hours of work per week. According to a recent Gallup poll (Saad, 2014), exactly half the US workforce works 40 hours a week or fewer; 11% average 41–49 hours, and the remaining 39% work 50 hours a week or more. Among salaried employees, the proportion working 50 or more hours a week pushes up to 50% (among hourly workers, only 23% work 50 or more hours in the average week). So by one common definition, two-fifths of all workers and half of all salaried workers are workaholics.

Other research has simply asked workers whether they self-identify as workaholics or not. About a third do (Hamermesh and Slemrod, 2005; Matuska, 2010).

Clark et al. (2014) have provided a recent and comprehensive summary of the correlates and outcomes of workaholism. The trait is related to achievement-oriented personality traits such as perfectionism and Type A personality, but largely unrelated to self-esteem, positive affect, or conscientiousness. So workaholism is *not* conscientiousness take to an extreme. Social background variables such as gender, marital status, parental status, and the like are weakly related, if at all, to workaholism. "Results also show that workaholism is related to many negative outcomes, such as burnout, job stress, work–life conflict, and decreased physical and mental health." So a workplace full of workaholics is not necessarily a good thing. Indeed, there is pretty solid evidence that "workaholism is best conceptualized as an *addiction* to work that leads to many negative individual, interpersonal, and organizational outcomes." The idea that compulsive working constitutes an addiction is widespread in the literature and at the heart of various efforts to treat the disorder.

It has thus become customary in the literature to differentiate between "work commitment" or "work engagement" and true addictive workaholism (see, e.g., Sussman, 2012). Work engagement is positively related to job performance, feelings of empowerment, positive affect, and good health. Work compulsion has the negative effects described above. Just where and when excess engagement turns into workaholism is a matter of intense debate. Sussman enumerates five characteristics that identify workaholism as a "negative addiction:"

- Excessive work hours
- Difficulty disengaging from work
- Frustration, anger, and resentment when prevented from working
- Inflexible, compulsive work style
- Associated negative life outcomes: Stress, low satisfaction, insomnia, burnout, poor health

True workaholics therefore often report miserable family lives (see also Yaniv, 2011), high levels of conflict and aggression at work (Balducci et al., 2012), and poor health outcomes (Shimazu et al., 2010). All in all, compulsive working does not seem to be any better than compulsive drinking, eating, or drug use.

How does workaholism in the US stack up against other advanced industrialized nations? One study compared the US with Belgium, Israel, Japan, and the Netherlands (Snir and Harpaz, 2006). The Japanese take pride of place as the most workaholic nation studied (and perhaps on earth). Japanese workers average almost 48 hours of work per week. "To the Japanese, work is an end in itself – what one does if one is human. It is the process of carrying out obligations owed to society and to oneself as a social being" (2006: 377). The Japanese word *karoshi* means literally death from work or overwork. Apparently, about 10,000 Japanese workers work themselves to death every year.

Belgium placed second in these standings, with an average workweek of 43.11 hours, followed by the US (41.65), Israel (41.49), and finally the Netherlands (39.37). So clearly, the US is not the only industrialized economy that harbors compulsive workers.

In sum: Many American workers voluntarily work extra unpaid hours on a regular basis. Many also decline to take vacations and in other ways exhibit a compulsive attachment to their jobs, usually at the expense of their health, social life, and marital relationships. This all makes me think that workers in general could use a little more sloth and a little less work compulsion in their lives, and that it is Eddie Cantor's advice that needs heeding the most. As author Sussman puts it at the conclusion of his review, after enumerating all the lacunae in the current literature on workaholism, "Clearly, there is much 'work' ahead; hopefully guided with some adequate personal time balance."

Closing Note: In Defense of Procrastination

A remarkable series of studies of the effects of procrastination has recently been described by Adam Grant in the *New York Times* (2016). Grant teaches management and organizational psychology at Penn's Wharton School of Business and describes himself as a "pre-crastinator," someone whose urges are always to start on a task immediately and get it done as quickly as possible. So he was surprised when one of his top students, Jihae Shin (now a professor at the University of Wisconsin) told him that all her really good ideas popped into her head at the last minute, after she had lingered at the task almost to the deadline. For her dissertation, Shin got access to a couple of companies, surveyed workers on their procrastination habits, and had their supervisors rate them on overall creativity. Result: "Procrastinators earned significantly higher creativity scores." Not satisfied with the one study, Shin designed a series of experimental studies where participants were asked to come up with some new, innovative business ideas. Participants were randomly assigned to two groups: One group started on the task immediately, while the second group was given an initial five minutes to play Minesweeper or Solitaire, and then begin. Again, the procrastinators were more creative – 28% more creative in Shin's studies.

The real world is full of extremely successful and creative chronic procrastinators, among them (according to Grant) Steve Jobs, Bill Clinton, Frank Lloyd Wright, and the screenwriter Aaron Sorkin who was notorious for putting off writing until the very last minute. When asked about this by Katie Couric, Sorkin is said to have replied, "You call it procrastination. I call it thinking…"

Grant warns, "Next time you're wallowing in the dark playground of guilt and self-hatred over your failure to start a task, remember that the right kind of procrastination might make you more creative." Sloths rule!

Notes

1 I am indebted to Paul Coelho's essay on sloth for the preceding points and for the Waugh reference. See http://paulocoelhoblog.com/2007/03/28/seventh-deadly-sin-sloth/.
2 https://stats.oecd.org/Index.aspx?DataSetCode=ANHRS.
3 www.bls.gov/cps/cpsaat08.pdf For evidence that "involuntary" part time workers are indeed involuntary, see Stratton, 1996.
4 www.usatoday.com/story/money/business/2014/01/21/states-people-working-two-jobs/4719485/.
5 My reference for this quotation is a web page maintained by democraticunderground.com and is probably not the most reliable source. Other sources refer to Yale rather than Harvard as the site of the utterance. And at least one source has Jeb Bush saying it, not George. Here's the link in any case: www.democraticunderground.com/discuss/duboard.php?az=viewall&address=389x8287771.
6 Watch it at www.addictinginfo.org/ 2015/12/03/steak-is-for-fucking-taxpayers-man-harasses-snap-recipients-steals-their-food-video/.
7 http://theweek.com/articles/449215/does-welfare-make-people-lazy.
8 The very first of the 76 million members of the Baby Boom generation is said to be one Kathleen Casey-Kirschling, born in Baltimore on January 1, 1946, at 12:00:01 a.m. In what turned out to be a media event of more than passing significance, Ms. Casey-Kirschling applied for Social Security benefits on October 15, 2007, at the age of 61 years 288 days. Many millions more have followed her lead.
9 www.theatlantic.com/business/archive/2015/06/ideal-retirement-age-work/396464/.
10 www.bankrate.com/finance/financial-literacy/americans-plan-to-work-through-retirement-1.aspx.
11 www.todayifoundout.com/index.php/2015/01/origin-trademarking-couch-potato/.
12 www.nbm.org/exhibitions-collections/exhibitions/diy.html?referrer=https://www.google.com/.
13 http://ghi-dc.org/index.php?option=com_content&view=article&id=1422&Itemid=1232.
14 www.statista.com/statistics/382623/most-popular-leisure-activities-among-adults-us/.
15 http://resources.woodlands-junior.kent.sch.uk/customs/questions/weekends.htm.

5

ANGER

I'm Mad as Hell and I am Not Going to Take It Anymore

Angry Voters

In *The Angry American* (subtitle: *How Voter Rage is Changing the Nation*), Susan Tolchin argues that American voters these days are consumed by rage. "[Political] scandals. The rise of militia and patriot groups. The proliferation of trash TV. Record US trade deficits. Isolated events, or is there some connecting thread?" The connection, of course, is electorate anger – "mainstream, inclusive, legitimate public anger... How to tap into this pervasive political anger and release its creative energy without being swept away by its force is the dilemma... for government leaders and citizens alike..."

An insightful dissection of the 2016 Presidential contest? Nope. The book whose arguments were just summarized was published in 1998 – almost two decades ago. *The New York Times* averred that 2016 was the "Year of the Angry Voter." But every election since 1964 has seen its share of angry voters. The "angry voter" meme seems to roll around like clockwork every four years.

1964? "Basically, Goldwater's hopes for victory have hinged on whether the voters were *angry* enough to want the drastic changes he has been proposing..." Evidently, they were not. The opinion piece just quoted was by Samuel Lubell and ran under the title *"Goldwater Isn't Able to Stir Voters' Anger."*[1] The anger was there, Goldwater just couldn't mobilize it.

1968? That was the year the *angry* "silent majority" elected Richard Nixon. Feisty George Corley Wallace, one of the last true segregationists, was also on the ballot in all 50 states.

> Like no candidate before, Wallace harvested the *anger* of white Americans who resented the progressive changes of the 1960s. Wallace supporters feared the urban violence they saw exploding on television. With tough

talk and a rough-hewn manner, Wallace inspired millions of conservative Democrats to break from their party....[2]

1972? The Democrats finally managed to nominate a candidate who was unequivocally opposed to the War in Vietnam. But McGovern's appeal was broader than that.

> McGovern's message echoed the public's *anger*. 'It is the establishment center,' McGovern proclaimed, 'that has erected an unjust tax burden on the backs of American workers, while 40 percent of the corporations paid no federal income tax at all last year'.

1976? Jimmy Carter was swept into power by a tide of "voter *anger* about Watergate."[3] 1980? American voters, *angry* at the "high inflation, high unemployment, and the low value of the United States dollar" and infuriated by the inability of the President to gain "the release of American hostages in Iran," elected Ronald Reagan to the Presidency.[4] 1992? "Voter choice in this three-candidate race [Bush, Clinton, and Ross Perot] [was] a function of economic perceptions, issue and ideological positions of voters and candidates, [and] *voter anger*" (Alvarez and Nagler, 1995).

1996? *Angry* Americans, faced with locked government offices and closed national parks, blamed the Republicans, forcing them to back down and pass a temporary measure to reopen the government on January 5, 1996. Voters who had once urged the Republicans onward in their attacks on big government now applauded Clinton for protecting their interests.

2000 and 2004? The run-up to the election of 2000 was pretty tame. But a great deal of anger surfaced when the Florida recount failed to produce a clear winner and the Supreme Court essentially gave the Presidency to Bush. A subsequent Gallup poll showed that among blacks and white Democrats, 68% and 55%, respectively, said they felt "cheated" by the outcome; 37% and 26% were "bitter" over the outcome, and 36% and 31% felt "*angry*."[5] In 2004, CBS News declared "*Anger* with Bush Drives Dem Voters,"[6] and *The American Thinker* opined that "While the ideological divide between the two sides often has been quite sharp, the current level of personal bitterness is unusually high, by recent historical standards."[7]

2008 and 2012? In 2008 (Obama vs. John McCain), voters (at least some of them) expressed fears about having a black man for President and a probable Muslim to boot. "I'm *mad*. I'm *really mad*. And what's going to surprise you, it's not the economy. It's the socialists overtaking our country."[8] One postelection headline read: "White Supremacist *Rage* Boils Over After Obama Victory."[9] In 2012, voters were asked to indicate how often they felt *angry* at the Democratic and Republican presidential candidates. More than two out of five Republican voters, 43%, reported feeling *angry* at Barack Obama either 'always' or 'most of the time.' By contrast, only 33% of Democratic respondents indicated a similar level of *anger* toward Mitt Romney.

Abramowitz and Webster (2015)

In the 2016 Presidential campaign, the Republican candidate Donald Trump rode a wave of voter anger straight to the Republican nomination and eventual Presidency, just as Bernie Sanders fashioned a credible campaign from populist anger on the left. Barely a political headline passed by that made no reference to the angry voters as the ones responsible for all this. "How Trump Dominated in Nevada, in one word: *ANGER.*" "Voter *Anger* Fueling Trump Phenomenon." "*Angry* White Males Propel Donald Trump – and Bernie Sanders." "Trump, Sanders and the *Angry* Voter." Examples could be multiplied almost without limit.

In their comment on the 2004 election, *The American Thinker* opined that "elections in which vengeful anger is the strongest motivating force for one or more sides deviate from the American norm." Hardly. Practically every election in the last half-century, and probably well before that,[10] has been driven by voter anger as a significant, if not always the strongest, "motivating force."

What, then, should we make of the consistency with which the angry voter meme appears in American political discourse?[11] Is it that the chattering classes are so bereft of analytic creativity that they have to recycle the same basic imagery year after year? Well, yes, that is certainly part of it. Find a couple of really pissed-off voters to supply a "man on the street" perspective, and your weekly commentary practically writes itself. But there is also an important residue of truth in the meme, namely, that without anger, there is no politics. Voters must have something sufficiently aggravating on their minds to get them out of the easy chair, away from the TV, and down to the polls to vote.

For many years, my research shop has done citizen surveys for local governments around Central Florida, usually to satisfy the "public participation" requirements in rewriting the municipality's Comprehensive Plan. These surveys always ask about satisfaction with local government and with its various responsibilities: the quality of police protection, code enforcement, local parks, sidewalks and street lighting, and so on. And we also always ask whether respondents have ever attended a meeting of the City Council or County Commission, whether they have ever spoken at a budget hearing, and whether they had ever written a letter or sent an email to a local elected official. Time after time and town after town, there is a strong correlation between any measure of direct participation in town affairs and the respondent's degree of dissatisfaction with local government. Happy, satisfied, "no worries" citizens simply do not take the trouble to go to a City Council meeting to express their contentment.

Only those who have a complaint bother. And ditto, it seems, for elections at all levels. *Of course,* angry voters dominate the political process. Happy voters could care less.

One useful indicator of the degree of anger in the American population might therefore be the overall level of political participation, and those levels tend to discount the "angry voter" theme. For starters, while estimates vary, somewhere between a quarter and a third of the politically eligible electorate (usually defined as US citizens over the age of 18) do not even bother *registering* to vote, a necessary first step. And among those who are registered, only about half vote in Presidential elections – sometimes a bit more than half, sometimes a bit less, but always in the vicinity of one out of two. Turnout in the off-year elections is even lower. Among the advanced Western democracies, voter turnout in the US ranks near the bottom. Those not registered and those registered but not voting comprise a sizable plurality in every election at all levels – Federal, state, and local. So it is not as though the large majority are just chomping at the bit to "throw the bums out" – the large majority simply subtract themselves out of the process. Unlike elsewhere, politics in America is largely a spectator sport.

Physical Violence

A recent project of some geographers from Kansas State University has been to map the seven deadly sins county by county all across the US. Obviously, such an undertaking requires ready-to-hand indicators, and the indicator chosen to represent anger (wrath) was the number of violent crimes (murder, assault, and rape) per capita. It is obviously true that there are more – many more – angry people in the US than there are murderers, assaulters, and rapists. And there are also legitimate questions about the proportions of murders, assaults, and rapes that are motivated by anger vs. by other motivators unrelated to anger (domination, revenge, pecuniary gain, etc.) Still, this gives us a place to begin.

Right off the bat, we confront a methodological question, namely, how does anyone know how many crimes are committed in the average year? Two methods predominate: one is to rely on the FBI's Uniform Crime Reports (UCR), which compile and report all the annual crimes that *are known to the police*; the other is to ask national survey samples whether crimes were committed against them in some previous time frame (typically the last year). Each method has advantages and disadvantages, discussed fully in Bureau of Justice Statistics (2014). We'll pick and choose as needed in the following discussion.

To begin, between the 1990s and the first decade of the 21st century, the overall crime rate, property crime rate, and violent crime rate all dropped precipitously, in what one expert describes as "the greatest crime decline in the twentieth century" (McCall and Hendrix, 2015). Why the crime rates fell so much is not precisely understood, but that they did is indisputable. So if the rate of crime, particularly the rate of violent crime, is indeed indicative of the overall level of anger in the society, we have become a dramatically less angry nation since the 1990s.

McCall and Hendrix examine three general classes of explanation for the crime rate decline: changing demography (fewer young people, more immigrants), changing criminal justice practices (incarceration policies, policing strategies, gun control), and changing social and economic conditions (waning crack-cocaine markets, economic boom times in the 1990s, impact of legal abortion on unwanted births). There is some evidence in favor of each factor but none is sufficient in itself to explain the entire trend. We are left with the conclusion that a concatenation of favorable circumstances brought the crime rate down to current low levels.

Just how low? As of this writing, the most recent year for which we have complete data is 2014, and in that year, 1,165,383 violent crimes were estimated to have occurred nationwide (and were reported to the police), which translates into a rate of 366 violent crimes per 100,000 population. So in any given (recent) year, 99.4% of the US population is *not* a victim of criminal violence. It is worth a further note that the 2014 violent crime rate was down 1% compared to 2013, down 6.9% compared to 2010, and down 16.2% compared to 2005.

Aggravated assault is by far the most numerous of the violent crimes. Assaults accounts for 64% of all the violent crimes that occur. Armed robbery is second at 28%, followed by rape (7%) and murder (1%). These are all UCR results and there is strong reason to believe that sexual assault is disproportionally under-reported to the police, so there is probably more rape "out there" – conceivably, a lot more – than these figures indicate.

In terms of raw numbers, 2014 witnessed 14,249 murders. Experts assume that almost all murders eventually come to the attention of the police, so this is probably a pretty solid number. In contrast, the 84,041 rapes that were reported to the police could conceivably be as little as a tenth of all the rapes that occur. The completeness of the data on armed robbery and aggravated assault is, well, anybody's guess. But since at least some, and perhaps, many of these crimes are not reported to the police, these UCR estimates are lower boundary estimates at best.

Experts in intimate partner violence (IPV) argue that rape is rarely a crime of rage or passion; rather, rape is how perpetrators exert power and control over their victims. This is nearly an article of faith among domestic violence researchers but has been challenged by Felson (2002), who has argued that the motives for violence against women – to control, to achieve retribution, to defend self-image – are the same as the motives for violence against men.

There is also an argument that most murders are spur-of-the-moment crimes of passion, rage, and anger, the typical evidence for which is that most murderers and their victims were known to each other prior to the murderous assault. But the more I explore this line of reasoning, the less persuasive it becomes.

The conclusion that most murders are not calculated or even premeditated, but rather are heat-of-the-moment slayings, as I say, is based on the common finding that victims and perpetrators know each other before the event. To many, it seems obvious that these altercations between associates turn deadly not so much because anyone intended them to, but because in a moment of passion or rage, a gun was at hand.

Evidence on victim–offender relationships in homicide is published annually by the FBI as part of the UCR. I first looked up these data back in the 1980s and I check back every so often to see if things have changed. One thing that *has* changed is that there are many fewer homicides these days than there were in the 1980s, before the crime rate began to drop. In 1988, to illustrate, there were something more than 18,000 murders reported to the FBI. In 2012, the year I focus on here, the number had dropped to 12,765, roughly a 30% decline.

In 2012, the FBI data on relationships between victims and offenders in homicide are reported in the UCR Report Expanded Homicide Data, Table 10. The 2012 patterns are effectively identical to the patterns that have been reported since the 1980s, and those patterns raise some serious doubts about the conventional depiction of victim–offender relationships. In 2012, we indeed find that "strangers" accounted for only 12.2% of the total. But this assuredly does not mean that the remaining 87.8% involved loved ones slaying one another.

To begin, the relationship between victim and offender is simply unknown in a very large percentage of cases. In 2012, "relationship unknown" was the case in 5,757 murders, or 45.1% of the total – almost half! This would obviously be the case for all the unsolved homicides, and perhaps, of some others (where, say, the relationship was too ambiguous to determine even though the offender was known).

The next largest category after "unknown" is "acquaintance," accounting for 21.3%. Since "friends," "boyfriends," "girlfriends," "neighbors," and all categories of relatives are tallied in other categories of their own, "acquaintance" cannot possibly be more than a casual acquaintance – it means that the victim and the offender had some idea of who each other were. This obviously does *not* imply lengthy, close, or affectionate relationships.

All categories of family and relatives combined (husband, wife, mother, father, son, daughter, brother, sister, and "other family") account for 12.5% of all murders – a mere one in eight. Persons described as "friends" or "neighbors" added another 8.9%. Altogether, then, family members, relatives, friends, and neighbors total barely one in five – 21.4%. It is definitely *not* the case that "most" murders involve persons who share some degree of intimacy or closeness. "Most" murders – almost 80% of them – are committed by casual acquaintances (21.3%), perfect strangers (12.2%), or persons unknown (45.1%).

That many murder victims know their killer beforehand is scarcely surprising. Ordinarily, the only people one would ever have any reason to kill would be people known to oneself. Contrary to the common assumption, some degree of prior acquaintance between victim and offender definitely does *not* rule out willful, murderous intent.

Actual family homicides, where victims and offenders are related by blood or marriage, comprise one-eighth of the total. Studies of these family homicides have shown that most of them involve families who have had previous domestic quarrels and disputes serious enough to bring the police to the residence. Indeed, most of the families in which family homicides occur have long histories of interpersonal violence and abuse going back years or even decades. These slayings, that is, are often *not* isolated outbursts of hatred or rage among normally placid, loving couples. Instead, they are the culminating episodes in long, violent, abusive family relations.

Obviously, a great deal turns on the actual relationship between victim and offender in the large percentage of cases where this relationship is unknown. Many presentations of these data simply omit all the "unknowns" and then re-percentage the data only for cases where the relationship is known. This, of course, changes the percentages drastically and it also assumes that the actual relationships in murders where the relationship is not known are identical to those where the relationship is known. But it seems very likely that homicides involving family members, close friends, or neighbors would be precisely the ones where the victim-offender relationship is most likely to be known; and very much less likely to be known if the offender was only a casual acquaintance or a complete stranger.

How many murders are committed in the stereotypical moment of rage? And how many result from an unambiguous, willful intention to kill? The fact is, nobody knows. An adequate answer depends on knowing what is going on inside the heads of murderers as they contemplate and then commit their offenses. The assumption that "heat of the moment" murders far outnumber willful murders has traditionally been justified with evidence similar to that considered here. Many interesting inferences can perhaps be drawn from such evidence, but inferences about homicidal motivations are not among them.

This leaves the armed robberies and the aggravated assaults. Pretty obviously, the motive in most armed robberies is economic gain, not uncontrollable wrath. In fact, in a study we did of incarcerated felons some years ago (Wright and Rossi, 1986), a main motive for carrying a gun in robberies was so that the victim would do what you wanted, and that way, you didn't have to hurt them. As for the assaults, the main precipitating factor seems to be what the FBI calls "altercations," which we can translate pretty accurately as bar fights over women, drink, or politics. In most assaults, the "victim" is whoever goes to the hospital and the "perpetrator" is whoever goes to jail.

So maybe violent crimes are not such a meaningful indicator of anger after all. In each case, as we have seen, the motivations of the perpetrators are at best ambiguous – perhaps rage, yes, but perhaps willful intent, economic gain, or sexual expiation. And in any case, if we insist that criminal violence *is* a meaningful indicator of anger, then it is one that leaves 99.6% of the US population untouched in the average year. That number ought to be considered in light of the percentage of all US households that possess a firearm, which is somewhere between a third and a half (Wright, 2016). Given that fact and the common depiction of "angry Americans," the remarkable thing about the US homicide rate would be not that it is so high, but that it is so *low.*

Spouse Abuse

Although counted as an assault when it is known to the police, wife battering and spousal abuse more generally warrant special consideration as instances of uncontrolled anger. One source describes the following scenario:

> Vandana, a middle class house wife, is a little late in coming home from the market. An enraged husband beats her up, giving her a black eye. Like all wife beaters, he needs only a flimsy excuse to physically abuse his wife. It could be because she has not cooked the vegetables properly, or has misplaced something in the house. When he is dissatisfied with her behavior, he simply uses his fist to 'discipline' her! What is frightening is that many victims of wife battering have sustained serious injuries, sometimes even resulting in their death.

This is from a story titled *"Wife Beating – men batter women for trivial reasons"* and appeared in a magazine article published on September 18, 2006.[12] A discerning reader would, I think, have two reactions: one, a reaction ranging from pity to rage that such things go on in this world, and two, a natural curiosity about just how common this sort of disgusting behavior is.

There is an immense research industry focused on what has come to be called IPV, although terms such as domestic violence or family violence are also commonly encountered. Alas, since the very first surveys were done in the 1980s and 1990s, each generation of researchers has added more and more behaviors to the IPV inventory and then has come up with progressively larger numbers of victims. In the most recent National Intimate Partner and Sexual Violence Survey (Black et al., 2011), for example, some of the things that are counted as sexual *violence* include:

- Kissed you in a sexual way (unwanted kissing)
- Exposed their sexual body parts to you (flashing)
- Harassed you in a public place
- Wearing you down by repeatedly asking for sex, or showing they were unhappy
- Left you unwanted messages? This includes text or voice messages.

- Made unwanted phone calls to you? This includes hang-up calls.
- Sent you unwanted emails, instant messages, or sent messages through websites
- Told you that you were a loser, a failure
- Called you names like ugly, fat, crazy, or stupid
- Made fun of you in front of others
- Tried to keep you from seeing or talking to your family or friends
- Kept track of you by demanding to know where you were and what you were doing
- Refused to use a condom when you wanted him to use one
- Slapped you
- Pushed or shoved you

To be sure, the items also include clear, unambiguous cases of serious physical violence: hit you with a fist, tried to choke you, beat you, burned you, or used a knife or gun on you. But beyond what most of us would think about when hearing the phrase domestic *violence*, the current conception includes all efforts to control sexuality, coercion, "expressive aggression," stalking, and pretty much any unwanted sexual expression, proposition, or innuendo you can imagine. When most people think about "violence against women," they are *not* thinking about expressive aggression or even stalking. So when we read, for example, that a third of all women and a fourth of all men have experienced "sexual assault" in their lifetimes, we don't realize that this includes unwanted kissing, name-calling, or the unappreciated slap on the butt. It doesn't help that the IPV specialists, like the drug economists, seem intent on coming up with the largest possible numbers no one will laugh at.

When I was in college, I knew an older man Vince who was married to a lovely and sophisticated woman whom I will call Rebecca. Vince was a devout Catholic, but he was also a mean, warped human being. His only route to sexual gratification was to mount Rebecca doggie-style and rape her in the anus while he beat her across the back with a piece of broom handle. After each such episode, Vince would hie himself off to church, tearfully confess his aggressions, promise that he would never do it again, and dutifully take a few spins around the rosary. And for a few weeks thereafter, he was a model husband. But then the hormones, rage, psychosis, or just plain meanness would well up in him again and there would be another anal rape, beating, and subsequent confession. As for Rebecca, she suffered numerous broken bones in her shoulders and ribs, a cracked spine a couple of times, a cracked skull once, and was permanently deformed because of her spinal injuries.

When I first encountered the research on domestic violence (as a graduate student in the late 1960s), I just naturally assumed that what we were talking about were situations like Vince and Rebecca, and when I saw the percentages of victims being reported in the studies, I was flabbergasted. But as

I later learned, we were also talking about my friends Dick and Eileen (Eileen got so frustrated one day that she threw a glass of lemonade on Dick – that counts as sexual violence), and about me and my college sweetheart (who sometimes had to be talked into intercourse – that's coercion and counts as sexual violence) or my other friends John and Jacquie (whose occasional marital disagreements turned into pretty vulgar shouting matches – that's verbal and emotional abuse and counts as sexual violence). And in the process of widening the definition of "abuse," we have pretty much lost track of cases such as Vince and Rebecca. So when we are told, for example, that "somewhere between 23% and 66% of American women are physically assaulted by a spouse or co-habitant lover during their lifetimes," we need to ask first why the range is so wide, and second, just what behaviors, exactly, are being counted as "physical assaults."

What I really want to know is how many Rebeccas or Vandanas are out there in the American population. How many women are physically beaten (not shouted at, pushed, or called names, but *beaten*) because they overcooked the green beans or got stalled in traffic on the way home from the gym or for some other trivial reason related to uncontrolled male rage? In the 2014 FBI homicide data, we find 539 murders of wives by husbands (about 4% of all murders). In the extreme case, then, fatal wife battering is pretty rare. Three of these wife-murders apparently resulted from an argument over money, eight involved some sort of love triangle, two were in drug- or alcohol-induced brawls, and all the rest were "others." Not too useful, I admit. But then, there *are* no truly useful data on the question whose answer we seek. Even a more narrowly construed concept such as *wife battering* includes psychological as well as physical and sexual assault.

Hate Crimes

A less ambiguous category of crimes of rage or anger is the "hate crime." For statistical purposes, the FBI defines a hate crime as "a criminal offense against a person or property motivated in whole or in part by an offender's bias against a race, religion, disability, sexual orientation, ethnicity, gender, or gender identity." An important proviso: "Hate itself is not a crime—and the FBI is mindful of protecting freedom of speech and other civil liberties."

FBI statistics register fewer hates crimes than almost any other category. In 2014, there were only 5,479 hate crime incidents reported to the police, involving 6,418 offenses and 5,176 known offenders. Murder is three times more numerous, and rape twenty times (just counting rapes known to the police). By focus of hate, racial bias was implicated in almost half of these incidents (47%), followed at some remove by sexual orientation bias (19%), religious bias (also 19%), ethnic hatreds (12%), and the remaining 3% from a miscellany of despicable dislikes.

Within these categories, the leading contributors were as follows:

- Race: anti-black bias (64%); anti-white bias (23%)
- Sexual orientation: anti-gay male bias (58%); anti-lesbian bias (14%); anti-same-sex relationship-of-any-sort bias (26%)
- Religion: anti-Jewish bias (58%); anti-Muslim bias (16%)
- Ethnicity: 48% anti-Hispanic bias; 52% bias against some other ethnicity

Some of these results merit a comment if only in passing. For all the anger surrounding the Black Lives Matter movement and the often-expressed fears of whites about the African-American population, anti-black prejudice generates almost three times more hate crimes than anti-white prejudice does. And rather remarkably in the current social and political climate, anti-Semitism accounts for 3.6 times more hate crimes than anti-Muslim prejudice does.

There were also 95 reported hates crimes in 2014 that were classified as resulting from "disability bias," of which 69 were directed against persons with mental disability and 26 against persons with physical disabilities. These crimes against the disabled have been called "the Invisible Hate Crime" (Levin, 2011) and often involve levels of sadism that are truly extraordinary. One case recounted by Levin involved a 30-year-old mentally disabled woman, who was kidnapped by six people and held hostage for days, during which her head was shaved, she was bound with Christmas decorations, beaten with a towel rack and vacuum cleaner hose, fed detergent, urine, and various medications, then was forced to write and sign a suicide note before her captors stabbed her to death.

What we learn from the incidence of hate crimes is that there are clearly enough bigoted and violent creeps out there ready, willing and able to perpetrate sadistic, hateful acts that we can expect a sizable annual stain on our certificate of membership in the community of civilized nations. But given the size of the US population, the ready availability of the instruments of violence, and the amount of ink spilt each year calling attention to Americans' residual hatreds – of blacks, Asians, Jews, Muslims, atheists, Hispanics, Arabs, immigrants, refugees, Cubans, gays, lesbians, the transgendered, the disabled, even Canadians, for heaven's sake (Harrison, 2007) – one would expect hate crimes to leave a much larger statistical trace in the UCR data than they seem to do.

Road Rage

Still another accretion of anger that is much discussed these days is road rage, defined as "violent anger caused by the stress and frustration involved in driving a motor vehicle in difficult conditions" – the kind of rage that wells up in the soul when you are sitting motionless in traffic after a long day, horns blaring, middle fingers extended, a snarling "Fuck you, you asshole!" hanging on every commuter's lip. A recent survey done by the American Automobile Association found that 80% of American drivers ranked "aggressive driving," both the cause and the effect of road rage, as a serious or extremely serious threat to their safety.

As one might expect, there is a pretty substantial literature on road rage, much of it produced by psychiatrists and psychologists who seem intent on depicting the phenomenon as a product of various personality disorders (vs. a response to situational frustrations). Indeed, in the current version of the Diagnostic and Statistical Manual, psychiatry's official listing of mental and personality disorders, road rage is mentioned as an example of "Intermittent Explosive Disorder" (DSM-5 312.34 in case you want more details).

> Because of the violent and intimidating nature of intermittent explosive disorder, the patient is likely to experience significant impairment in many areas. Common behavioral manifestations of intermittent explosive disorder include road rage, domestic violence, child abuse, and property damage.

Barry Glassner, whose work we consider in detail below, calls this "psycho-blather."

Lustman et al. (2010) link aggressive driving to narcissism and anger; Sansome et al. (2010) find a correlation between road rage and borderline personality disorder. The latter also report that about a third of their subjects self-reported road rage, and that road rage was correlated, although not strongly, with the number of prior driving citations (but not with automobile accidents or DUI episodes). The relationship between road rage and prior citations is also reported in Sansone et al. (2012). And there is some evidence (from Spain) that road rage is also associated with alcohol and illicit drug use (Fierro et al., 2011).

It appears, moreover, that automobile drivers do not have a monopoly on road rage. A study of serious bicyclists in Australia (O'Connor and Brown, 2010) quotes one interviewee as follows:

> ... all of the people that I ride with have road rage instances often, its full-on... They're always having problems... and they [fellow cyclists] go off 50 times worse than I do in regards to road rage... we chase down cars, I bang on roofs. Usually if I go down the bike lane and if there's a car in the bike lane, I grab their mirror...so that they think they've hit me...

When respondents in this study were asked whether cycler arrogance is often the cause of abuse from drivers, the majority indicated moderate agreement.

Just how big a problem is road rage? Asbridge and Butters (2013) describe the problem as "a key criminal justice and public health concern." Survey estimates of road rage (basically, the percentages of various samples who self-report incidents of road rage) range from 5% to 40% but seem to average about a third – in short, common enough but well short of a majority of drivers (Sansone and Sansone, 2010). Studies also show that road rage seems to be a property mainly of younger males; women and seniors do not seem prone to the behavior. Other nonpsychological correlates include number of miles driven per day, traffic congestion and density, and, somewhat alarmingly, carrying a firearm in the car. So the next time you get cut off on the freeway, choose your response carefully or the miscreant might open up with his .38.

Barry Glassner's chapter on "Dubious Dangers on Roadways and Campuses" in his book on *The Culture of Fear* is a delightful corrective to the evident moral panic that has come to surround the topic of road rage. His dissection begins with a recounting of some of the more vivid media presentations of the road rage meme. An Oprah Winfrey segment on road rage contained the remark, "We've all been there. It starts out with a tap of the horn, an angry gesture, a dirty look…" This was followed by "a few actual incidents in which the outcome was a shooting or a fistfight." The unspoken but obvious truth: Every day, there are thousands or hundreds of thousands of horn beeps, angry gestures and dirty looks, but there are not thousands of shootings or fist fights, not hundreds, not even dozens. Stringing together the common with the exceptional is a quick route to moral panic.

Another example comes from a story in the *Los Angeles Times* about road rage, "an exploding phenomenon across the country."

> Only after wading through twenty-two paragraphs of alarming first person accounts and warnings from authorities did the reader learn that a grand total of five drivers and passengers had died in road rage incidents in the region in the previous five years.
>
> *(p. 4)*

Glassner refers readers to a study done by the American Automobile Association showing that of about 250,000 people killed on highways between 1990 and 1997, a mere 218 deaths could be attributed to angry drivers – fewer than one in a thousand. Year after year, he notes, "drunk driving causes about 85 times as many deaths as road rage."

Rage and Anger Surveys

The incessant media babble about the angry American voter prompted *Esquire Magazine* and NBC News to team up on a survey of "American Rage," results of which were published by *Esquire*'s editors on January 3, 2016.[13] The bold-faced front tag on the story read:

> We the people are pissed. The body politic is burning up. And the anger that courses through our headlines and news feeds—about injustice and

inequality, about marginalization and disenfranchisement, about what they are doing to us—shows no sign of abating. Esquire teamed up with NBC news to survey 3,000 Americans about who's angriest, what's making them angry, and who's to blame.

This is by no means the most sophisticated survey you'll ever come across but there are some useful nuggets that are revealing about rage in America today.

The key question in the survey asks: "How often do you hear or read something in the news that makes you angry?" Note: This does not ask how often something happens to you that makes you angry. So the question would seem to exclude road rage, passing insults, waiters' snubs, extended time spent "on hold," long lines, indifferent receptionists, and a great deal more that would anger most people most of the time. It also specifies "in the news." So really, we are talking about anger resulting from local, national or world affairs, not anger at one's spouse or children, anger at the price of milk, anger over the stupidity of commercial TV, anger at the school board's decision to end bus service to your subdivision, or anything of the sort, just anger over "something in the news."

So let's ask first, how many people even watch the evening news, read a newspaper, or keep up with local, state, national, and international affairs on the web. Not too many, it appears. About 20 million people watch the evening news on one of the three major commercial networks (ABC, CBS, or NBC). Cable news networks (CNN, MSNBC, Fox News, CNBC, etc.) have total markets numbering in the hundreds of thousands (at best, a bit more than a million). Fewer than one American in four reads a daily print newspaper, an all-time low. If we assume that people who do not follow the news are never angered by what they see, read, or hear there, then among those who do, the number who find themselves angered almost daily would have to approach 100%!

In fact, the results for the question were as follows:

About how often do you hear or read something in the news that makes you angry?

A few times a day	31%
Once a day	37%
Once a week	20
Once a month	5
Rarely	6

So about two-thirds of the population say they find something in the news that makes them angry once a day or more often. Since this evidently exceeds the percentage of the population that follows the news, one is entitled to wonder just what this result means.

At least once a day, the news has an item on some terrorist horror some-where in the world, some horrific murder at home, some sleazeball politician being indicted for corruption, some local business that has been ripping off its customers, some government agency that has inflicted some new bureaucratic inanity on "we, the people." The remarkable thing about the results from this survey is not that two-thirds get angry at least once a day but that anyone who follows the news does not. These results reflect more on the state of the world than on the psyche of the American population.

Anger has apparently increased since last year. Forty-eight of respondents say they get angry more often than they did a year ago, 42% get angry about as often, and 8% get angry less often. It is possible, and perhaps likely, that these results reflect where we were in the Presidential election cycle in 2014 vs. when this survey was done (mid to late 2015).

Anger was unevenly spread over the income distribution. The least angry income brackets, surprisingly, were those at the bottom ($15,000 or less per year) and those at the top ($150,000 and up per year). The angriest were those in the middle, the so-called "middle class" ($50,000–75,000 a year). Just what they have to be angry about compared to those at the very bottom of the income distribution is anybody's guess.

One obvious source of anger is the lingering effects of the Great Recession, and this made itself felt in the American Rage survey. A bit more than half said that "I'm worse off today than I thought I would be" when I was younger; one in four was better off; another one in four was "about where I thought I'd be…"

There was also a long series of questions on just what makes people so angry. The things that make Republicans angry were a dysfunctional Congress, mas-sive consumer fraud, and cops shooting unarmed black men. The latter was first on the Democratic list, followed by massive consumer fraud, and a "billionaire vowing to spend $500 million on the 2016 elections." The gender differences were also of interest: Men are angrier than women about global warming and gay marriage; women are angrier than men about police violence against black people and billionaires buying elections.

Who has a right to be angry about how they are treated? Blacks led this list (47% of the total population felt that blacks had a right to be angry about how they are treated), following by LGBT people (45%), women (42%) and Hispanics (37%). Further down the list: Muslims (34% – a surprisingly strong showing), white men (18% – c'mon guys, get off it!), and at the very bottom, atheists (16%). Interestingly, in a population depicted as seething with rage, not one group achieved a majority consensus that they had a right to be upset. So is that the story: Everyone's pissed but no one has a right to be?

A final question of note asked, "Do you think elected officials generally enact policies that favor the interests of all Americans or mainly the wealthy?" The 78% consensus was that policies favor the wealthy.

Studies in the Sociology of Emotions

Having seen what media mavens come up with when they feed on the anger meme, let's next ask what serious scholars have to say about the topic. One such is Scott Schieman, a self-described analyst of the emotions who has written a helpful overview of what we know about the emotion of anger (Schieman, 2010). Anger, Schieman helpfully reminds us, "provides drama; rage enlarges it." Continuing,

> Anger can sharpen one's critical perspective and creative edge. Its expression can stimulate the lifeless and detached. While there is little doubt that anger can be personally and socially destructive – if it is too intense, enduring, and misdirected – anger can motivate and mobilize efforts against the injustices of everyday life.
>
> *(2010: 329)*

Too, anger is less a personality trait than a response to anger-inducing situations. Sure, we all know people who seem to have "angry" personalities and who are enraged by the slightest insult. And the psychologists have described an "anger disorder" that is considered to be a borderline personality disorder. But then, the DSM describes people who spell poorly as suffering from "disorders of the written expression," so we do well not to take them all too seriously. For most people most of the time, anger is a stress response to aggravating situations.

Most people, it seems, have little trouble distinguishing between anger and other emotions such as sadness or fear, but there are "anger-like" emotions – frustration, reproach, resentment, and the like – where the distinctions are less clear. In research on anger, terms such as annoyance, outrage, and anger tend to be used interchangeably.

A common measure of anger that has been deployed in numerous national surveys asks how often people "felt annoyed" in the past week. Different surveys give sharply different results, but in general population surveys (as opposed, for example, to surveys of workers), somewhere around 40% will say that "they did not feel annoyed at all" in the past week, while as many as 25% feel annoyed nearly every day.

A similar question about how often people feel angry gives largely similar results. In most surveys, about 40% say they were angry on no days of the past week, a similar number say they were angry on one or two days, with the remainder being angry more frequently.

Annoyance and anger questions have been included in national surveys since the 1990s, so it is possible to look at trends. Interestingly, annoyance has apparently increased pretty substantially, while anger (or better, the frequency with which people feel angry) has been virtually constant. Schieman attributes this to various social changes in the past two decades: "the proliferation of loud-speaking users of cell phones in public spaces, increasingly congested traffic, and the constant stream of unpleasant news about terrorism, an unpopular war in Iraq, and global warming." To this list, I would add the always unpleasant news about ISIS, the global immigrant crisis, the worldwide sexual exploitation of children, and a large number of other annoyances. Again, the surprise is not that so many are annoyed by these developments but that anyone is not.

Being annoyed or angry is one thing; doing something about it is another. The one angry behavior that has been studied in some depth is yelling, which is far less frequent than experiencing feelings of anger or annoyance – "probably because of the greater intensity and severity of anger that yelling represents, as well as its social consequences" (2010: 332). Obviously, other responses to anger like punching someone out or shooting them are rarer still.

We have also learned a fair amount about how anger is distributed in society. To begin, there is a great deal of research showing that "emotion-related experiences (negative and positive) are typically linked to relationships in work or family roles" (2010: 334) and, moreover, that within families, the presence of children is a major stressor. So we would naturally expect that the "epidemiology of anger" would hew pretty closely to exposure to work and family stressors. And here, the data do not disappoint.

Consider age. Younger people, just starting out in their careers, will generally have worse jobs and more work-related stressors than middle-aged people at the peak of their earning power; retired people will have none. So the expectation is that younger people will be angrier, middle-aged people less angry, and the old will be the least angry at all. And this indeed is what the research shows. "There is also evidence that older adults experience lower levels of other social causes of anger, including economic hardship, work-home conflict, job dissatisfaction, and interpersonal conflict in the workplace."

Ditto education and income: More education = better jobs = less workplace aggravation = less anger. And likewise, more income = less hardship = less stress = less anger. Interestingly, while the research consistently supports both these generalizations, "there is an unusual and small blip in level of anger among individuals with earnings between $60,000 and $79,000" – just what the American Rage survey showed. (On possible nonlinearities between anger and occupational status, see also Collett and Lizardo, 2010.)

Results for gender generally do not support that men are angrier than women, or vice versa. Men and women experience anger at about the same rate. The gender difference is in how anger, once experienced, gets processed. "Once angered, women think about the anger more, talk more to the person they feel angry with, and take longer to stop feeling angry." Also, "men tend to see anger as taking control of a situation while women tend to experience anger as losing control of themselves." It has also been shown that among women, persistent anger is associated with higher rates of depression (Simmons and Lively, 2010) – reminiscent of the theory that depression is "anger turned inward," a topic we take up in detail below.

Other reasonably consistent research findings: Children (any age) are anger-inducing to parents; "average parents report high levels of anger with their children, the need to... control their anger, and fear that they will at some time lose control and harm their children." Anger-engendering conflicts between work demands and home life are more often reported by women. Economic hardships and perceived inequities are often sources of anger for many people.

Schieman also reports his own intriguing multivariate analysis of anger. The analysis holds constant the socio-demographic effects we have just discussed (specifically age, gender, education, race, marital status, household size, and a few others) and then looks at other factors that might generate (or mollify) anger: economic hardship, feeling rushed for time, negative life events (deaths, divorces, job losses), home–work conflicts, interpersonal conflicts at work, job satisfaction, trust, and religiosity. While all these variables performed pretty much as expected (thus, economic hardship and negative life events increase anger whereas job satisfaction, trust, and religiosity decrease it), the most powerful determinant of anger among those listed (by a substantial margin) was feeling rushed for time. "The sense that one has insufficient time to deal with demands, expectations, and responsibilities in core social roles is likely to be one of the most frustrating, chronic conditions of everyday life" (2010: 336).

The "Frustration-Aggression" Hypothesis

Sanford Lyman's (1978) discussion of anger dwells at some length on a theory originally developed in the 1930s by John Dollard that has come since to be known as the "frustration–aggression hypothesis." Subsequently refined by Neil Miller and Leonard Berkowitz (see Berkowitz, 1969 for the history), the theory in its simplest form states that aggression is the result of blocking, or "frustrating" persons' efforts to attain their goals. The original formulation was intended to help understand black-white confrontations and violence in the Depression-era South.

The hypothesis stimulated a great deal of research, much of it experimental, on topics such as scapegoating, violence, and a wide variety of other aggressive behaviors. Alas, the theory has been more or less abandoned in recent years because, as stated in a recent essay on the social psychology of aggression, "it quickly became obvious that frustration does not always lead to aggression, and that not every act of aggression can be traced back to frustration" (Warburton and Anderson, 2015). Basically, frustrations are situational disturbances, whereas aggression is learned behavior. People, that is, learn to respond to frustrating situations with a behavioral repertoire, of which aggression is at best a small part.

"Depression Is Anger Turned Inward"

It is commonly asserted that the notion, "depression is anger turned inward," originated with Sigmund Freud and his (1917) paper on "Mourning and Melancholia." But I am unable to find "anger," "depression," or "inward" anywhere in the original text and in no passage is there an implication that melancholia results from the internalization of anger. I am also unable to find the phrase in any of the usual secondary discussions of Freud's paper. Perhaps Freud has been mistaken for Alexander Pope, who did say, "to be angry is to revenge the faults of others upon ourselves." In any case, at least one commentator (Trimarchi, 2012) infers from the Pope passage that "Anger turned inward is depression."

The general sense of the passage, doubtlessly true, is that emotions of all sorts require expression and expiation, and if they go unexpressed – if they are held inside, repressed, allowed to eat away at the psyche – then some sort of "boil and pop" reaction is likely. Emotions turned inward, anger included, erode mental well-being. In one study illustrating the process, Umberson et al. (2002) found that men who suppress or avoid conflict, feel threatened by conflict and repress their feelings of stress tend toward more violent domestic outbursts than men who directly confront their stresses.

Another version of the meme is that depression results from "unexpressed wants that have been swallowed" or "a collection of unfinished business that has been haunting you" or "an invitation to be more creative with your life."[14] Unfortunately, these variations do not appear in legitimate psychology or psychoanalytic journals. They tend instead to be standard fare in pop psychobabble outlets, "holistic mind-body healing" outlets, and related sources of dubious reliability. Let's see instead what an authoritative source, "Harvard Health Publications," the newsletter of the Harvard Medical School (2009), has to say about "What causes depression:"

> It's often said that depression results from a chemical imbalance, but that figure of speech doesn't capture how complex the disease is. Research suggests that depression doesn't spring from simply having too much or too little of certain brain chemicals. Rather, depression has many possible causes, including faulty mood regulation by the brain, genetic vulnerability, stressful life events, medications, and medical problems. It's believed that several of these forces interact to bring on depression. To be sure, chemicals are involved in this process, but it is not a simple matter of one chemical being too low and another too high. Rather, many chemicals are involved, working both inside and outside nerve cells. There are millions, even billions, of chemical reactions that make up the dynamic system that is responsible for your mood, perceptions, and how you experience life.

So please, let's have no more of "depression is anger turned inward." While the quoted passage makes it clear that depression has multiple complex causes, some biochemical, others genetic, some involving nerve cell communication, still others involving temperament or stressful life events, at no point do the good doctors from Harvard implicate internalized anger specifically as a source of depression. Indeed, the word "anger" is not even mentioned anywhere in the article.

Positive Aspects of Anger in Society

We are evidently conditioned to think of anger as a bad thing, as something that should be avoided or repressed, but it is obvious from the preceding discussion than anger serves a number of useful social functions. First, as we have seen, anger drives our political system. Political systems that do not allow for the existence or expression of anger are authoritarian and totalitarian systems where anger is ruthlessly repressed. Democracies, in contrast, encourage and channel anger in politically useful ways. Granted, the outcome is not always ideal. In 1933, German anger at Jews, Communists, Catholics, and economic hardship (along with a great deal more) got Adolph Hitler elected to the Presidency. But in general, angry voters are engaged voters, and engaged voters are essential to the progress of democracy. As the American abolitionist Wendell Phillips said, "Eternal vigilance is the price of liberty" (a phrase mistakenly attributed to Thomas Jefferson, and Philips was not the first to use it either).

On a personal level, as Scott Schieman reminds us, "anger provides drama and rage enlarges it." Without drama, life would be boring. Anger, as Schieman also says, "stimulates the lifeless." It gets the blood boiling, it gets us up and out of the easy chair. Anger is probably the leading reason why we are not even more of a nation of couch potatoes than we already are. It is thus a leading antidote to sloth.

The relationship between anger and having children in the household also suggests a link between anger and the socialization of children. If we didn't get angry at children's misdeeds, we would not bother to correct them and there would be even more under-socialized children than we already have, children who have never been taught what is proper behavior and what is not. In a larger sense, anger is therefore an important mechanism of social control. An under-recognized constraint on exuberant or improper behavior is the fear of incurring the wrath of persons whose respect we crave. Assistant professors, to give an obvious example, do what they need to do in part because they don't want to make senior professors angry.

More generally, as Fischer and Roseman (2007) conclude,

> People recalling experiences in which they got angry evaluated a majority of the overall effects of anger episodes as beneficial because they got the object of their anger to change his or her attitude or behavior or because it helped them realize their own strengths or faults.

Anger, they say, can be seen as "a means of trying to get something done."

Tori DeAngeles, writing in the American Psychological Association News-letter *Monitor on Psychology*, puts it this way. "Anger can help clarify relationship problems, clinch business deals, fuel political agendas and give people a sense of control during uncertain times." The idea that anger is always bad, that it never pays, is largely restricted to "the Bible, the great philosophers, and Chinese fortune cookies."

What About...?

In the hopes of deciding what I might cover in this concluding section of the chapter, I googled the antonyms of "anger" but got such a profusion of alternatives, it was no help. If you are not angry, you might be calm, cheerful, comforting, delighted, at ease, gleeful, full of goodwill, happy, joyful, kind, loving, peaceful, agreeable, content, good-natured, pleasant, or any of a number more. Some of this has already been covered in the concluding sections of chapter one on pro-social behavior, charity, and volunteering. No sense being redundant here.

One obvious topic for our concluding reflection is the "Random Acts of Kindness" movement (although calling it a "movement" probably overstates). In 1993, one Anne Herbert (an archetype of the holistic "alternative thinkers" who have clogged up contemporary discourse) came across a discussion of the Rodney King business in Los Angeles that contained the phrase, "random violence and senseless acts of cruelty." In a rather clever play on words, Herbert transformed that phrase into "random kindness and senseless acts of beauty" and published a children's book with that title. A later publication morphed the phrase into "Random Acts of Kindness" and urged people to engage in selfless acts of assistance to those in need or to cheer people up who seemed to be sad, or to be polite, volunteer, compliment, and forgive as a preferred mode of being in the world.

There is now a Random Acts of Kindness Foundation with its own Face-book presence, a place where random practitioners of unsolicited kindnesses can share stories about their virtuous behaviors, post photos, and share quota-tions along the general lines of "What is Done in Love is Done Well – Vincent van Gogh" or "It's OK to Bite off More than You Can Chew. Especially When Being Kind" (unattributed) or "Be You, No One Else Does It as Well." There is also a nonprofit organization called Random Acts that "is aiming to conquer the world, one random act of kindness at a time." Under the section of their web page titled Get Involved, one finds a button to click if you want to "Do-nate to Random Acts," "Fund Raise," or "Perform a Random Act." Curious, I clicked on the latter and learned that

> If you wish to perform an act of kindness that's sponsored by us we can provide you with fliers or some business cards depending on your need.

Simply fill in an Act Proposal Form and select 'no' for funding and 'yes' for promotional material. Please allow up to 4 weeks for your proposal to be reviewed and processed.

Good grief.

The Wikipedia entry on "Random acts of kindness" has a section on "Negative Effects."

There have been several documented cases when random acts of kindness failed to produce good outcomes and have even worsened the situation. For example, in the case of the 2014–15 floods in Southeast Asia and South Asia in Malaysia, random acts of donations were not reaching their intended targets, rather [they were] being strewn about, becoming street-side rubbish that further complicated planning, cleanup, and relief efforts. Additionally, people claiming to help others randomly took selfies on social media, sparking a disastrous tourist frenzy of *I was there helping*, whereby actual relief vehicles were delayed by the excessively clogged traffic. Additionally there was some theft of relief supplies by pilferers pretending to be among those helping.

There are dozens of additional examples of random acts of kindness that back-fired. Middle school students in Janesville, Ohio, undertook a class project to go to the local mall and leave coins and small stuffed animals scattered around everywhere with short notes saying, "Random act of kindness. Pass it along." Shortly after students left, mall employees gathered up all the notes, coins and stuffed animals. Mall management then released a statement saying:

We regret what has happened. Janesville Mall also practices Random Acts of Kindness. However, we schedule those through the mall office so the mall team is well informed which allows us to provide a comfortable, convenient and enjoyable shopping experience for our customers.

In another example, this out of Tulsa, Oklahoma, a motorist saw that a woman was having trouble pulling out of a drugstore parking lot, so stopped and waved her into his lane. The woman, however, needed two lanes, pulled out, but failed to notice the oncoming school bus in Lane Two. Luckily, none of the 32 students riding in the bus was injured in the ensuing crash.

It is easy to be snarky about saccharine "feel good" things such as Random Acts of Kindness and to take a perverse delight when these sophomoric good intentions go bad. So in fairness it has to be admitted that little acts of kindness – letting the woman with the nearly empty grocery cart cut in front of you in the line, switching seats on the airplane so that mother and daughter can sit together, dropping a few bucks into the Salvation Army kettle – doubtlessly do far more to enhance the quality of life than diminish it. And if people are more likely to do these things when they think they are marching under a slogan, then Practice Random Acts of Kindness isn't a bad one. The road to hell, they say, is paved with good intentions, but over on the other side, where the road is paved with evil intentions, the road to hell is a six-lane super-highway.

There is also a well-developed social science of happiness (Veenhoven, 2015).

> The number of scientific publications on happiness has grown steeply since the 1960s… [leading to] the World Database of Happiness Research (2013), which currently involves some 20,000 findings, some 5,000 'distributional' findings on how much people like the life they live, and about 15,000 'correlational' findings on things that go together with the subjective enjoyment of life.
>
> *(2015: 524)*

The social science of happiness is sometimes referred to as positive psychology (although social scientists from a vast array of disciplines other than psychology have contributed to this literature). For psychology specifically, "positive psychology" has to be seen as a repudiation of the discipline's roots.

> For much of its history, psychology has seemed obsessed with human failings and pathology. The very idea of psychotherapy, first formalized by Freud, rests on a view of human beings as troubled creatures in need of repair. Freud himself was profoundly pessimistic about human nature, which he felt was governed by deep, dark drives that we could only tenuously control. The behaviorists who followed developed a model of human life that seemed to many mechanistic if not robotic: humans were passive beings mercilessly shaped by the stimuli and the contingent rewards and punishments that surrounded them.
>
> *Lambert (2007)*

Positive psychology, in contrast, although not denying humanity's many flaws, focuses instead on peoples' strengths and virtues as the starting point for analysis. Rather than study alcoholics, perhaps we learn more by studying those who have successfully overcome their alcohol addiction; rather than seeing religion as an "illusion," as Freud did, perhaps we should understand spirituality as a positive force in the human experience.

★★★★★

Huey et al. (2014) interviewed a group of self-mutilating homeless women in Manchester and Liverpool, England. Social stressors of a deplorable variety were the distal causes of self-cutting in most cases, but the anger generated by these stressors was the proximate villain.

I had a lot of anger and that's what kind of led me to cutting myself. It was my mom. I have a lot of anger in me and I can't let it out on her, so I used to hurt myself, thinking that it would affect her.

Self-injury provided relief from anxiety and anger – the anger at an emotionally frozen mother, about sexual abuse suffered as a child, or over the unkindnesses of strangers when pleas for help were met with a cold shoulder. There is probably less anger in society than media depictions would suggest and a great deal of personal and social good that anger and the release of anger accomplishes. But when your anger reaches the point where you grab the nearest sharp object and start slashing away at your veins, anger has yielded to bitterness. To paraphrase Maya Angelou, anger is like fire – it burns clean. But bitterness is a cancer. It feeds upon its host.

Notes

1 https://news.google.com/newspapers?nid=1298&dat=19641028&id=PuxNAAA AIBAJ&sjid=jYoDAAAAIBAJ&pg=7331,2422881&hl=en.
2 http://americanradioworks.publicradio.org/features/campaign68/d1.html.
3 www.manythings.org/voa/history/220.html.
4 www.manythings.org/voa/history/222.html.
5 www.gallup.com/poll/2188/black-americans-feel-cheated-election-2000.aspx.
6 www.cbsnews.com/news/anger-with-bush-drives-dem-voters/.
7 www.americanthinker.com/articles/2004/01/the_myth_of_the_stolen_electio. html.
8 www.cnn.com/2008/POLITICS/10/10/mccain.crowd/.
9 http://archive.adl.org/presrele/extremism_72/5387_72.html#.VuGeLPkrJhE.
10 The election of 1824, for example, was thrown to the House to decide when none of the five candidates received a majority of the Electoral College vote. A backroom deal between Quincy Adams and Henry Clay gave the Presidency to Adams. "[Andrew] Jackson's disgust with Adams's 'theft' of the election of 1824 was then part of a broader *anger* over the degradation of America's political processes..." (www.shmoop.com/jackson-era/politics.html). One senses that a sufficiently diligent search would turn up angry voter memes in every Presidential election since the first in 1788.
11 There is a related meme involving the imagery of the "perpetually angry activist" that has been analyzed by Gentile (2015). "News coverage of protests and the activists which engage in them forms into patterns; media tends to highlight the extreme, irrational, angry, and violent segments of collective action..." That most protest is peaceful and that most activists are sober, calm, concerned citizens just does not meet the requirements for an eye-catching headline.
12 https://nitawriter.wordpress.com/2006/09/18/wife-beating/.
13 www.esquire.com/news-politics/a40693/american-rage-nbc-survey/.
14 http://therapyideas.net/depression-expectations-are-connected.htm.

6

ENVY

Keeping Up with the Joneses, the Smiths, and Everyone Else

American journalist and author John Tierney, writing in *The New York Times* in 2011, wondered whether envy was the most useless of the deadly sins, a torture to experience, hard to own up to, and without any long-term benefit. He alluded to evolutionary psychology that would find logic in the act of seducing a neighbor's wife or stealing his goods – both sins themselves – but, he asks, "what's the point of merely coveting them?"[1]

There are dozens of Biblical verses that warn against envy, covetousness, and jealousy (these terms tend to be used interchangeably) but not one that provides an answer to Tierney's question, namely, what is so sinful about being envious? Envy is desiring that which you don't already have, but what is so sinful about that? If this is indeed the meaning, then envy demands to be understood as the mother of aspiration and, therefore, the grandmother of accomplishment. It is the source of motivation to get up, work hard, and succeed. It is, one would think, the sort of trait that should be urged on people at every opportunity. But no, the Bible warns against envy in dozens of passages. Why?

Envy, it is said, is a challenge to God because to be envious is to question God's decisions about who merits their unequal shares (Leach, 2008). But this, it seems to me, only sanctifies social inequality. Venturing into theological mysteries is hazardous for any social scientist, but I find it hard to escape the suspicion that Biblical admonitions against envy are intended to promote acceptance of the status quo ante (God's "divine distribution of good fortune," as Leach puts it), to convince the large mass of believers that they should be happy with what they have and not be taken in by those who promote change. "Render unto Caesar that which is Caesar's, and unto God the things that are God's." And while theologians also argue over the intended meaning of this passage (e.g., Barr, 2010), does it not seem a pretty obvious endorsement of leaving the basic structure of society intact? In some respects, the warnings against envy are basically recommendations to dwell always in the spiritual realm and not to be overly concerned with material well-being. The warnings against greed seem largely in the same vein. The basic message is that the grass is never greener "over there," so shut up and be happy with what you have. What kind of world would we live in today if people had hewn closely to this advice for the past 2,000 years?

What Is Envy?

My online dictionary defines envy as "a feeling of discontented or resentful longing aroused by someone else's possessions, qualities, or luck." Listed synonyms are jealousy and covetousness. So our rendition above, "desiring that which you don't already have," comes pretty close. But we need to add "and that others do have..." to be complete. Many people might wish they could fly, but none do, so the wish to do so is not true envy. Many people do have large bank accounts and luxurious homes, so the wish to have these things too is clearly envious.

Ironically, in one account of the Biblical differences between envy and jealously, envy is defined as "anger turned inward..." (Wellman, 2014), clearly an overworked phrase! But in the case of envy, the anger is focused on "something that someone has like status, possessions, power, or wealth that [the envious] don't have but wished that they did." Jealousy, in contrast, is the resentment one feels against the "haves." As Tierney expresses the difference,

> Envy involves a longing for what you don't have, while jealousy is provoked by losing something to someone else. If you crave a wife like Angelina Jolie, you're envious of Brad Pitt; if you're upset about losing your wife to him, you're jealous...

Or as Richard Smith phrases the difference, "envy is a two-person situation whereas jealousy is a three-person situation. Envy is a reaction to lacking something. Jealousy is a reaction to the threat of losing something (usually some*one*)" (2011).

Smith (2015) makes a further important distinction between benign and malicious envy (see also Belk, 2011). Biblical admonitions against envy are really warnings about malicious envy. The two forms differ mainly in how we tend to process each. Suppose we notice that a friend has obtained the latest iPhone, it is clearly superior to our iPhone, and so we envy the new phone. What do we do? In most cases, we find the means to buy ourselves a new iPhone too – and that's benign envy. Suppose instead we club our friend over the head and take his phone for our own. That's malicious envy. The difference is that benign envy stimulates "leveling up" motivations while malicious envy is all about leveling down.

Yet another emotion that is close to malicious envy is *Schadenfreude*, a German word that means taking joy in someone else's pain or misfortune. Psychologists have created a pretty substantial literature around *Schadenfreude*. A recent entry in this literature is Cikara and Fiske (2013), who observe that "one potent predictor of envy is *Schadenfreude*." In other words, the tendency to take pleasure in another's misfortune is largely restricted to others whom we envy, certainly not those with whom we empathize. One experiment showed that people smiled more often when witnessing the misfortunes of "high status competitive targets," people who, in another ordinary language phrase, "got their comeuppance." Another experiment showed that people are more likely to endorse harming those same high-status targets compared to other targets that were not envied. The authors infer from their results that part of America's "image problem" around the globe is that we are seen as a "high status" target envied by most; thus, the invariable glee, often thinly disguised, when American interests take a serious hit. (A helpful review of the psychology of *Schadenfreude* is Powell et al., 2008.)

Like all other features of human existence, envy can be seen as an evolved trait that persists because it confers some sort of survival value on individuals. "At first glance, envy appears to be a maladaptive emotion" (Hill and Buss, 2008). But envy is one emotion that alerts us that we may not be as competitive against our nearest rivals as we should be; thus, envy may be an evolved "emotional adaptation that has been shaped by selection to signal strategic interference [or inadequacies] in the quest for resource acquisition" (2008, p. 62).

Property Crime

If envy is wanting what other people have, and malicious envy is acting viciously on that desire, then the principal expression of malicious envy in modern society has to be property crime. (This is the indicator of envy used in the Kansas State University project mapping the seven deadly sins.) As we saw in the chapter on anger, violent crime is often ambiguously motivated, but property crime – burglary, robbery, theft, stealing cars, and the like – is pretty clearly a result of wanting what other people have and you don't.

Although violent crime is what people fear most, property crime is far more common. (All that follows is based on UCF crimes known to the police. Criminal victimization surveys will always yield larger numbers.[2]) In 2014, as reported earlier, there were 1,165,383 violent crimes reported to the police and a violent crime rate of 366 violent crimes per 100,000 population. In the same year, there were 8,277,829 property crime offenses and a property crime rate of 2,596 per 100,000 population. In percentages, that is 2.6% of the population experiencing a property crime in 2014, almost eight times the percentage experiencing a violent crime. Still, that leaves 97.4% of the US population who were not victimized by property crime in 2014.

Like the violent crime rate, the property crime rate has fallen sharply since the early 1990s. The 2014 property crime rate was down almost 12% from 2010 and down 24% since 2005. Still, in 2014, property crimes resulted in losses of about $14.3 billion. In this connection, we can also call attention to the so-called "clearance rates," the percentage of offenses that eventuate in an arrest. In 2014, the clearance rates were 23% for larceny and theft, 14% for burglary, and 13% for motor vehicle theft. The old saw that "crime doesn't pay" is evidently wrong. Property criminals net $14 billion annually but property criminals only run about a one in five chance of being caught, which seems like a pretty profitable enterprise, particularly given the low capital costs of getting into the crime business in the first place.

The most common property crime is larceny-theft, accounting for about 71% of all property crimes. Burglary (or breaking and entering) was second at 21%, with car theft accounting for the remaining 8%. Interestingly, in 2003, the most commonly stolen automobile was the Cadillac Escalade. Can you feel the *Schadenfreude* rising? (More recent data show that older cars are now the more common target for car thieves than newer cars, presumably because of more sophisticated anti-theft systems on the newer models.)

By region, property crime is generally more common in the South than outside it and least common in the Northeast, but these are not large or categorical differences.

Probably the most important takeaway from this brief discussion is that if the property crime rate is our best indicator of overall envy, then envy has fallen off pretty sharply in the last quarter century.

Envy and Social Stratification

In his book *Categorically Unequal* (2007), the sociologist Douglas Massey argues that people carry around cognitive schema in their heads that sort others into categories (usually stereotypical categories) and that these schema form the basis of social stratification (the unequal distribution of wealth, income, power, prestige, or other valued items across the social structure). These schema, Massey argues, are aligned across the two dimensions of competence and warmth. Persons and groups perceived as both warm and competent define our "esteemed in-group," the people to whom we feel attracted, people we respect. The warm but incompetent are the "pitied outgroup" – the disabled, the elderly, the mentally challenged. Those neither warm nor competent are the "despised outgroup." "Being neither likable nor capable, people within these outgroups are social despised, and the dominant emotion is disgust" (p. 13) – these are the drug dealers, the chronically homeless, the lazy welfare recipient. Then finally we have those recognized as competent but not warm – they are the "envied" outgroup and certainly the ones whose misfortunes stimulate *Schadenfreude*. "In a stable social structure, people show public respect for and defer to members of envied outgroups," but in times of turmoil they are the easy targets of scapegoating and "may become targets of communal hatred and violence."

In Massey's theory, "human beings are psychologically programmed to categorize the people they encounter" along these dimensions and "to use these categorizations to make social judgments." These social judgments in turn form the basis for how socially valued things get distributed. Taking these points into simultaneous consideration, the implication is that envy will exist in any society that does not have a perfectly egalitarian distribution of resources, which is to say in every society. Envy is the inevitable result of social inequalities of all sorts.

These themes are elaborated by the Princeton psychologist Susan T. Fiske in her book *Envy Up, Scorn Down: How Status Divides Us* (2012). Both envy and scorn, Fiske argues, have distinctive cognitive, emotional, and behavioral characteristics, all resulting from the hard-wired need to compare one social group with another. These comparisons and the resulting categorizations form the basis for status and class in society. The book's title suggests the general result: Those above us in the status hierarchy are envied, and those below us are scorned (or sometimes pitied, depending on whether they are perceived as warm or cold). In times of social turmoil, the resulting rancor often leads to devastating outcomes.

In the same vein, envy can be seen as the emotion that drives social mobility. As one researcher quoted by Tierney (2011) puts it, "It's much like a car crash we can't stop looking at. We can't get our minds off people who have advantages we want for ourselves." The theory is that by paying more attention to the people we envy, we learn to mimic their success strategies – and become more successful ourselves. Or as the poet de Mandeville put it, "Envy itself, and vanity, were ministers of industry."[3] As I have already stated, envy is the root of aspiration and, therefore, of success. Only in the (nonexistent) condition of perfect equality will envy not be a visible emotional element of social interaction and structure.

It is often stated that the preference for a more egalitarian society is related to the degree of envy. Churchill himself said, "Socialism is the gospel of envy" (quoted in Kemp and Bolle, 2013). And many writers ranging from Friedrich Hayek to John Rawls have intimated that envy is a major force that drives the social and economic thinking of the left. Kemp and Bolle's research generally contradicts this position. Their "dispositional envy" scale was quite strongly (and negatively) correlated with general life satisfaction scores (more envy = less life satisfaction) but not correlated at all with preferences for living in societies with more egalitarian income distributions. "Both questionnaire and experimental studies show a tendency for more envious people to prefer more equal distributions [of income] but the tendency is neither large nor consistent" (2013, p. 60).

Still, as Boris Johnson put it in his recent Thatcher Lecture, "I don't believe that economic equality is possible; indeed, some measure of inequality is essential for the spirit of envy and keeping up with the Joneses that is, like greed, a valuable spur to economic activity."[4]

Envy in the Workplace

A key source of envy in modern society is "when people believe they compare unfavorably with others in their workplace" (Duffy et al., 2008). Every workplace embraces some sort of internal process of evaluation and, thus, provides endless opportunities for employees to compare themselves with their peers. Often, these comparisons are carried out in public, which can amplify the shame, anger, and envy for those whose performance is weak. Often, the forces unleashed in these comparisons can be destructive of morale and productivity. So consultants offer numerous seminars and workshops to organizational managers on how to manage envy in work settings.

Alas, organizational science has not paid the topic an equivalent amount of attention, or indeed, very much attention at all (Veiga et al., 2014). So we don't (yet) know very much about the specific organizational factors that promote (or retard) workplace envy. It is not yet clear, for example, whether objective assessments (based on specific performance criteria) stimulate more or less envy than subjective assessments (based, for example, on supervisors' feelings about whose contributions are most meritorious). More competitive reward structures (for example, where pay raises are based on performance assessments) appear to generate more envy than less competitive ones (for example, where pay raises are across-the-board), although evidence favoring this conclusion is described as "relatively modest" (Duffy et al., 2008: 171). Many aspects of supervisors' behaviors have also been shown to reduce (or increase) employee envy; for example, when supervisors are perceived as "friendly and approachable," their assessment decisions generate less envy. "Considerate managerial behaviors are a signal of fairness" (p. 172) and are therefore perceived as more just.

More is known about the workplace consequences of employee envy that about the causes. Envy threatens workplace self-esteem, job satisfaction, and willingness to stay. Envy also degrades coworker relationships and employees' commitment to the organization. Various studies also link envy to absenteeism and sabotage. In contrast, the possibility that envious employees work harder in order to move up in the organizational status hierarchy has received very little research attention. High on the list of matters for further research is whether "under certain circumstances invidious reactions to others' success may ultimately motivate performance and self-efficacy" (2008, p. 185). It remains an open question whether workplace envy can somehow be harnessed "to become a source of productivity and initiative."

One effort to parse the potential upside of workplace envy is Tai et al. (2012). "Although envy has been characterized by resentment, hostility, and ill will, researchers have begun to investigate envy's benign manifestations."

Conceptualizing envy as "pain at another's good fortune" allows these authors to explore both positive and negative consequences. Findings show that the effects of envy on job performance and workplace relationships are moderated by (depend on) self-evaluations and perceived organizational support. Research by Eissa and Wyland (2016) also suggests that the workplace "undermining" characteristic of the envious is moderated by relationship conflicts. That is, if envy is accompanied by positive (non-conflictual) workplace relationships, it does not lead to undermining.

Envy and Aggression

"For centuries, scholars have argued that envy is the source of much aggressive behavior as well as the root cause of much unhappiness." So says Richard Smith in the introduction to his (2008) book on *Envy*. And indeed, it is very easy to find *arguments* that this must be so, that envy, particularly intense, malevolent envy, rapidly turns into anger and then aggression. What is much harder to find are empirical studies supporting this supposed relationship.

An illustration of the point is the paper by Efrat and Shoham (2013) on determinants of aggressive driving. "Previous studies," they say, "have established a relationship between envy and aggression." Yet in a paper published in 2013, only three studies are cited as proof of the point: One published in 1969, another published in 1957, and a third (an analysis of Peruvian truck drivers) published in 1979. The 1969 paper does not present any direct new evidence on the relationship between envy and aggression; it is, rather, a "critical review of the status of the envy concept" as used in psychoanalysis. The 1959 citation is to a book titled *Envy and Gratitude: A Study of Unconscious Sources*. Insightful though these sources might be, none of them presents any compelling evidence that envy is a fundamental progenitor of aggression. In fairness, the study of truck drivers in Peru did suggest "a positive relationship between envy and aggressive driving." But the measure of envy was derived from truck drivers' mottos and was obviously confounded with "an ethos of *machismo,* the later understood as a combinations of beliefs, values, attitudes, emotions and behavioral patterns" (2013, p. 461).

Efrat and Shoham (2013) demonstrate a definite positive relationship between aggressive driving and *materialism,* the latter, in turn, comprising envy, possessiveness, and non-generosity. But since the materialism measure is a single index, we have no way of disaggregating the result to see how much of the aggressive driving is due to envy, how much to possessiveness, and how much to non-generosity. More generally, it is hard to see how envy *per se* would make people drive aggressively, unless the thing desired but not possessed happened to be the other fellow's place in the line of traffic.

Levesque (2014) reminds us that envy exists in many different forms. Some forms of envy lack any overtones of hostility; other forms are marked by sharp hostility "that turns into frustration, fear, aggression, prejudice, anger and hostile behavior." Thus, "Envy can compel an individual to achieve, while it can also produce hostility, unhappiness, and considerable destruction."

In reviewing this literature, one quickly senses that generalizations such as "envy leads to aggression" are out of place without specification of the form of envy being considered and the situational and environmental factors that must be present to precipitate specific behavioral outcomes. As Wu and Chang (2012) conclude, "Envy influences physical and mental health leading to aggression, *Schadenfreude*, as well as prosocial behavior." Which outcome is realized in any particular case will depend on situational factors too diverse and varied to sustain any easy generalizations.

Envy and Health

The Levesque paper cited above remarks that

> envy also has been linked to negative physical health outcomes, links that are attributed to such factors as hostility's reducing sources of emotional support as well as the creation of negative emotions that contribute to stress that eventually leads to ill health.
>
> *(2014)*

A very detailed and comprehensive review of the literature on this point is Smith et al. (2008) and the discussion below follows their presentation closely.

Commentators since Ovid have stressed that envy can make you sick and unhappy (that is, both physically and emotionally ill). "There is very little research to support or reason to believe that transient feelings of envy... might detract from health" (p. 291), but *chronic* envy is another matter. But why would even chronic envy be injurious to well-being? Our authors posit several connecting mechanisms. First, the presence of chronic envy implies a more or less constant unfavorable comparison between the self and those above the self in a social hierarchy; in all social mammals including humans, "lower ranking is associated with poor health" (p. 292). More generally, as numerous analysts have concluded, inequality is inherently unhealthy, and envy is the inevitable result of inequality (see, e.g., Barr, 2014; Evans et al., 1994; Marmot and Wilkinson, 2005). So envy, inequality and poor health exist in some sort of linked triad.

Too, chronic envy seems to come in a package that also includes ill will, anti-social tendencies, hostility, anger, frustration, pettiness, meanness of spirit, shame, feelings of inferiority, and resentment. Wandering through life with this package of negativity cannot possibly be *good* for one's health. The hypothesis is that these negative emotional states increase the stress of everyday life, and the effects of excess stress on health are too well documented to require further comment here. "When envy is dispositional, its frequency, intractability, and ill effects may become a way of life and its presence akin to a malady" (p. 295).

Still another pathway from chronic envy to poor health is via the effects of chronic envy on personal and social relationships. Functional relationships depend on the norm of reciprocity, which in turns requires gratitude and recognition of a responsibility to reciprocate. Chronically envious people, it appears, are largely incapable of gratitude; as such, their social networks deteriorate and with it, their sources of social support. And lack of social support is reliably linked to poor health outcomes in any number of studies.

Whatever the specific causal mechanisms, the outcomes are pretty clear: Envy has been linked to a variety of health outcomes in multiple studies – to enhanced risk of cardio-vascular disease, hypertension, sleep disorders, and various emotional and psychiatric disorders, among others. Given these findings and the uncertain consequences of obesity for health, it is possible that envy is worse for you than gluttony, however hard that may be to believe.

Penis Envy

Freud was of the opinion that the psychosocial development of women was interrupted by the anxiety experienced when women realize they do not have a penis. The onset of penis envy, Freud argued, marked the transition from attachment to the mother to competition with the mother for the attention of the father. Penis envy was an essential element in the transition to mature female sexuality and gender identity.

No one seems to take Freud's theory too seriously anymore, save for a few recalcitrant, hard-core Freudian psychoanalysts, and the opinion of feminist scholars is that "the theory of 'penis envy'—as conceived by Freud—has arguably done more harm to women's psychology than any other psychological or philosophical theory in the 20th century" (Kass, 2014). Despite the prominence of Freudian theories and concepts in the larger culture, as an academic research program or paradigm, "it's pretty much dead" (Dvorsky, 2013). "He was totally, utterly wrong about gender. And his notion of 'penis envy' is now both laughable and tragic." So about the apparently fictitious penis envy, nothing further need be said.

Positive Aspects of Envy in Society

We normally think of envy as a bad thing, a deadly sin, a maladaptive emotional state, but as several authors considered earlier have suggested, there is also a strong upside to envy that a complete account needs to consider. Probably the most obvious has already been mentioned at least twice before, namely, that envy creates aspirations and, therefore, drives achievement. One wonders what inventions would have lain undiscovered, what cures never found, what works of art never realized, without the envies of inventors, doctors, and artists? Would there have been a Mozart without Salieri? Edison without Tesla? Lavoisier without Priestly? Rivalry, and, therefore, envy, are essential features of the process of discovery (White, 2001).

Again, it is important to distinguish between benign and malignant envy.

> We tend to feel malicious envy towards another person if we think their success is undeserved. This is the type that makes us want to strike out at the other person and bring them down a peg or two. However when another's success feels deserved to us, we tend to feel a benign envy: one that isn't destructive but instead motivates.[5]

The Psyblog post noted earlier lists "four ways benign envy is good for you." They are, first, that envy motivates; second, benign envy can generate hopefulness – if others do better and are successful, maybe we can too; third, benign envy stimulates creativity; and finally, benign envy can make you smarter, more alert to opportunities that will reduce the status differential between you and those you envy.

Belk (2009) makes the further important observation that virtually the entire point of marketing and advertising is to make people want what they don't have; thus, all marketing is essentially a process of creating envy. In the modern world, "others' consumer goods have arguably become the chief source of people's envy" (p. 211). What, after all, do we really know about the models who are featured in advertisements, brochures, catalogs, and window displays? Only that they are "young, attractive, popular and glamorous, and that they have what we lack." Advertising is based on the sleight-of-hand thought that if "we had what they have, we would be more like them." More generally, "mass media images open a window on lives that seem more attractive than one's own." These images are not truthful, of course, and neither is the subliminal marketing message: If you come to own what "they" own, your life will be more attractive too!

A materialistic culture is one where a person's worth is measured by what he or she is able to consume. In the end, rampant materialism probably makes people less happy, not more. Robert Wuthnow (1994) found that "blaming materialism has replaced blaming the Devil for the ills of society" (Belk, 2009, p. 217). Still, studies show that even people who condemn materialism as a source of evil will say later in the same interview that they want bigger homes, nicer cars, and more income. Consumer envy, in short, drives the world economy forward. Marketing assists this process by creating or provoking consumer envy. Without envy and greed, there could be no capitalism.

At the same time, social and economic resources are very unevenly distributed in capitalist societies, most of all the United States. And this implies, in turn, a class of perpetually envious poor people. If the consumer envies of the poor turn from benign to malicious, and if there is the will and the means to act on that malice, "then it is possible that consumer envy might undo capitalism as effectively as it undid communism" (p. 223).

What About Satisfaction?

The antidote to envy is to be satisfied with what one has. So who is? As it happens, almost everyone. Yes, despite all the concern with envy and rampant dissatisfaction, one of the most remarkable findings of present-day social science is that most people are mostly satisfied with most aspects of their lives.

The National Opinion Research Center's General Social Survey (GSS) is the data source of record for measures of the satisfactions and discontents of modern American life. One question included in every wave of the GSS asks: "Taken all together, how would you say things are these days – would you say that you are very happy, pretty happy, or not too happy?" If, as prior discussions suggest, envy is a source of unhappiness, then the envious would be among the mere 12% of the US population who describes themselves as "not too happy." About one in three say they are very happy; the remainder, 56%, are at least somewhat happy. General happiness bottomed out in 2010, in the middle of the Great Recession, and has since come back up to pre-recession levels (Smith et al., 2015).

What is true of life in general is equally true of the various domains of life. Over the years of the GSS (1972 to date), about 63% describe their marriages as very happy; only 3% say they are "not too happy." Majorities approaching 90% say they derive "a very great deal," "a great deal," or "quite a bit" of satisfaction from their family life. Questions on job satisfaction find that nearly half are "very satisfied" and another two-fifths are "somewhat satisfied." Those "not too satisfied" or "not satisfied at all" with their jobs amount to barely one in ten. These days, half the people in the country described their lives as "exciting" (as opposed to routine or dull). In a society said to be riven with anger, envy, frustration, and discontent, life proves to be happy, satisfying, and exciting for most.

Smith and his associates also report on the demographics of general psychological well-being, as indexed by these and related questions. "Men and women differ little in their psychological well-being" (2015: 1). Older people are generally happier than younger people, but the pattern is not consistent over time (and is not strong at any time). Finally, by any measure, the more educated you are, the happier and more satisfied you will be.

Concluding Thoughts

Envy, it seems, has gotten a bad rap, perhaps because it is an emotion scorned in virtually all religious, ethical, and philosophical systems of thought. But as we have seen, envy is a strong motivator and basic to the economics of consumer society. And in an inegalitarian society, envy is doubtlessly inevitable. As the ancient Greek dramatist Aeschylus put it, "It is in the character of very few men to honor without envy a friend who has prospered." Or, if you prefer, we can conclude with an observation due to Pindar: "To be envied is a nobler fate than to be pitied."

Notes

1 Full article: *Envy May Bear Fruit, but it Also Has an Aftertaste,* by John Tierney (*The New York Times,* Oct. 11, 2011): www.nytimes.com/2011/10/11/science/11tierney. html?_r=0.
2 National criminal victimization surveys suggest that only about a third of all property crimes are ever reported to the police; reporting of most violent crimes is higher. With respect to property crimes, however, all the numbers reported in this paragraph will be closer to the true values if you multiply them by three. But even that leaves well more than 90% of the US population unaffected in any given year.
3 Quoted in Belk (2009).
4 Quoted at http://makewealthhistory.org/2013/12/04/is-envy-a-good-thing/.
5 www.spring.org.uk/2012/06/4-ways-benign-envy-is-good-for-you.php.

7

PRIDE

Does Self-Esteem Solve Everything? Anything?

There seems no end to the prominences who have had something erudite to say about pride. St. Augustine opined that "It is pride that changes angels into devils; it is humility that makes men as angels." Khalil Gibran's *The Prophet* observes that "generosity is giving more than you can, and pride is taking less than you need." Dante asserts: "Pride, envy, avarice – these are the sparks that have set on fire the hearts of all men." Even Shakespeare has his say: "My pride fell with my fortunes."

Nor is the erudition reserved just for the classics. The pop songstress Taylor Swift observes: "One of the things people don't really recognize about the similarities between country and hip-hop is that they're celebrations of pride in a lifestyle." The comedian Penn Jillete observes: "Religion is often just tribalism: pride in a group one was born into, a group that is often believed to have 'God' on its side." And here are the words of Johnny Cash:

> The things that have always been important: to be a good man, to try to live my life the way God would have me, to turn it over to Him that His will might be worked in my life, to do my work without looking back, to give it all I've got, and to take pride in my work as an honest performer.

Clearly, pride is an outsized topic: One scarcely knows where to begin!

It is, first of all, immediately obvious that there is good pride and bad pride. Good pride is Johnny Cash taking pride "in my work as an honest performer" and the Prophet "taking less than you need." Bad pride is Dante's "pride, envy and avarice," the pride "that changes angels into devils" – more generally, the "pride that goeth before the fall."[1] But what's the difference? Perhaps only that some pride is deserved and, therefore, good or at least tolerable, whereas at other times, pride is undeserved, unjustifiable, and, therefore, sinful. Good pride is when you do the best you can, give it your all, and are rightly pleased with your accomplishment. Bad pride is when you break your own arm patting yourself on the back.

Bad pride goes by many different names: Hubris, arrogance, narcissism, obnoxiousness, vanity, haughtiness, and self-love are a few synonyms that come to mind. And these days, good pride has another name too: We call it *self-esteem*. Deficient self-esteem (self-loathing) is said to be responsible for a wide variety of social ills, and so enhancements to self-esteem are said to be the cure, although there are good reasons to be skeptical of both propositions.

Alert: The empirical materials we have to work with in this chapter are rather thin. Pride is known to psychologists as a "self-conscious emotion," and "the study of self-conscious emotions has only recently begun."[2] So the following is somewhat more speculative than would otherwise be desirable.

What Is Pride and How Does It Differ from Hubris and Arrogance?

The online dictionary tells us that pride is

> a feeling of deep pleasure or satisfaction derived from one's own achieve-
> ments, the achievements of those with whom one is closely associated
> [e.g., students, children, family members, a work team], or from qualities
> or possessions that are widely admired.

One can therefore be proud of one's deeds, one's associates' deeds, one's temperament or intelligence, or one's possessions. Sam is proud that he graduated from college, Jill is proud of her grandchildren, Richard is proud of his stamp collection, Lionel is proud of his race, Zoe is proud of her nation, Ron is proud that he seldom responds harshly to provocation. Are all these different manifestations of pride equally sinful? Sinful at all?

Multiple Biblical passages tell us that God wages war against the proud. "When pride comes, then comes disgrace" (Proverbs 11:2). "God opposes the proud but gives grace to the humble" (James 4:6). "The eyes of the arrogant will be humbled and human pride brought low; the Lord alone will be exalted in that day" (Isaiah 2:11). Such passages can be multiplied nearly without limit (All quotes are from the NIV Bible).

A posting on "Why is Pride a Sin?" by S. Michal Houdmann begins to shed light on why pride is sinful, or rather, what kind of pride is a sin.[3] Houdmann poses the central question thus: "Why is pride a sin? Why is it a sin to feel proud of something you have accomplished? It is very important to understand what precisely is the pride that God hates." Later in the posting we get the answer. To the believer, nothing in which we might take pride could possibly exist without God's hand in creating it.

That seems to be the key distinction between 'good' pride and 'bad' pride. Sinful pride is refusing to recognize God's sovereign role in everything. 'Good pride' is recognizing that apart from God, you can do nothing, and, therefore, giving God the glory for the things that you accomplish.

Aha! When believers take pride in their accomplishments or possessions or other things and qualities without recognizing God as the ultimate source of all good, they are committing a sin. They are expropriating God's glory for their own. So when Jeff Gordon hops out of his winning race car, grins from ear to ear, fist-pumps the air but then takes pains to thank "the Man upstairs" before he thanks his crew, his sponsors and his fans, he exhibits good pride, but if he overlooks the role of "the Man upstairs" in his expressions of gratitude, he is being sinful.

God, it seems, not only demands to take credit for all the good in the world, He evidently demands that His role be specifically acknowledged in every instance. You must explicitly recognize that nothing you possess or accomplish would be possible without God. Failure to do so is prideful and condemns your mortal soul to death. That this seems terribly vengeful on the part of what people believe to be a kind and loving God shall pass without further comment.

Alas, while this explains why pride is considered a sin, it does not explain why the good things in life – accomplishment, intelligence, money, good health, material well-being – are so unequally distributed. If God is responsible for making the rich rich, and the rich in turn owe thanks to God for their good fortune, is He not equally responsible for keeping the poor in poverty, and should the poor therefore thank God each night for their miseries? If good health is to be acknowledged as God's doing, then what about poor health? Is that God's doing too? If pride is a sin, human agency would itself appear to be sinful. Either God has endowed us with free will, or He hasn't. If the former, then surely we can take such pride as we wish in what we willfully accomplish. And if the latter, then there can be no pride because no one can be blamed (or credited) for anything they do.

Evolutionary psychologists think that

> pride may have evolved to motivate people to achieve social status in a socially valued domain. Pride makes people feel good about *themselves*. Children are quick to associate pride with domains in which they feel competent, and are driven to further pursue those domains. In contrast, those who continually receive negative feedback in a domain quickly lose their motivation for achieving in that domain.
>
> *Cheng et al., (2010) and Kaufman (2012)*

In short, with pride comes achievement, and with achievement comes progress. Some degree of pride seems essential to drive social systems forward, whether it is the pride of the early Cro-Magnon who was better at mammoth hunting than his peers, the pride of the die-cast operator who makes rate at every shift, or the pride of the college professor whose papers stimulate lots of citations.

Psychologists generally view pride as a "positively valenced moral emotion," as opposed to shame, guilt, or embarrassment, which are "negatively valenced" (Tangney et al., 2007). The obvious social function of pride is that it "serves to enhance people's self-worth and, perhaps more importantly, to encourage future behavior that conforms to social standards of worth or merit."

Self-Esteem and the Self-Esteem Industry

The many Biblical admonitions against pride are very hard to square with the now half-century fixation of the therapeutic community on self-esteem. As the psychologist Elizabeth Venzin has put it, "We live in a world where there is an epidemic of low self-esteem. It affects almost every aspect of our lives, from how we think about ourselves to the way we think about or react to life situations" (2014). From the 1980s forward, low self-esteem has been blamed for obesity, eating disorders, teen pregnancy, smoking, alcoholism, drug addiction, truancy, bullying, crime, delinquency, child abuse, domestic violence, dropping out of school, poor academic performance, aggression, adverse health outcomes, marital discord – even the present-day urge to take selfies![4] – and probably a great deal more. And the universally proposed solution to all these ills has been to raise people's self-esteem.[5]

An entire industry has grown up around these presumed causal connections, an industry based on four dubious propositions: (1) Low self-esteem indeed characterizes all the miscreants responsible for the laundry list of social problems just noted. (2) We know how to raise self-esteem. (3) Once we get persons' self-esteem up to some critical point, they will cease their villainous ways and become normal human beings. Therefore (4), self-esteem can never be too high. Nice theory, but all four of these propositions are wrong.

My suspicions about self-esteem as the all-purpose panacea were first raised in a passage from Rossi et al. (2004: 83). The passage was discussing a program that intended to address the problem of juvenile delinquency by raising self-esteem. "Examination of the applicable social science literature, however, will reveal that juvenile delinquents generally do not have problems with self-esteem and moreover, that increases in self-esteem are not generally associated with reductions in delinquency among juveniles." That rang true to me: Most of the juvenile delinquents I had interacted with in my life seemed to entertain unrealistically high impressions of themselves, indeed, narcissistically so. What they really needed was to be convinced that they were worthless, mean-spirited little creeps who needed to stop what they were doing and figure out some way to make a positive contribution to the human condition, not to have their already-inflated egos puffed up even more.

The theory seemed equally implausible when applied to other social problems. Just what is the causal sequence presumed to connect low self-esteem to teen pregnancy, for example? Many of the young pregnant girls that I worked with in the public housing communities of New Orleans (Kreutziger et al., 1999) were *proud* of their pregnancy, *pleased* that they were able to show the world that someone had found them sufficiently attractive to have sex with them, *confident* in the knowledge that their baby would qualify them for a unit of their own, probably food stamps, a Medicaid card, and possibly even a monthly welfare check. I seriously doubt that *any* of their pregnancies resulted from telling the fathers, "I am a worthless human being, so go ahead and have your way with me." It just does not ring true.[6]

Mark Tyrrell is a UK therapist who follows the scientific literature on self-esteem and has recently posted the *"Top Ten Facts about Low Self-Esteem"* that other therapists, psychologists, parents, and people in general need to be aware of.[7] Number One on the list: Low self-esteem is *not* to be blamed for being bad or doing bad things. At one time, those who suffered from low self-esteem were lumped together with "bullies, narcissists, criminals and child abusers." What research has shown since the 1980s, when the self-esteem craze started, is that people with low self-esteem tend to treat themselves badly, not other people. Studies of attempts to reduce bullying by raising self-esteem, for example, show them to be failures because bullies are not low on self-esteem to begin with. "Lifting self-esteem doesn't raise academic performance either." More generally, "Low self-esteem is not to blame for nearly as many problems as has traditionally been thought."

To the contrary (and this is Tyrrell's second point), there is now substantial scientific evidence that inflated self-esteem, not a deflated sense of self-worth, is what generates delinquency and criminality (Baumeister, 1996; Baumeister et al., 1996). As Tyrrell puts it,

> Hundreds of pieces of reliable research now show that bullies and many criminals are much more likely to suffer from unrealistically high self-esteem and impulse control problems than low self-esteem. An exaggerated sense of entitlement – expecting much from many situations – is more likely to lead to frustration and aggressive, antisocial, or even criminal behavior.

This, as Roy Baumeister puts it, is the "dark side" of self-esteem. The idea that self-esteem can never be too high is just silly. Unrealistically positive self-opinions are at least as destructive as unrealistically negative ones, and probably more so.

Not all agree, of course; there are quite a number of psychologists and therapists who continue to believe that low self-esteem is just about the worst calamity that can befall someone. Consider, for example, the paper by

Donnellan et al. (2005), titled *"Low self-esteem is related to aggression, anti-social behavior, and delinquency."* The study acknowledges the controversy surrounding the links implied in the title and presents new evidence on the negative consequences of low self-esteem. Alas, as is often the case in these matters, the new evidence is well short of compelling. One study was based on 292 11- and 14-year-olds from two schools in northern California; a second study surveyed about 1,500 children from a town in New Zealand; a third study was a survey of 3,000 undergrads at a university in northern California. All three studies provide some empirical support for the relationships mentioned in the paper's title, but the generalizability (or "external validity") of the findings is obviously questionable. Alas, it is largely from such tatters that the fabric of modern psychology is woven.

Another study in the same vein is Mann et al. (2004), where low self-esteem is linked to various elements of mental and social well-being.

> Evidence is presented illustrating that self-esteem can lead to better health and social behavior, and that poor self-esteem is associated with a broad range of mental disorders and social problems, both internalizing problems (e.g. depression, suicidal tendencies, eating disorders and anxiety) and externalizing problems (e.g. violence and substance abuse).
>
> *(p. 357)*

Quite a shocking indictment of poor self-evaluations until one realizes that "can" also implies "but might not." Here too, correlation is pointedly not cause; the authors themselves acknowledge that "low self-esteem can also be considered as an important *consequence* of such disorders and behavioral problems" (p. 368), i.e., that people might exhibit a high sense of self-worth *because* they are happy, healthy, well-adjusted, doing well in school, and not spending their recess time bullying their peers.

Some data also suggest that increasing a person's self-esteem is a more complicated business than sitting children in a circle and pouring bottles of self-esteem over their heads (see below). "These results suggest that efforts to improve self-esteem in children require both supportive social surroundings and the formation and acceptance of realistic personal goals in the personally relevant domains" (p. 367).

Still another misunderstanding of the self-esteem craze was the idea that low self-esteem could be "cured" by bombarding people with positive messages, as many self-esteem interventions try to do. (This is Number Five on Tyrrell's list.)

> Telling someone they are great or wonderful when they are constantly negative about themselves will not work. Imagine if you really detest yourself and someone tells you that you're lovely even as they are

telling everyone else the same thing. In fact people with low self-esteem can be upset by disconfirming feedback. Healthy self-esteem needs to emerge subtly, not as a sudden result of hearing you are 'really special' or 'fantastic'.

The point about "telling everyone else the same thing" deserves emphasis. Many esteem-enhancement interventions consist of gathering up a group of kids in a circle and chanting "I am a lovable person" or "I accept myself completely" in unison, as if the mere act of saying positive things about the self makes them true. "Everyone's a winner" works fine for elementary children who play T-ball in the summer, but as adulthood approaches and it becomes increasingly obvious that in the adult world, there are both winners and losers, "everyone's a winner" becomes a meaningless slogan.

The evidence that self-esteem can somehow be successfully manipulated (i.e., that there is some method to increase self-esteem among those who lack it) is mixed at best. One study (Biddle and Asare, 2011) asked whether physical activity would enhance self-esteem. "Physical activity can lead to improvements in self-esteem, at least in the short term. However, there is a paucity of good quality research." Many other esteem enhancements have been tried out, sometimes with success (at least in the short term), sometimes not. At least one line of theoretical reasoning is that self-esteem is a "relatively stable aspect of personality" that changes very slowly in the process of development, not something that can be artificially stimulated by artful "feel good about yourself" strategies (Brown, 1993; see also Juth et al., 2008). For all the emphasis on "improving self-esteem" as a therapeutic intervention, the evidence on how to do this, or even whether it can be done, is surprisingly thin and unconvincing.

The things that have been reliably linked to low self-esteem are social withdrawal, lack of social skills, eating disorders (one of the few social problems that is in fact exacerbated by low self-esteem), self-neglect, negativism, worry, reluctance, and low expectations about life. Many of these are serious, counter-productive character traits and deserve attention. But they are not the traits that lead to aggression, bullying, delinquency, or other untoward social consequences.

If self-esteem is synonymous with pride, and if the self-esteem movement were correct in its assessment that lack of self-esteem is the source of many of the problems that beset us, then it would not be pride but rather the *absence* of pride that would be sinful and problematic. But since, with the prominent exception of eating disorders, the link between low self-esteem and other social problems is so tenuous, perhaps all that should be urged on people is to have a realistic assessment of one's worth – adding, perhaps, that faced with a behavioral choice, the best decision is the one you'd be proudest of (or, better, that your mother would be proudest of). As for giving God the credit He is due, I have to conclude that much of Creation is shameful (poverty, misery, disease, bigotry, cruelty, hatred – need I go on?) and if the Deity insists on credit for all that is good, He has to own all that is bad too.

Pride and Productivity

Many of the personality nuances associated with self-esteem (at least in some studies) would seem to make those of low self-esteem (those who lack pride) very poor bets as employees. According to the Counseling and Mental Health Center at the University of Texas, Austin, low self-esteem can lead to anxiety, stress, loneliness, and depression, can create problems with friendships and romantic relationships, will often impair academic and job performance and might pose an "increased vulnerability to drug and alcohol abuse."[8] The Center further explicates the Three Faces of Low Self-Esteem:

1. The Imposter: Acts happy and successful, but is really terrified of failure. Lives with the constant fear that she or he will be found out. Needs continuous successes to maintain the mask of positive self-esteem, which may lead to problems with perfectionism, procrastination, competition, and burn-out.

2. The Rebel: Acts like the opinions or good will of others – especially people who are important or powerful – don't matter. Lives with constant anger about not feeling good enough. Continuously needs to prove that others' judgments and criticisms don't hurt, which may lead to problems like blaming others excessively, breaking rules or laws, or opposing authority.

3. The Victim: Acts helpless and unable to cope with the world and waits for someone to come to the rescue. Uses self-pity or indifference as a shield against fear of taking responsibility for changing his or her life. Looks repeatedly to others for guidance, which can lead to such problems as unassertiveness, underachievement, and excessive reliance on others in relationships.

Now ask yourself: Do you know imposters, rebels, and victims in your workplace? I certainly do, and so do most of the other people that I have queried about the matter. Are these your favorite coworkers? Are they consistently your most productive coworkers? Do you look forward to having them speak up in group meetings? And with these answers in mind, ask finally who is the better employee – the coworker who takes pride in his or her ability to get things done, or the one who is constantly kvetching about the injustices of life?

Other compendia of symptoms and correlates of low self-esteem lead to the same conclusion. Among these are depression, mistrust, self-doubt, rigidity, passivity or passive-aggressiveness, poor communication skills, shyness, and so on.[9] In most cases, sensible employers would look for the precise opposite traits in potential employees. Indeed, the source just cited lists as some of the "signs of healthy self-esteem" the following:

- Looks ahead, setting both long-range and short-range goals
- Establishes goals that are reasonable and likely attainable
- Doesn't procrastinate/is not a perfectionist/is a self-starter
- Accepts his/her own weaknesses and lack of skills
- Is highly motivated and determined to succeed
- Bounces back after a setback, moving forward again
- Trusts own ideas, perceptions, and opinions
- Has the courage to say what he/she truly feels and believes
- Is able to hear and benefit from constructive criticism
- Can make timely decisions after considering the options
- Displays good social skills
- Has a history of far more successes than failures in meeting goals
- Keeps moving to achieve goals in difficult times
- Is open to both positive and negative feedback
- Learns from past mistakes rather than repeating them
- Is willing and able to take risks
- Is willing to cut his/her losses when a project seems doomed to fail
- Can change course when it is necessary to do so
- Is generally positive, energetic, and assertive
- Takes people at their word unless or until there is reason to do otherwise

Low self-esteem (lack of pride in oneself and one's accomplishments) leads to workers who are morose, withdrawn, and neurotic. High self-esteem (*realistically* or *healthfully* high self-esteem, not narcissism) leads to workers who are confident, outgoing, and flexible. It makes one wonder what would happen to the productivity of the American workforce if pride were somehow eliminated! As the English novelist Julian Barnes has it in *Flaubert's Parrot*, "Pride makes us long for a solution to things – a solution, a purpose, a final cause; but the better telescopes become, the more stars appear."

There is a small academic literature on the effects of pride on productivity. In most cases, the link is taken as self-evident, but to the extent that it has been researched, the consensus is clear: Increasing employee pride, self-respect, and self-worth increases productivity (e.g., Sahoo and Das, 2011). Indeed, many workplace innovations that increase worker productivity or morale are assumed to work mainly through the mechanism of increasing employee pride in the employer, the product, or the work being done.

But here too, there may be a "dark side" of workplace pride that needs to be mentioned. A study by Braithwaite and Ahmed (2015) distinguished between "narcissistic pride" and "humble pride," much as we did earlier in this chapter. Narcissistic pride is self-aggrandizement and "leads individuals to feel that they are better than others." "Humble pride," in contrast, "flows from personal and internal satisfaction of having mastered a challenge central to one's identity, while being aware of one's limitations and of the importance of collaborative relationships to one's achievements" (p. 5). It would seem to follow from the definitions of the terms that narcissistic pride is bad and humble pride good, and that is indeed what the data show.

> Those who identified themselves as having bullied others [in the work-place] were pride-focused, not shame focused. They were more likely to express narcissistic pride over their work success, lauding their feats over others, and were less likely to express humble pride, sharing their success with others.

Moreover, there is evidence that the nature of the workplace matters.

> Where work norms, incentive schemes and management styles create hierarchical and competitive work environments, a message is sent to workers about how they should manage their pride and shame if they want to get on. That message does not encourage shame and pride management that builds teams and promotes a healthy work environment, that is, shame acknowledgment and humble pride. Instead it promotes shame displacement and narcissistic pride and fuels workplace disharmony.
>
> *(p. 16)*

Pride and Social Relations

Among psychologists, pride is known as a self-conscious or self-reflective emotion, much like shame, guilt, or embarrassment – emotions that are stimulated by self-reflection and self-evaluation (Tangney et al., 2011). Authentic pride (what we have called good pride) is "fueled by the emotional rush of accomplishment, confidence, and success, and is associated with prosocial and achievement-oriented behaviors, extraversion, agreeableness, conscientiousness, satisfying interpersonal relationships, and positive mental health" (Kaufman, 2012). Clearly, good pride *improves* interpersonal relationships. Bad pride, or narcissism, on the other hand, "is fueled by arrogance and conceit, and is associated with anti-social behaviors, rocky relationships, low levels of conscientiousness and high levels of neuroticism, narcissism, disagreeableness, and poor mental health outcomes." Bad pride is destructive of interpersonal relationships. (Of some interest to today's readers, Kaufman's *Psychology Today* essay has a photo of John Lennon to illustrate authentic pride and a photo of Donald and Melania Trump to illustrate hubristic pride.)

Thus we see, as elsewhere, that pride is a two-edged sword. So long as pride is "authentic," "deserved," or "good," it is a social lubricant that improves pro-social behavior and betters social relations. But when pride degenerates into arrogance or hubris, it is destructive of social relationships and promotes anti-social behaviors, mainly dominance and aggression. "Pride has always received mixed reviews. The ancient Greeks viewed pride as 'the crown of the virtues' whereas the early Christian philosophers viewed pride as the 'deadliest of the Seven Deadly Sins.' Pride is quite the polarizing emotion!" (Kaufman, 2012).

A recent posting on pride and dieting illustrates the two sides of pride. If you take authentic pride in your efforts to lose weight – pride in exerting some measure of self-control, for example – then the warm fuzzies that spring from pride help keep you on track. But if you take false pride in the effort – hey, I've lost five pounds, I'm halfway to my goal – your pride tells you that you have earned the right to indulge. The author of the post, Meghan Walsh, asks in her title, "Is Pride Making You Fat?"[10]

Pride and Prejudice: Ethnic Pride, Nationalism, and Other Horrors

Although Jane Austen intended no deep meaning in the title of her famous novel (the title was apparently chosen for commercial reasons), it seems fairly obvious that pride found in some things can lead to prejudice against other things. What I have in mind specifically are two of the most destructive forces of the modern era: Pride in one's ethnicity or origins (which can lead to xeno-phobia, racism, and ethnic hatred) and pride in one's country, or nationalism (which in its most benign form is simply patriotism but in its malignant form is the source of ferocious world wars).

It is easily forgotten that the modern nation-state is very much a product of the 19th century. When the United States of America was formed in the late 18th century, it was intended as a loose federation of autonomous states, not as the powerful super-state is has become. Even today, many Constitutional scholars doubt that the Constitution grants to the nation-state all the powers it has assumed. Prior to 1871, "Germany" as we know it did not exist. What is now "Germany" was in the early 19th century the Holy Roman Empire of the German Nation, a loose coalition of some 500 independent states and principalities, many of them regularly at war with the others. The independent nations, duchies, principalities, and Papal States of the Italian peninsula were not integrated into the Italian nation-state until 1871, when Rome became the capital of the newly formed Kingdom of Italy. Spain was a unified nation-state much earlier (by 1512) but one with internal nationalistic sentiments that con-tinue to threaten Spanish unity even today, as Catalonia threatens to secede from the state and the Basques agitate for their own autonomy.

Tribal animosities (which have evolved over the millennia into ethnic iden-tities and hatreds) go back much further, of course – back to the time when the tribe on the far side of the river decided that the antelope were tastier "over there" and sent its strongest men into battle to secure and defend their newly appropriated antelope rights. The very notion of an ethnic group presupposes an "us" and a "them." "We" are those of like origin, language, technology and mind. "They," simply, are "other," different, strange and, therefore, to be feared and hated. To protect "our" interests – our territory, women, resources, whatever – "we" need to be wary and suspicious of "them," and likewise, they of us. The idea that we might trade our catfish or our wheat for their antelope so that in the end we are all better off is a later development. Commerce awaited the dawn of agricultural society about 10,000 year ago; recognizably modern humans have been around for some 200,000 years. Warfare and brutality have much deeper roots than commerce and exchange!

Even today – and sharply in contrast to the Marxian epigram that all conflict is class conflict – the world is riven with ethnic, religious, linguistic, and nationalistic divisiveness and hatred. The long struggle in Northern Ireland was between Catholics and Protestants, who not only worship the same God but recognize Jesus Christ as their Savior. Much of the Middle East can only be understood as a conflict between Shia and Sunni Muslims, the rest as a conflict between Muslims and Jews. The Kurds sprawl out over a territory that spans five independent nations and seek to become an independent nation of their own. The Dutch-speaking Belgians have little to do with the Flemish; francophone Canada keeps trying to secede from its English-speaking neighbors. In the Great Lakes region of Africa, there has been a bloody civil war for decades between the Hutus and the Tutsis. In the United States, racial tensions between blacks and whites remain intense a century and a half after Emancipation. Throughout East Asia, there are conflicts involving the Chinese, the Koreans, and the Japanese. On several occasions, the Chinese and Japanese have been within a whisker of going to war over the ownership of about three square miles of uninhabited rock in the East China Sea. Why? Not so much because the Senkaku Islands are of much strategic importance or even resource rich. No, their contested ownership derives from a sense of national *pride*.

Donald Kagan, professor of history and classics at Yale, delivered a paper on "National Honor" at a foreign policy conference in 1996. In that paper, he remarked:

> For the last 2,500 years, at least, states have conducted their affairs and often gone to war moved by considerations that would not pass the test of "vital national interests."... Honor is the name of one category of concerns and motives that has dominated relations among peoples and states since antiquity.[11]

American nationalism has been particularly virulent in the last half of the 20th century. Our sense of pride, national honor, and national interests have involved us in countless and largely pointless but highly destructive wars around the globe: In Korea, Vietnam, Panama, Iraq, Afghanistan, Kuwait, Lebanon, Grenada, Somalia, Kosovo – this list goes on. We enter these wars, usually, with the surface rationale that we are safeguarding "democracy," the implication being that our values (democracy, freedom, pluralism) should be the world's values whether the rest of the world is ready for them or not. We proudly declare that we are "the land of the free and the home of the brave" but, really, are we any freer than the Dutch or the Canadians? Any braver than the Aussies or the Brits? Many nations can stake a claim to freedom and bravery. The national anthem of Belize is entitled, "The Land of the Free." And yet the idea that we, the United States, are the freest and bravest of them all is an inherent part of our civil religion.

Americans are taught that we are the best nation on earth, a sentiment loudly proclaimed by political candidates in their stump speeches. But the Norwegians believe that Norway is the best country on earth, the Spanish think that of Spain, Brazilians couldn't imagine living anywhere but Brazil, and on around the globe. Not only are we instructed that we are the best nation on earth, we also believe that all other nations should try to be more like us. And when they don't – when they drift off toward some ideology we do not embrace – we think we have every right to bomb their cities and kill their citizens. Do we, really? Where's the international charter that grants us these rights? Are we truly the greatest nation on earth, the greatest that has ever existed? Or are we just international bullies, full of national hubris, quick to take offense and even quicker to retaliate? Just what has our national pride accomplished? And at what cost?

Will McAvoy is the fictional newscaster in Aaron Sorkin's *Newsroom* and in the very first episode, McAvoy is asked by a student at Northwestern University, "What makes America the greatest country in the world?" His reply has become a classic:

Just in case you accidentally wander into a voting booth one day, there are some things you should know. One of them is: There is absolutely no evidence to support the statement that we're the greatest country in the world. We're 7th in literacy, 27th in math, 22nd in science, 49th in life expectancy, 178th in infant mortality, 3rd in median household income, number 4 in labor force and number 4 in exports. We lead the world in only three categories: number of incarcerated citizens per capita, number of adults who believe angels are real and defense spending - where we spend more than the next 26 countries combined, 25 of whom are allies. Now, none of this is the fault of a 20-year-old college student, but you, nonetheless, are without a doubt a member of the worst period generation period ever period, so when you ask what makes us the greatest country in the world, I don't know what the FUCK you're talking about!... Yosemite?

Not that American nationalism is uniquely bad on a world-historical scale. German and Italian nationalism have done their fair share to make the 20th the bloodiest century on record (so far); Russian nationalism, likewise. Spanish and Portuguese nationalism colonized the world; British nationalism did it again a century or two later. French, German, British, Italian, and even Belgian nationalism carved up the African continent. And all in the name of national *pride*. As at the level of individuals, whole nations exhibit both authentic pride and hubris. Authentic pride is the justifiable gratification that results from real achievement – landing on the moon, for instance; national hubris has slaughtered people by the millions.

In 2008, the National Opinion Research Center released a survey identifying the world's most and least patriotic (nationalistic) countries. The ten most patriotic countries were (in order) Israel, The Philippines, New Zealand, Chile, Canada, Austria, South Africa, Australia, Venezuela, and, leading the list, the United States. The least patriotic (also in order): Czech Republic, Switzerland, France, Taiwan, (former) West Germany, Slovakia, Poland, Sweden, Latvia, and (former) East Germany.

When not riven by worldwide warfare, the 20th century was a century of mass genocide, all of it perpetrated in the name of national honor, ethnic purity, or some other equally bogus principle of pride. It began early in the 20th century when the fading Ottoman Empire and its ruthless Sultan Abdul Hamid decided that the Christian Armenians were the source of the Empire's decline. In the three years from 1915 to 1918, one and a half million Armenians in Turkey were slaughtered. A bit later in the century, Stalin decided that the Ukrainians were un-loyal and dangerous to the Revolution and so engineered a famine that left seven million of them dead. The invasion of Nanking by the Japanese in 1937 saw the wanton murder of 300,000 Chinese – half the entire civilian population. Then came Hitler, the Third Reich, the Holocaust, and six million dead Jews, along with numerous gypsies, homosexuals, and other despised outgroups. (Some estimates put the Holocaust death toll as high as twenty million.) In the late 1970s, the Cambodian Communist Party leader Pol Pot slaughtered two million innocents in a forced effort to convert Cambodia to a Communist peasant society, apparently in an effort to emulate Mao's Cultural Revolution (which itself took the lives of a million and a half Chinese). Toward the end of the century, a million died in ethnic conflict in Rwanda. In Bosnia-Herzegovina in the early 90s, conflict between the Serbs, Croats, and Muslims left a quarter million Muslims dead. The worst genocide of the 21st century (so far) has been the indiscriminate slaughter of a half-million ethnic minorities in Darfur by the Sudanese government – well short of the mass genocides of the 20th century, but it is still early. The Syrian civil war has almost certainly topped the Darfur toll but the estimates of the Syrian death toll are all over the place. And who knows what horrors are still to come?

In sum, just as individual hubris and arrogance are almost unreservedly bad, so too is the unrestrained hubris of whole nations and their leaders. It is worth underscoring that none of the genocides of the 20th century succeeded. There are still a hundred thousand Christian Armenians in Turkey, the Japanese do not occupy Nanking, the Third Reich was defeated, Ukraine remains an autonomous nation (for now), Cambodia is an increasingly modern society. What bizarre, twisted, murderous mentality convinced the perpetrators of these genocides that their actions were somehow workable strategies, that something worthwhile would be accomplished? Racial, ethnic, and national pride lies at the root of this insanity. That, plus the presumed moral certainty that as the superior group, the perpetrators of genocide had a natural right, an obligation almost, to slaughter all who appeared to stand in the way. Has history known a more destructive force than ethnic or national pride run rampant?

How About Shame? Guilt? Humility?

The opposites of pride are shame, guilt, and humility, although the notion of "humble pride" casts some doubt on the status of the latter. Let's take these up in order.

Given the recent emphasis in the therapeutic community on enhancing self-esteem as a solution to many of life's ills, it is remarkable that shaming has also received some attention as a therapeutic intervention. We brushed up against this topic in our discussion of workplace pride. Valerie Braithwaite, a psychologist whose work we reviewed, is the spouse of the Australian John Braithwaite, originator of an important theory in criminology (and since applied elsewhere) known as "reintegrative shaming." For a time in the 1990s, this was probably the hottest topic in criminology.

The general idea behind reintegrative shaming is simple: The criminal justice system imposes a sanction on an offender that is designed less to punish than to strengthen the moral bond between the offender and the community. Thus, the sanction "shames" the offender in such a way that he (or she) becomes "reintegrated" into the community's norms and values. The emphasis, clearly, is on the offender's behaviors, not on the offender himself (or herself). In some respects, then, reintegrative shaming is just behavior modification brought into the criminal justice system.

The underlying psychological basis for the theory is that shame is an intensely painful emotion that demands resolution; offenders change their behaviors so as to reduce or eliminate shame. An example would be the shoplifter whose "punishment" is that he has to apologize to the store owner for his crime and undertake some form of restitution (say, stocking shelves or sweeping up – something commensurate in value to what was stolen). Those who see an obvious link here to "restorative justice" perceive correctly.

Bazelon (2012) acknowledges that "shaming had a particular power – exposing the wrongdoer to the public gaze was different from hiding him behind prison walls or imposing a fine he could quietly pay." And the theory did claim some early successes (see, e.g., Kahan and Posner, 1999). Indeed, reintegrative shaming worked quite well for offenses like shoplifting, public urination, and driving under the influence (see, e.g., Tyler et al., 2007), and perhaps, even with more serious offenses such as sexual offenses (McAlinden, 2005) or domestic violence (Koss, 2000). Its major remaining expressions in criminal justice today are probably "communitarian conferencing" (where the victim, offender, the offender's family, the police, and a convenor conference to discuss the offense, its impact, and a just punishment) and the tendency to sentence minor, nonviolent offenders to hours of community service rather than to do time in jail or pay a fine.

When it came to serious hard-core violent offenders, however, reintegrative shaming was a bust, mainly because serious predatory offenders are largely impervious to shame and because it proved impossible to "scale" shaming to the magnitude of the offense. A shoplifter can be made to apologize and render proper restitution, but what do you do with a murderer or a serial rapist or a habitual armed robber? For this end of the criminal spectrum the policy has not been reintegrative shaming but rather "three strikes and you're out." When all sense of decency is gone, "shaming" is no longer possible.

Another version of shame as behavior modification is so-called "fat shaming," the effort to get obese people to lose weight by making them ashamed of their weight. One item on the matter appeared in the *Huffington Post*, which reported that a British group called Overweight Haters Ltd. had been handing out fat-shaming cards to women on the subway. The cards read in part: "It's really not glandular, it's your gluttony. Our organisation hates and resents fat people. We object to the enormous amount of food resources you consume while half the world starves." In related incidents, we have airlines refusing to sell tickets to people over a certain size, doctors who use fat-shaming as a strategy to get obese people to lose weight, and employers who make overweight employees enroll in wellness and weight reduction programs. Some of this was discussed earlier in the chapter on gluttony.

Alas, "Science Confirms: 'Fat Shaming' Just Makes Things Worse." So said an Internet posting by an outfit called Authority Nutrition.[12] The post remarks, "Psychologists have done a lot of research on this, and the evidence is very clear. Fat shaming does NOT motivate people, but makes them feel terrible about themselves and actually causes them to eat more and gain more weight." Part of the problem is that most obese people are *already* ashamed of their weight, have tried numerous times and methods to lose weight, but always fail. Many decide instead to just be comfortable with who they are, rolls of fat and all. Said one:

Being fat is not the worst thing you can be. There are an infinite number of things you could be that are so much worse than fat. For example: racist, sexist, bigoted, mean to people on the Internet, mean to babies, mean to cats, that person who takes up two parking spaces, that person who uses 23 hashtags after every Instagram picture.

And some counter-punch with "skinny shaming" – the parallel and equally cruel effort to shame seriously underweight women to give up their body obsessions and tuck into a plateful of cheeseburgers and fries.

Just as pumping up self-esteem is often thought to resolve many social issues, so too do many people seem to believe that miscreants of all sorts can be shamed out of their offensive behaviors. Thus, one can find items on the Internet that deal with teenage pregnancy shaming, college dropout shaming, cigarette smoker shaming, bullying shaming, and on ad infinitum.[13] There is practically no serious scientific evidence that any of this works, so one wonders why people even bother. Perhaps these people are not, as they often say, "just trying to help" but rather are indulging their private mean streaks. The cruelty one discovers in reading the Internet postings on shaming (such as those mentioned above) is – shall we say? – shameful.

Humility

The problem with writing about humility – how much of it there is, who is humble and who not – is that truly humble people wouldn't make any effort to let you know how humble they are. It is the essence of humility, I guess, to be quiet about one's humble deeds. That point notwithstanding, humility has been described as the only true source of joy, the foundation of a successful marriage, and the sole path to a virtuous life.[14] "Humility," St. Augustine reminds us, "is the foundation of all the other virtues. Hence, in the soul in which this virtue does not exist there cannot be any other virtue except in mere appearance."

How odd, then, that the verb form of humility is *humiliate*. So if you have set out to spread humility among your peers and associates (to humiliate them, in other words), you are (it seems) trying to make people look foolish or ashamed by destroying their dignity and deflating their self-respect. From this we learn at least one important lesson, namely, that the line between humility and shame is thin indeed. We also learn that humility inflicted on you by others is far less virtuous than humility that wells up from within.

False humility is much easier to come by. Indeed, it has even been given a name: *Humblebrag*. The concept of a humblebrag appears to have originated with the comedian Harris Wittels, a writer for the sitcom hit *Parks and Recreation*. Wittels has gathered up his favorites and published them in a book: *Humblebrag: The Art of False Modesty* (New York: Grand Central Publishing,

2012). Basically, a humblebrag is a boast disguised as self-deprecation. Example: "I hate my Lamborghini. The police are ALWAYS pulling me over just because I drive a Lambo. They always think I am speeding but I'm not!! Then they let me go." Another: "Just in case you think all this has gone to my head, within 36 hours of winning the Oscar, I was back home plunging a clogged toilet." Yet another: "Why do men hit on me more when I am in sweatpants?" Or the common response of job applicants when asked to describe their greatest weakness: "I sometimes work too hard on projects."

The humblebrag is a strategy to boast about an event, feature, or accomplishment by trying to make it seem bad. There's no need to envy me, my car, my awards, my good looks, my clothes, or my sexual conquests – they all have a downside you wouldn't believe! A humblebrag, then, is "an ostensibly modest or self-deprecating statement whose actual purpose is to draw attention to something of which one is proud" (in the above examples, my car, my Oscar, my butt).

Henry Alford, a commentator for *The New York Times*, has observed that "social media status updates are basically selfies, humblebrags, and rants." "Most humblebrags," Alford observes, "are attempts to convey one of three messages: 'I have too much work;' 'I am an idiot/impostor;' or 'I have firsthand knowledge of the gritty gilt to be found inside the gilded cage.'" The latter seems by far the most common.[15]

What's the difference between a humblebrag and outright bragging? Clearly, a brag is intended to generate awe among one's associates. A humblebrag is intended to generate both sympathy and awe.

Remarkably, humblebragging has already attracted some scholarly attention (Sezer et al., 2015):

> Humblebragging – bragging masked by a complaint – is a distinct and, given the rise of social media, increasingly ubiquitous form of self-promotion. We show that although people often choose to humblebrag when motivated to make a good impression, it is an ineffective self-promotional strategy. Five studies offer both correlational and causal evidence that humblebragging has both global costs – reducing liking and perceived sincerity – and specific costs: it is even ineffective in signaling the specific trait that that a person wants to promote. Moreover, humblebragging is less effective than simply complaining, because complainers are at least seen as sincere. Despite people's belief that combining bragging and complaining confers the benefits of both self-promotion strategies, humblebragging fails to pay off.

News from the Front: The very day the above passages were written, the MSNBC news website featured an item, "12 Things You're Doing That Make People Dislike You Immediately." No. 8 on the list: Humblebragging. A study mentioned in the post declared that more than three-quarters of their research participants humblebragged when asked in a mock interview situation to describe "their biggest weakness." Among the humblebrags: "I work too hard" and "I'm a perfectionist."[16]

Guilt

Guilt, it is said, is the most useless of the emotions. The handmaiden of shame, guilt can be paralyzing or a catalyst for concerted action. The manipulation of guilt is likewise the handmaiden of shaming – and probably about as effective.

Transforming nouns into verbs is an affliction of the age, but yes, people can certainly be "guilted" into doing something they might not otherwise do, sometimes to their detriment and sometimes to their benefit. Parents are guilted into certain child-rearing practices; new mothers are guilted into breastfeeding; householders are guilted into recycling; shoppers are guilted into buying organic versions of products at two or three times the price. Manipulation of guilt has thus become a favorite way of encouraging people to do the things we (or someone) want them to do – guilt is the sharp edge of the sword of today's moral certainty.

There seems to be no end to the things people can be made to feel guilty about. Anyone found shopping in, say, Sears or Walmart or the local supermarket can be guilted by "fair trade" advocates (and with good reason: See the concluding chapter). Gun owners can be guilted by their presumed association with the National Rifle Association. Articles have been written on mothering guilt (Sutherland, 2010), eco-guilt (Hesz and Neophytoum, 2010; Mallett, 2012), food guilt ("The new eating disorder you might not realize you have;" Damassa, 2013), relationship guilt (Valor-Segura et al., 2014), migration guilt (Ward and Styles, 2012), fat guilt (Salk and Engeln-Maddox, 2012), exercise guilt (Streuber et al., 2015), and on through virtually the entire repertoire of human behaviors. In this matter, apparently, we must cede the floor to Voltaire: "Every man is guilty of all the good he did not do." Or perhaps to the cartoonist Bill Watterson, whose character Calvin remarks to his stuffed tiger Hobbes, "There's no problem so awful, that you can't add some guilt to it and make it even worse."

Since we are largely conditioned to think of guilt as bad (indeed, everything is bad: Pride, shame, guilt, the entire gamut!), it is worth concluding on the point that guilt also does a great deal of good (e.g., Plante, 2013). A *soupcon* of guilt, Plante reminds.us, makes us "more likely to help our neighbors, care for loved ones, act honestly and with integrity, offer gracious and kind expressions to others, recycle, and so forth." Guilt is that little nagging feeling deep in our consciousness that reminds us to do the right thing at the right time. We drink less, eat more healthily, and work out at the gym because not doing these things makes us feel guilty. Guilt also motivates a great deal of pro-social and charitable behavior. Absent at least a little guilt from time to time, our world would be much more challenging, narcissistic, and generally unpleasant.

Notes

1 Pride that "goeth before the fall" is how the passage from Proverbs 16:18 is usually rendered, but in the KJV, the passage reads, "Pride goeth before destruction, and a haughty spirit before a fall."
2 http://psychology.jrank.org/pages/564/Self-Conscious-Emotions.html.
3 www.blogos.org/gotquestions/pride-sin.html.
4 www.adweek.com/socialtimes/selfies-narcissism-addiction-low-self-esteem/147769.
5 See, e.g., Crocker, Luhtanen, and Sommers (2004): "This tremendous interest in self-esteem has been fueled by the suggestion that low self-esteem plays a causal role in social problems and that raising self-esteem may help to solve those problems" (p. 134).
6 For a compelling and sustained argument that "it just does not ring true," see Twenge and Campbell, 2009.
7 www.self-confidence.co.uk/articles/top-ten-facts-about-low-self-esteem/.
8 http://cmhc.utexas.edu/selfesteem.html.
9 www.getesteem.com/lse-symptoms/emotional.html.
10 www.ozy.com/acumen/is-pride-making-you-fat/65354.
11 www.cs.utexas.edu/users/vl/notes/kagan.html.
12 https://authoritynutrition.com/fat-shaming-makes-things-worse/.
13 http://nymag.com/thecut/2015/05/teen-moms-need-support-not-shame.html; www.telegraph.co.uk/comment/columnists/bryonygordon/3559126/There-is-no-shame-in-dropping-out-of-university.html;http://thoughtcatalog.com/jameson-dumaurier/2015/01/stop-smoker-shaming/; www.quora.com/Is-ostracizing-and-publicly-shaming-a-bully-considered-an-effective-form-of-therapy.
14 See among many other postings www.foryourmarriage.org/humility-foundation-for-marital-happiness/or www.opusdei.org/en-us/article/humility-source-of-joy/.
15 www.nytimes.com/2012/12/02/fashion/bah-humblebrag-the-unfortunate-rise-of-false-humility.html?_r=0.
16 www.msn.com/en-us/lifestyle/smart-living/12-things-youre-doing-that-make-people-dislike-you-immediately/ss-BBrifTN#image=8.

8

CONCLUDING OBSERVATIONS

And thus we come to the end of our ramble through American manners and morals here in the early decades of the 21st century. What we have learned is that without anger, there is no politics, no drama, no zest; without greed, no economy, no accumulation of productive capital (but probably no inequality); without gluttony, no real pleasure; without envy, no motivation; without lust, no reproduction, no next generation; without pride, no genuine accomplishment; and without sloth, no rejuvenation, no distinction between work and play. As one wag put it in commenting on the Seven Deadlies, "These days, for all but the most devout, Pope Gregory's list seems less like a means to moral behavior than a description of cable TV programming."[1] Or as the songster Jon Foreman (lead singer of the rock band *Switchfoot*) has put it, "Greed, envy, sloth, pride and gluttony: these are not vices anymore. No, these are marketing tools. Lust is our way of life. Envy is just a nudge towards another sale." Whatever else might be said about life without the Seven Deadlies, it would surely be boring!

To conclude that the seven deadly sins no longer seem to provide a proper moral basis for the modern society and economy – indeed, are fundamentally incompatible with all sense of *modernity* – is thus to beg the question: Well, if not the seven deadly sins, then what? What would be reasonable moral principles around which to organize a modern society or one's personal life? At the risk of venturing into philosophical and moral questions where I am largely bereft of expertise, let me conclude by presenting and briefly commenting on Mahatma Gandhi's alternative moral framework, called appropriately the "Seven Social Sins," first published by Gandhi in his weekly newspaper *Young India* in 1925 nearly a century ago.[2] And here they are:

Wealth without Work
Pleasure without Conscience

> Knowledge without Character
> Commerce without Morality
> Science without Humanity
> Religion without Sacrifice
> Politics without Principle

Some of these have an obvious relationship with the Seven Deadlies. "Wealth without work" conjures up both greed and sloth; "pleasure without conscience" is one meaning of lust. So there are certainly allusions in Gandhi's list to traditional moral virtues. But this list also takes us well beyond the original Seven Deadlies, and in what seem to me morally appropriate ways. So we'll conclude with an explication of and some comments on Gandhi's Seven Social Sins.

Wealth Without Work

Many huge fortunes have been acquired without working for them, via inheritances, investments, outright crime, corruption, or plain good luck. The problem of wealth without work is that it creates a sense of entitlement – you don't deserve your wealth because you worked for it, strove toward it, sacrificed in order to attain it, but rather because it was given to you as your entitlement. It is therefore right and natural that the wealth be yours. On a societal level, wealth and entitlement bring waste – just as one is entitled to wealth, so is one entitled to discard that which wealth brings. Little wonder, for example, that food waste is most pronounced in the most affluent nations, and likewise, in the most affluent households (Pearson et al., 2013). Wealth without work and the entitlement it brings are largely responsible for what has been called the "disposable society" or the "throwaway society." Having acquired lots of "stuff" without labor, we become indifferent to the value of our stuff and throw lots of it away. Not needing to work to obtain stuff, all sense of its material value evaporates, much to the detriment of the environment and society as a whole.

The contemporary predations of global capitalism are a blight on the conscience of all right-thinking people. Capitalism as an economic system was intended as a means to harness the productive capital of an economy to the benefit of all, the benefit of society as a whole. Granted, the assumption is always that everyone will behave so as to maximize their own self-interest, but the point of capital accumulation was to add value to the aggregate social product, not just to swell the coffers of the super-rich at the direct expense of the well-being of ordinary men and women. The triumph of capitalism over Communism was not that self-interest is an inherently better economic principle than "from each according to ability, and to each according to need." The triumph was that the Communist societies never developed a workable and equitable method of determining everyone's abilities and needs.

The various get-rich-quick schemes that have at times threatened to bring the global capitalist economy to ruin over the last three or four decades have all been strategies to accumulate wealth without working for it. "Wealth without work" is a pretty accurate description of today's upper 1%. Indeed, as Steven Covey has observed,

> today, there are entire professions built around making wealth without working, making much money without paying taxes, benefiting from free government programs without carrying a fair share of the financial burdens, and enjoying all the perks of citizenship of country and membership of corporation without assuming any of the risk or responsibility.[3]

The rational pursuit of self-interest coupled with productive work indeed bestows wealth, and should. The social wage – the minimum income that society decides is necessary to live an acceptably decent life, conferred as a right of citizenship rather than as the benefit of employment – has always been less than the minimum wage, so that people toward the bottom of the income distribution will always be better off by working than not working. And while some (e.g., Blau, 1992) question this as a principle, I do not. Work confers dignity, purpose, and identity as well as income and, thus, has value that exceeds the earned wage. So, all who can work should continue to make some sort of contribution to the larger whole.

There are, of course, many who cannot work: The elderly, the very young, the disabled, often mothers caring for dependent children, and others. For better or worse, we (and everyone else in the world) have evolved a society with a permanently dependent class of people for whom "self-sufficiency" will always be a pipedream. It thus falls to us as a civilized society to decide what the minimum income of such persons should be, which amounts in essence to defining a lifestyle below which no one should be allowed to fall. It is a characteristic of the more advanced societies that their social wage is higher, whereas in the developing societies it is lower. These days, our American minimum acceptable lifestyle is several pegs lower than that enjoyed in the social democracies of Europe.[4] At the same time, we lead the world in the number of billionaires and multi-billionaires. Surely, any version of "self-interest" must be satiated once you have a thousand million dollars or more to your credit.

Pleasure Without Conscience

Pleasure without conscience is not a bad definition of lust and carries overtones of gluttony as well, but Gandhi's admonition goes well beyond the advice to avoid prurient sex or gluttonous consumption. When Gandhi warns against pleasure without conscience, he is advising us to appreciate the evils that may have gone into the production of our enjoyment. It is a useful habit that few Americans seem to have ever developed.

To illustrate, many people sit down in the morning to a nice cup of hot chocolate, or perhaps end their day with a slice of chocolate cake. But something like 70% of the world's chocolate is made from cacao beans grown in West Africa, mainly Ghana and Cote d'Ivoire, where child labor and even child slavery are common practices in the cocoa industry. Cocoa farmers earn, on average, only a few dollars a day and are thus reduced to using child labor to be economically competitive. In many cases, children as young as five are kidnapped in neighboring countries such as Mali or Burkino Faso (two of the poorest nations on earth) and indentured to the cocoa farmers, in many cases, never to see their families again. Harvesting the cacao bean is hard dangerous work that requires climbing high into trees and whacking open ripe cacao pods with heavy machetes. Most cocoa workers are covered with scars resulting from this practice.

My point here is not to denude your morning cocoa of all pleasure or to make you feel guilty for not being aware of the dubious agricultural practices that make your cup of hot chocolate possible. My point is only to illustrate what goes on in the world to generate your and my pleasures. "Pleasure without conscience" is another blight on our humanity.

Alas, there is scarcely a product that you can consume – not coffee, not beef, not clothes, not cars, not cell phones – nothing! – that does not trace its lineage somewhere through a nasty cesspool of evil. Consider your cell phone and your many other electronic devices. The manufacture of these devices requires a range of exotic minerals (germanium, tantalum, cobalt, gadolinium, and a bunch of others) that are mined in places like the Democratic Republic of the Congo, China, Afghanistan, and elsewhere. In the Congo, there is an open civil war that feeds off the global demand for these minerals, so much so that the CEO of Intel has referred to "conflict minerals" in a speech to the electronics industry. An item in *Dissent* remarks:

> It's no secret by now that the supply chain feeding our smartphones and laptops is not pretty. Thanks to a flurry of media coverage of Foxconn and other Chinese manufacturers, we know about the dismal conditions at the factories that churn out iPhones. Less is known about what happens to our phones and computers and those clunky old monitors when we throw them away. Many of them are shipped to places like Guiyu, China, or to the slums surrounding cities like Delhi and Accra, where men, women, and children make a living dismantling them with hammers and blowtorches. The metals stripped out of old circuit boards become fodder for new circuit boards, and the cycle continues.
>
> *Kinniburgh (2014)*

Or think about the clothes on your back. In lecturing undergraduates on globalization, I invite students to inspect the garment labels on their hats or t-shirts and tell me where their clothes were manufactured. As I sit and write, I am wearing a t-shirt made in Nicaragua, a pair of chinos manufactured in Bangladesh, and a pair of sneakers made in China. When students in my classes do this exercise, they call out The Philippines, Sri Lanka, China, Honduras, India, Pakistan, and so forth. It is a rare student who wears even a single piece of clothing manufactured in the USA and when one does, they shout out "America!" as if they had won the lottery. It certainly makes the point that we live in a globalized economy, often without even recognizing it.

But how much do any of us know about the Chinese or Indian or Honduran manufacture of clothing for export to the American market? What wages are paid? What are working conditions like? Are children exploited in this process? Are these industries environmentally neutral? We shop for quality or price, but rarely do we shop to clear our conscience of duplicity in abetting dubious practices of which we are usually not even aware.

What is true of electronics, cocoa, and clothes is unfortunately true of almost everything. Most of the food you eat is produced in monocultural factory farms engaged in environmentally destructive and wasteful production practices. Most of the clothes you wear come from Third World sweat shops. Indeed, the book you hold in your hands is very likely to have been printed on paper containing illegally harvested wood fibers, wood fiber from endangered and old growth forests, fiber from tropical forests in Indonesia and elsewhere, and fiber from other dubious and contentious sources.

The point, of course, is to consume with conscience when it is possible to do so, and to at least be aware of the issues surrounding the production of your pleasure when it is not. With some effort, you can restrict your consumption of chocolate to that made from cacao harvested in Latin America, where no cases of child slavery have yet been documented (not the same as saying they do not exist). Free trade coffee (and many other free trade products) are available as a pricy alternative to major brands. Some electronics companies now advertise that their products are made from "conflict-free" minerals; some book manufacturers (for example, HarperCollins) have policies concerning environmentally sustainable fiber use. And with some investment of effort, you can also figure out which brands of imported clothing are humanely manufactured and which are reprehensible.

It is even possible to consume pornography more responsibly, if you choose. There is a porn outfit called Hump the Bundle which offers "artisanal" pornography (meaning mainly that their products do not exploit women against their wishes) and channels a portion of their profits to charitable organizations. Consumers even get to choose where the profit from their download goes. Another outlet specializes in eco-porn, with a share of the profits on each download donated to efforts to preserve the rain forest.[5]

Very few people have the time, money, or resources to be fully aware of the origins of everything they consume; doing so would turn any shopping trip into a very elaborate research exercise. But whenever you find yourself enjoying something, it is not a bad idea to ask, At whose expense has this pleasure come? A great many of the pleasures we enjoy have come at the expense of the planet as a whole and consume resources that can never be replaced. As one commentator on the issue of pleasure without conscience has put it:

> Think about golf courses and the chemicals that are required to maintain them. Often times, golf courses are sited on what were beautiful lands, sometimes lands open to the public, or home to numerous other creatures, who as the lawns become progressively more manicured drive out and even poison those other creatures. We cannot mask the horrors of our human failings. We must be honest on all levels in order to truly appreciate what it means to have pleasure with conscience.[6]

Knowledge Without Character

Alexander Pope wrote that "a little learning is a dangerous thing. Drink deep, or taste not the Pierian Spring."[7] (In Greek mythology, the Pierian Spring was sacred to the Muses and seen as the source of all knowledge.) Gandhi reminds us that *all* knowledge can be a dangerous thing if not deployed with principle, morality, and character. This is an admonition to use knowledge for good, not for harm or manipulation.

A great deal, perhaps the larger share, of humankind's knowledge has been deployed senselessly and immorally – to wage war, to enslave whole societies, to deplete resources, or to destroy the natural environment. Indeed, we often recount the progress of the species via the evolution of the instruments of destruction: The Stone Age, the Bronze Age, the Iron Age, and then, much later, the Nuclear Age, each stage being marked by a greater capacity for domination and violence than the one before. Is the true mark of our progress the evolution of our destructive capability?

Apparently, our civilizing capacities have not kept pace with our destructive potential. We accumulate knowledge but often deploy it in evils ways. In the words of Jack Varnell,

> the central paradox of our time is that despite our powerful intellectual skills and our ingenious engineering and medical achievements, we still lack the ability to live wisely. We send sophisticated satellites into space that beam us startling information about the destruction of the environment, yet we do little, if anything, to stop that destruction.[8]

Or quoting Martin Luther King, Jr., instead, "we live in a world of guided missiles and misguided men."

There seems to be no scientific or technical challenge that is beyond our grasp. Put a human on the moon? Sure, no problem! Map the human genome? Yep. Build a transcontinental railroad? Give us a few years. Defeat Communism? All in a half-century's work. But end poverty, racism, hunger, discrimination, or homelessness? Nope, sorry. Why are these fundamental human problems always on the list of things we *can't* do? Do we lack the knowledge of how to do these things? The money? Or do we simply lack the moral imperative and political will?

What could be more fundamental than figuring out how to share the planet in peace and harmony with all its other inhabitants, both human and otherwise? And yet 200,000 years of human evolution have left us warlike and belligerent. Despite our advanced brainpower (and for all we know, the human brain is the most remarkable and complex three-pound chunk of matter to be found anywhere in the Universe), we prove incapable of changing how we think, act toward one another, or live.

Gandhi's implication is assuredly not that we are fundamentally evil in our character, or that we have learned too much for our own good. The point of "knowledge without conscience" is that we have not yet learned what our real needs are – real needs that will not be solved by technology or chemistry or economics (these will come along as needed) but by accepting our moral calling to be responsible stewards of the planet and all that is found upon it.

Commerce Without Morality

It is said that "the market has no heart," no morality, and watching how many big businesses operate these days, it is hard to quarrel with the sentiment. In the recent financial meltdown, we witnessed investment advisors driving their own clients into bankruptcy for personal gain. Commerce without morality has given us false and misleading advertising, sweatshops, "bait and switch," unsafe factories, environmental devastation, drug cartels, human trafficking, child slavery, pink slime, Ponzi schemes, pyramid schemes, and Bernie Madoff. "Commerce without morality" means conducting business without regard to what is right and wrong, making profits by any means possible regardless of who gets hurt in the process.

Much has been made over a couple of decades now on the need to regulate Wall Street and the banks. Why do they need more regulation? Precisely because they operate without morality.

Everyone knows about (or thinks they know about) Adam Smith and *The Wealth of Nations*, where the fundamentals of capitalism were first adumbrated, but few know his earlier book, *Moral Sentiment*, which argued that a moral foundation was necessary for a successful economic and political system, a foundation that governed how we treat one another, how we conduct commerce, and the absolute necessity of benevolence toward one another. To Smith, each and every business transaction was a moral challenge to assure that all parties benefitted from the transaction. All parties have certain rights, and all parties are obligated to respect those rights. How far this is from the "cowboy capitalism" that Smith is said to have favored!

These days, most business schools feel obligated to offer courses on "business ethics," on the proper and improper ways that business gets done. So these days, and for at least the last twenty years, MBAs have been exposed to the topic to some degree. But to what effect? For all practical purposes,

> the codes of conduct for corporations are practically non-existent. Witness how Enron subverted their entire ethics process to allow the company to pursue almost unlimited degrees of immoral and unethical behavior. In most corporations, the ethics statements are followed only when convenient and never if they conflict with the prime directive: Make Money.
> *(Persico, 2013)*

Yawning your way through a boring required course in business ethics is one thing; developing an understanding that commerce without morality is not business but thievery is quite another.

The Nobel Prize winning economist Milton Friedman is famous for criticizing the very idea of "business ethics" and corporate social responsibility, this on two grounds: First, business people are not ethicists and, therefore, they lack the knowledge base or experience to make ethical judgments. Second, left to its own, the invisible hand of the market (everyone maximizing his or her best interests) will, in the end, always bring about the greater overall good. The first of these is the equivalent of arguing that murderers can be excused of their murderous acts because they have not read Immanuel Kant. And in a world riven with poverty, inequality, disease, hunger, and all manner of immiseration, the second is self-evidently false.

Another line of argument is one we broached in the early pages of this book, namely, that "morality" presupposes a value system upon which all will agree, and no such system exists. This can be granted in the abstract but is hogwash at the level of everyday business transactions, where one would expect a near-universal agreement that kindness, fairness, dignity, reciprocity, and integrity are to be preferred over meanness, exploitation, humiliation, thievery, and dishonesty. Is it really too much to ask that commerce be conducted on the basis of these few simple principles?

Science Without Humanity

Here, the Mahatma is calling for the vast scientific resources of the species to be directed toward the betterment of the human condition. Huge moral debates surround many topics of current and intense research interest, none more illustrative, perhaps, than stem-cell research. Stem cells are human cells with two critically important features: One, they are capable of self-regeneration even after long periods of inactivity, and two, under certain conditions, they can be induced to develop into tissue-specific or organ-specific cells with very different functions: They can become skin cells, pancreas cells, heart cells, etc. In other words, stem cells are not specialized themselves but can give rise to specialized cells.

Stem cells are harvested from human embryos that have been fertilized *in vitro* and donated to science, always with the informed consent of the donors. Often, women undergoing *in vitro* implantation of embryos for purposes of becoming pregnant create many more fertilized embryos than can be implanted. The "spares" are either discarded or used for scientific research. Using these embryos for research on cell development, to develop replacement organs, or to help find cures for all sorts of diseases (all seemingly promised by the technology) seem a far better fate than flushing them down the laboratory sink. At the same time, we are talking about fertilized human embryos that contain all the genetic material to become a fully-fledged human being. So stem cell research poses the possibility of engineering humans to predetermined design standards. "We'll take a blue-eyed, blond boy of greater than average stature and much greater than average intelligence." The mind boggles at the moral and demographic implications.

Medical science is almost universally of the opinion that stem cell research has the potential to help us understand and cure all sorts of diseases (spinal cord injuries and Parkinson's disease are the two most widely cited examples), but various religions condemn the practice vociferously. Jews are generally OK with embryonic stem cell research but Baptists believe that humans are created in the likeness of God and creation begins at the moment of conception; Catholics oppose the practice as "an absolutely unacceptable act;" Methodists, Pentecostals, and other denominations also oppose the practice on various religious grounds, most having to do with the belief that human life begins at conception. That these fertilized embryos, of which there are some 400,000 in storage in America today, are otherwise to be discarded does not seem to factor into anyone's thinking.

Stem cells are not the only arena of scientific inquiry where science comes up against fundamental religious and humanitarian issues: Genome mapping, much of modern biology, the causes of global warming, mobile phone surveillance, what people should and should not eat, medical tourism, the safety of genetically modified food for human consumption – this list continues indefinitely. Even once the scientific issues are settled (vaccines do *not* cause autism, nuclear power *is* safe, climate change *is* real and man-made), controversy over the human implications continues.

It is probably safe to say that most practicing scientists "these days" are aware of and sensitive to the moral, human, and philosophical implications of their work, but the history of science is riddled with evils and cruelties of an almost unimaginable variety. The grotesque medical experiments of Nazi scientists need not be described here in any detail. In 1932, Einstein himself rationalized research on atomic weapons with the comment, "There is not the slightest indication that nuclear energy will ever be obtainable. It would mean that the atom would have to be shattered at will." A mere thirteen years later, Hiroshima and Nagasaki were destroyed by bombs that did indeed shatter atoms at will. The infamous Tuskegee Syphilis Experiment denied effective treatment (penicillin) to a sample of syphilitic black men because to treat them would have ruined the design of a long-term observation study on what it was about syphilis that caused death. Remarkably, this experimental study continued into the 1970s.

No one (not even self-styled "futurists") can predict the future and so it is hopeless to insist that science always understand all the ethical implications of research before it be allowed to proceed. But it is not unrealistic to demand that scientists *think about* what some of the implications might be before embarking on a particular line of inquiry. All research universities now have "Institutional Review Boards" (IRBs) whose task is to review all university-based research for its adherence to certain basic ethical standards. How well the IRBs discharge this task is an open question, but the system almost certainly intercepts the most seriously abusive science before it even begins.

Religion Without Sacrifice

The Sanskrit word *yajña* is variously translated as sacrifice, offering, oblation, or worship, so Gandhi's sixth social sin is variously rendered as religion without sacrifice, worship without sacrifice, worship without offering, and so on. In Sanskrit, the term usually refers to the offering of material goods (ghee, grain, spices, etc.) while chanting the sacred mantras, but clearly, Gandhi had something more in mind here than simply reminding church goers to toss a few bucks into the collection plate at the end of the service.

My limited study of Gandhi's social thought (largely restricted to an undergraduate research paper I wrote 50 years ago plus some refresher Googling) suggests to me that the best rendering, the one that hues most closely to the true meaning, is "religion without compassion," of which we find a great deal in the contemporary world. Here is the description from the Gandhi Institute for Non-Violence on which my interpretation is based:

> **Worship without Sacrifice**: One person's faith is another person's fantasy because religion has been reduced to meaningless rituals practiced mindlessly. Temples, churches, synagogues, mosques and those entrusted with the duty of interpreting religion to lay people seek to control through fear of hell, damnation, and purgatory. In the name of

God they have spawned more hate and violence than any government. True religion is based on spirituality, love, *compassion*, understanding, and appreciation of each other whatever our beliefs may be.[9]

"Meaningless rituals practiced mindlessly" certain describes much of what seems to pass for religion these days. I would add to this "ancient slogans mindlessly uttered, misinterpreted and used to justify bigotry." A huge debate is currently raging in the United States over whether people can discriminate against gays and lesbians because of their "religious beliefs" that homosexuality is sinful. Several states have passed laws ensuring this "right." "God hates homosexuals!" read one placard I saw on TV. "Bible says: Homosexuality a sin!" read another. Devout born-again evangelicals use various Biblical passages to justify their hatred of and disgust with everyone in the LGBT community.

But here's a problem none of them seem to realize. The concept of "homosexual" *did not even exist* when the Bible was written. The very word homosexual was not coined until 1869 by the Hungarian physician Karoly Benkert. And while there are words in classical Aramaic, Greek, and Hebrew, the languages in which the Bible was written, whose connotations might include consensual sex between same-sex partners, these are not the words in the original Biblical text. One Hebrew word sometimes translated as "homosexual" is *kedah*, which means "temple prostitute," i.e. someone who hung around the temple looking to sell sexual favors, whether homoerotic or not. A Greek word sometimes translated as sodomite or homosexual, *malakos,* is better translated as effeminate or perhaps pederast (a common Greek practice of older men having sex with young boys, certainly not consensual sex between same-sex peers). Another ambiguous Greek term is *arsenokoitai*, which appears one time in the Bible (1 Corinthians) and seems to mean male prostitute (again, not consensual sex between same-sex peers), although admittedly the "true meaning" of the word is still fiercely debated by Greek scholars. The passage in Jude 7 sometimes translated as "homosexual flesh" literally means "strange flesh." In the context of the passage, this clearly describes the flesh of angels sent to evaluate Sodom and Gomorrah.[10]

The theologian Mel White says that the word *homosexual* first appears in an English translation of the Bible in 1958, in a ham-handed translation of the New Amplified Bible. English Bibles published prior to 1958 use an assortment of translations of *arsenokoitai* (sodomites, prostitutes, etc.) but none use the word homosexual. White believes that Paul intended the term to imply same-sex behavior but acknowledges that Greek scholars really don't know *what* it means. He comments:

> In the past, people used Paul's writings to oppress women and limit their role in the home, in church, and in society. Now we have to ask ourselves,

'Is it happening again? Is a word in Greek that *has no clear definition* being
used to reflect society's prejudice and condemn God's gay children?'

(1994: p. 18)

In short, there is very little serious Biblical evidence to justify use of the Bible to
condemn or discriminate against gays and lesbians. The passages interpreted to
mean that God hates homosexuals only reflect the bigotries of translators. Alas,
many true believers seem to believe that the Bible they read in English translation is in fact the original and don't understand that the original is in classical
Aramaic, Greek, and Hebrew, and was translated multiple times before King
James and his scribes produced the first English language version, and has been
retranslated many, many times since. In fact, one born-again of my acquaintance took great, noisy umbrage when the elders of his church debated the
purchase of Spanish-language Bibles for their Hispanic proselytes. "If English
was good enough for Jesus, it's good enough for me!"

And it is not just gays and lesbians who incur the religious bigot's wrath.
African-Americans are sometimes derided as the Lost Tribe of Israel, forsaken
by God and, thus, deserving of their fate. Mental illness is sometimes understood as demon possession and can only be treated by exorcism. Indeed, it has
been said with some justification that "religious bigotry may well have been the
most common form of bigotry for much of Europe's history."[11] And certainly
today, there is much more religious conflict around the world than, say, Marx's
class conflict. When it all gets added up, my bet is that religion is the leading
cause of death in human history.

Why the seemingly robust association between religion and bigotry? To a
social scientist, the connection is obvious and authoritarianism is the common
factor. Authoritarians have strong feelings of inadequacy which they resolve
by believing they were created in God's image; anyone who doesn't look like
them must therefore be godless and, thus, hateful. Thus does self-loathing get
directed outward to the loathing of all difference. How else do we explain
the Crusades, the Holocaust, or Jihad if not as the vicious loathing of people
different from ourselves?

Nearly all religions, and certainly Christianity, counsel their believers to
"love thy neighbor." In Mark 12:13, it is written that you should "love your
neighbor as yourself. There is no commandment greater than these." Elsewhere
we are told to "do unto others as you would wish others to do unto you" (this
is the Golden Rule). Almost all religions have an equivalent saying:

Buddhism: "Hurt not others with that which pains yourself."
Judaism (from Leviticus): "Thou shalt love thy neighbor as thyself."
Hinduism: "One should always treat others as they themselves wish to be treated."
Zoroastrianism: "Whatever is disagreeable to yourself, do not do unto others."
Confucianism: "What you do not want done to yourself, do not do to others."[12]

Nowhere in any religion is there a proviso that says, "except if your neighbor is gay, or black, or manic-depressive, or Muslim, or Hindu, or Irish, or..." – well, you get the point. In a globalizing society, we are *all* neighbors, and to preach this and its moral and spiritual implications is the essence of worship with compassion, of religion with sacrifice. Faith without compassionate deeds is useless; religion without compassion is yet another blight on human civilization.

And finally:

Politics Without Principle

The word principle has numerous meanings, and so we need to be clear on just what "principle" or "principles" politics needs. Every election season, we are deluged with cant about "Democratic Party principles" and "Republican Party principles," as though anyone in the electorate has the foggiest idea about what these "principles" are. In this sense, "principles" are just firmly held beliefs about which there can be no discussion or negotiation. Politics without *these* principles would be a relief.

There are other "principled" beliefs that have caused more than their share of horrors. We do not negotiate with terrorists "on principle." We do not challenge the fundamental tenets of capitalism "on principle." We believe we have a "principled" right to inflict our version of democracy on nations around the globe. The Monroe Doctrine says that "on principle," any threat to any nation of the Americas is a direct threat to the interests of the United States. The North Atlantic Treaty Organization established that same "principle" with respect to Western Europe. Many of these are "principles" we could do nicely without.

There are several dozen synonyms for "principle" in every thesaurus and dictionary. The one that in my opinion comes closest to Gandhi's true meaning is the second definition given in Merriam-Webster's: The code of good conduct for an individual or group, with listed synonyms ethos, morality, morals, norms, ethics, and standards. What Gandhi is calling for is a politics driven by ethical understandings.

One must then ask, is there anywhere in the world where politics is practiced with principle in this sense of the word? Maybe not: At base, politics is about power and its acquisition, and as Lord Shaftesbury warned, "Power corrupts, and absolute power tends to corrupt absolutely." This being the case, we have to wonder whether politics with principle is even possible.

Certainly, the political gamesmanship one sees in the US political process – the flip-flopping, negative campaigning, sloganeering, name-calling, guilt by innuendo, deceit, and outright prevarication – makes one wonder if principled politicking is not an oxymoron – or possibly just plain moronic. Republican Joe Scarborough (the Joe of *Morning Joe*) recently published a column, "Don't Cry for Us, We're Not Argentina," [13] decrying the ridiculous exaggerations of contemporary politicians. One item he mentions: President Obama renamed a post office to honor a deceased Bronx politician whereupon a Republican congressman took the podium to announce, "Tonight freedom has died a bloody death!" He calls this "Republican hyperventilation" about "the existential threat Barack Obama posed to family, freedom and the very fabric of Our Great Republic."

We seem to have lost all sense of political perspective. As preposterous as the claims against Obama may have been, "Democrats did the same during the Bush years. And before that, Republicans ...sometimes lost their better judgment during Clinton's stay in the White House." A later confession in the same essay: "time has taught me that the 'Chicken Littles' among us are always wrong. The sky never falls on America."

Every four years, we have allegations that the incumbent President has driven us to the brink of ruin and that the only solution is to elect the opposition, coupled with assurances from the other side that the incumbent has us on the right track and just needs another four or eight years to accomplish what was promised. In the process of trying to get elected, politicians will make all sorts of crazy promises knowing full well they can never be kept. Bush 41 piously promised "no new taxes" and then raised taxes; Obama promised to close Gitmo, which remains open; Clinton promised to reform the national health care system but was rebuffed. And while it is probably true that most Presidents try to do something about most of the promises they issue during the campaign, their failures are what we remember most.

Scarborough's essay refers to

> decades of screamers on talk radio and cable news, and the legions of angry partisans who spend their days and nights predicting America's collapse. These nattering nabobs of negativism that pollute our not-so-new-media landscape have embarrassed themselves for 30 years by constantly predicting the collapse of a country that has to date survived two world wars, slavery, a bloody civil war, countless recessions and Spiro Agnew as vice president. (The phrase "nattering nabobs of negativism" was coined by Agnew's speechwriter William Safire; hence Scarborough's allusion).

Clearly, the 24–7 news cycle has contributed mightily to the debasement of political discourse. Principled politics will rarely get one on CNN.

In the aggressive pursuit of power, ethics often takes a backseat. Fact checkers and Truth-o-Meters routinely expose the near lies and outright falsehoods that are bandied about in political debates, and yet no one seems to mind and the prevaricating candidate quickly recovers. Sex scandals pretty routinely drive politicos off the stage (think Gary Hart, Anthony Weiner, David Petraeus, John Edwards), but when's the last time a political career ended because a candidate told an outright lie?

If "party principles" are in fact unprincipled and political ideologies are just the lies we tell ourselves, then what "principles" would a principled politician want to follow? John Perkins has provided the answer in his essay on Humanism and Morality:[14]

Non-malificence: Do not harm yourself or other people.
Beneficence: Help yourself and other people.
Autonomy: Allow rational individuals to make free and informed choices.
Justice: Treat people fairly: treat equals equally, unequals unequally.
Utility: Maximize the ratio of benefits to harms for all people.
Fidelity: Keep your promises and agreements
Honesty: Do not lie, defraud, deceive or mislead.
Privacy: Respect personal privacy and confidentiality.

Perhaps a politics that respects these eight simple maxims will never happen – to return to an earlier point, power is corrupting, perhaps inevitably so. But surely, such a politics is not too much to hope for.

I am fond of a story (possibly apocryphal) about Gandhi, who had just returned from his first trip to the West, specifically to England, and was asked by a reporter what he thought of Western civilization. The Mahatma is alleged to have replied: "I think it would be a good idea." Or, as Sitting Bull said when he was asked what he thought of Christianity, "From what I have read it is an admirable religion, however I do not see any white people practicing it."

To conclude: If we let our lives and affairs be governed by our civilizing tendencies and our true humanistic inspirations, we will find that we have no need for moralistic and outdated lists of do's and don'ts such as the original seven deadly sins or even the Ten Commandments. Modern life is far too nuanced and complex, and the choices life presents to us are far too subtle, for such lists to be of much use in any case. Just what behaviors are sinful and what behaviors are not is no longer as obvious as perhaps it once was; what is sinful from one perspective can be perfectly acceptable behavior from another. And certainly, the promise of eternal salvation or the threat of eternal damnation no longer carry the moral weight they did even a century ago. If we no longer aspire to Heaven or fear Hell, what compels us to act in ethically responsible ways? Only our aspirations to be admitted to citizenship in the community of civilized beings. Those aspirations may be a thin thread from which to hang all human morality, but it's apparently all we have to work with.

Notes

1 www.openculture.com/2014/11/mahatma-gandhis-list-of-the-7-social-sins.html.
2 It appears that the Seven Social Sins were not entirely original to Gandhi either, but had been published some six months earlier in a sermon delivered at Westminster Abbey. A mutual friend sent the list to Gandhi who then republished the list. To be

sure, Gandhi's newspaper article makes the origin of the list clear, but the name of the Westminster sermonizer is evidently lost to history and these seven are known universally as Gandhi's.

3 www.mkgandhi.org/mgmnt.htm.

4 Or even elsewhere in North America. Per capita, the Canadians spend about five times more money than we spend safeguarding the well-being of their seniors and there are similar differentials for child welfare, housing assistance, and, most of all, subsidized medical care.

5 www.ozy.com/presidential-daily-brief/pdb-69030/giving-it-away-69037.

6 www.revja.com/worship-and-celebrations/28-worship-and-celebrations/sermons/110-seven-deadly-social-sins.html.

7 The common version of Pope's iamb is "A little knowledge is a dangerous thing," but alas, that is a misquotation of the original.

8 http://goodmenproject.com/good-feed-blog/gandhi-on-knowledge-without-character/.

9 This passage was called to my attention by John Persico's blog on the sixth social sin: https://agingcapriciously.com/2013/05/30/gandhis-sixth-social-sin-worship-without-sacrifice/.

10 My exceedingly helpful source for the above is an unattributed posting from a site called Our Spirit: http://ourspiritnow.org/2009/04/more-testing-misues/ For the record, Google translates the Greek malakos as malleable and does not even recognize arsenokoitai as a current Greek word.

11 www.religioustolerance.org/relbigot.htm.

12 www.thegoldenrule.net/quotes.htm.

13 www.washingtonpost.com/blogs/post-partisan/wp/2016/04/12/dont-cry-for-us-we-arent-argentina/.

14 http://home.alphalink.com.au/~jperkins/humoral.htm.

REFERENCES

Abel, Steve, 2015. Fat on trial. *Obesity*. Available at www.doctorabel.us/obesity/fat-on-trial.html.

Abramowitz, Alan, and Steven Webster, 2015. The angry American voter. *Sabato's Crystal Ball*, August 6, 2015. University of Virginia Center for Politics.

Adler, Alfred, 1927. *Understanding Human Nature: The Psychology of Personality*. New York: George Allen and Unwin.

Albrecht, Morgan, 2014. Alcoholism is not a disease. In Nora Ishibashi (ed.), *Arguing with the DSM-5*. Privately printed.

Alvarez, R. Michael, and Jonathan Nagler, 1995. Economics, issues and the Perot candidacy: Voter choice in the 1992 Presidential Election. *American Journal of Political Science* 39(3): 714–744.

American Psychological Association, 2007. *Report of the APA Task Force on the Sexualization of Girls*. Washington, DC: APA.

American Psychological Association Zero Tolerance Task Force, 2008. Are zero tolerance policies effective in schools? *The American Psychologist* 63(9): 852–862.

Ariely, Dan, and Aline Grüneisen, 2013. The price of Greed. *Scientific American Mind* 24 (November–December): 38–42.

Armstrong, Miranda E. G., Jane Green, Gillian K. Reeves, Valerie Beral, and Benjamin J. Cairns, 2015. Frequent physical activity may not reduce vascular disease risk as much as moderate activity: Large prospective study of women in the United Kingdom. *Circulation* 131(8): 721–729.

Asbridge, Mark, and Jennifer Butters, 2013. Driving frequency and its impact on road rage offending and victimization: A view from opportunity theory. *Violence and Victims* 28(4): 602–618.

Axelrod, Robert, 2006. *The Evolution of Cooperation*. New York: Basic Books.

Balducci, Cristian, Monica Cecchin, Franco Fraccaroli, and Wilmar B. Schaufeli, 2012. Exploring the relationship between workaholism and workplace aggressive behavior: The role of job-related emotion. *Personality and Individual Differences* 53: 629–634.

Banerjee, Abhijit, Rema Hanna, Gabriel Kreindler, and Benjamin Olken, 2015. Debunking the stereotype of the lazy welfare recipient: Evidence from cash transfer programs worldwide. HKS Working Paper No. 076. Available at SSRN: http://ssrn. com/abstract=2703447.

Barr, Donald A., 2014. *Health Disparities in the United States: Social Class, Race, Ethnicity and Health.* Baltimore, MD: Johns Hopkins University Press.

Barr, Jeffrey F., 2010. Render unto Caesar: A most misunderstood New Testament passage. www.lewrockwell.com/2010/03/jeffrey-f-barr/render-unto-caesar-amost misunderstood-newtestamentpassage/.

Barss, Patchen, 2010. *The Erotic Engine: How Pornography has Powered Mass Communication, from Gutenberg to Google.* Doubleday Canada.

Baumeister, Roy, 1996. Should schools try to boost self-esteem? Beware the dark side. *American Educator* 20: 14–19.

Baumeister, Roy, Laura Smart, and Joseph M. Boden, 1996. Relations of threatened egotism to violence and aggression: The dark side of high self-esteem. *Psychological Review* 103: 5–33.

Bazelon, Emily, 2012. Shame on you! Published in *Slate.* www.slate.com/articles/news_ and_politics/crime/2012/02/shaming_drug_offenders_in_new_orleans_and_drunk_ drivers_in_ohio_and_minnesota_.html.

Bearman, P., and Bruckner, H., 2001. Promising the future: Virginity pledges and first intercourse. *American Journal of Sociology* 106(4): 859–911.

Bekkers, Rene, and Pamala Wiepking, 2007. *Generosity and Philanthropy: A Literature Review.* Department of Sociology, Utrecht University; Department of Philanthropic Studies, Vrije Universiteit Amsterdam. http://papers.ssrn.com/sol3/papers. cfm?abstract_id=1015507.

Belk, Russell W., 2009. Marketing and envy. In Richard H. Smith (ed.), *Envy: Theory and Research,* 211–226. Oxford: Oxford University Press.

Belk, Russell W., 2011. Benign envy. *AMS Review* 1: 117–134.

Berkowitz, Leonard, 1969. *Roots of Aggression.* New York: Atherton Press.

Betzig, Laura, 1989. Causes of conjugal dissolution: A cross-cultural study. *Current Anthropology* 30(5): 654–676.

Biddle, Stuart J. H., and Mavis Asare, 2011. Physical activity and mental health in children and adolescents: A review of reviews. *British Journal of Sports Medicine.* Published Online August 1. http://bjsm.bmj.com/content/early/2011/07/31/bjsports-2011-090185. full.pdf+html.

Bielefeld, Wolfgang, Patrick Rooney, and Kathy Steinberg, 2005. How do need, capacity, geography, and politics influence giving? In A. C. Brooks (Ed.), *Gifts of Money in America's Communities,* pp. 127–158. Lanham, MD: Rowman & Littlefield.

Black, Michele C., Kathleen C. Basile, Matthew J. Breiding, Sharon G. Smith, Mikel L. Walters, Melissa T. Merrick, Jieru Chen, and Mark R. Stevens, 2011. *The National Intimate Partner and Sexual Violence Survey: 2010 Summary Report.* Atlanta, Georgia: CDC National Center for Injury Prevention and Control.

Blank, Cornelia, Veronika Leichtfried, Wolfgang Schobersberger, and Claudia Möller, 2015. Does leisure time negatively affect personal health? *World Leisure Journal* 57(2): 152–157.

Blau, Joel, 1992. *The Visible Poor: Homelessness in the United States.* Oxford University Press.

Blizzard, Rick, 2004. Americans and alcohol: Drink, drank, drunk. *Gallup,* August 24, 2004. www.gallup.com/poll/12790/americans-alcohol-drink-drank-drunk.aspx.

Boudreaux, Don, 2007. The politics of prohibition. *Reason Magazine.* July 31, 2007. http://reason.com/archives/2007/07/31/the-politics-of-prohibition/.

Bradley, Jayson D., 2014. Overcoming the seven deadly sins: Gluttony. Available at http://jaysondbradley.com/2014/07/09/overcoming-the-seven-deadly-sins-gluttony/#sthash.ArFlXIWi.dpbs.

Braithwaite, Valerie, and Eliza Ahmed, 2015. *The Personal Management of Shame and Pride in Workplace Bullying.* Australian National University: RegNet Research Paper Series Number 96.

Braswell, Sean, 2016. How pornography saved civilization. *Ozy,* January 4. www.ozy. com/flashback/how-pornography-saved-civilization/40480?utm_source=dd&utm_medium=email&utm_campaign=01042016&variable=c65fd537397caf4e6312d 0c07defebe7.

Brecher Edward M., and the Editors of Consumer Reports, 1972. *Licit and Illicit Drugs.* Mount Vernon, NY: Consumers Union.

Bridges, Ana J., Robert Wosnitzer, Erica Scharrer, Chyng Sun, and Rachael Liberman, 2010. Aggression and sexual behavior in best-selling pornography videos: A content analysis update. *Violence Against Women* 16(10): 1065–1085.

Brown, Jonathon D., 1993. Self-esteem and self-evaluation: Feeling is believing. In Jerry Suls (ed.), *Psychological Perspectives on the Self. Vol. 4: The Self in Social Perspective,* Chap. 3. New York: Psychology Press.

Bureau of Justice Statistics, 2014. *The Nation's Two Crime Measures.* Washington, DC: BJS. www.bjs.gov/content/pub/pdf/ntcm_2014.pdf.

Bureau of Labor Statistics, 2013. *A Profile of the Working Poor, 2013.* Washington, DC: BLS Reports.

Bureau of Labor Statistics, 2015. *American Time Use Survey—2014 Results.* Department of Labor: BLS, USDL-15-1236.

Bushman, Brad J., 2005. Violence and sex in television programs do not sell products in advertisements. *Psychological Science* 16(9): 702–708.

Campbell, Angus, Philip E. Converse, and Willard R. Rogers, 1976. *The Quality of American Life: Perceptions, Evaluations, and Satisfaction.* New York: Russell Sage Foundation.

Campos, Paul, Abagail Saguy, Paul Ernsberger, Eric Oliver, and Glenn Gaesset, 2006. The epidemiology of overweight and obesity: Public health crisis or moral panic? *International Journal of Epidemiology* 35(1): 55–60.

Centers for Disease Control, 2015a. *Fetal Alcohol Spectrum Disorders.* Atlanta: CDC. www.cdc.gov/ncbddd/fasd/facts.html.

Centers for Disease Control, 2015b. Insufficient sleep is a public health problem. *CDC Features,* September 2015. www.cdc.gov/features/dssleep/.

Center on Budget and Policy Priorities, 2015. Policy basics: Where do our federal tax dollars go? www.cbpp.org/research/policy-basics-where-do-our-federal-tax-dollars-go.

Cheng, Joey T., Jessica L. Tracy, and Joseph Henrich, 2010. Pride, personality and the evolutionary foundations of human social status. *Evolution and Human Behavior* 31(5): 334–347.

Choi, Namkee G., and Jinseok Kim, 2011. The effect of time volunteering and charitable donations in later life on psychological wellbeing. *Ageing and Society* 31: 590–610.

Cikara, Mina, and Susan T. Fiske, 2013. Their pain, our pleasure: Stereotype content and *Schadenfreude. Annals of the New York Academy of Sciences* 1299: 52–59.

Clark, Malissa A., Jesse S. Michel, Ludmila Zhdanova, Shuang Y. Pui, and Boris B. Baltes, 2014. All work and no play? A meta-analytic examination of the correlates and outcomes of workaholism. *Journal of Management* 20(10): 1–39.

Clarren, Sterling, and Jocelynn L. Cook, 2013. Dose-response effect of alcohol consumption during pregnancy and prenatal alcohol exposure: A brief review. http://fasd.alberta.ca/dose-response-article.aspx.

Collett, Jessica L., and Omar Lizardo, 2010. Occupational status and the experience of anger. *Social Forces* 88(5): 2079–2104.

Crabtree, Vexen, 2006. Altruism is an illusion. Available at www.humantruth.info/altruism.html.

Crews, Ed, 2007. Rattle-skull, stonewall, bogus, blackstrap, bombo, mimbo, whistle belly, syllabub, sling, toddy, and flip: Drinking in colonial America. *Trend and Tradition: The Journal of the Colonial Williamsburg Society* (Winter). www.history.org/foundation/journal/ holiday07/drink.cfm.

Crocker, Jennifer, Riaa K. Luhtanen, and Samuel R. Sommers, 2004. Contingencies of self-worth: Progress and prospects. *European Review of Social Psychology* 15: 133–181.

Curioni, C., André, C., and Veras, R., 2006. Weight reduction for primary prevention of stroke in adults with overweight or obesity. *Cochrane Database of Systematic Reviews* (4): CD006062.

Damassa, Kelsey, 2013. The new eating disorder you might not realize you have: Food guilt. *Health*. www.hercampus.com/health/new-eating-disorder-you-might-not-realize-you-have-food-guilt.

Daneski, Katherine, Paul Higgs, and Myfanwy Morgan, 2010. From gluttony to obesity: Moral discourses on apoplexy and stroke. *Sociology of Health & Illness* 32(5): 730–744.

deAngelis, Tori, 2003. When anger's a plus. *APA Monitor on Psychology* 34(3): 44.

Decety, Jean, Jason M. Cowell, Kang Lee, Randa Mahasneh, Susan Malcolm-Smith, Bilge Selcuk, and Xinyue Zhoi, 2015. The negative association between religiousness and children's altruism across the world. *Current Biology* 25: 2951–2955.

Degenhardt, Louisa, Wai-Tat Chiu, Nancy Sampson, Ronald C. Kessler, James C. Anthony, Matthias Angermeyer et al., 2008. Toward a global view of alcohol, tobacco, cannabis, and cocaine use: Findings from the WHO world mental health surveys. *PLOS Medicine*. Available at http://journals.plos.org/plosmedicine/article?id=10.1371/journal.pmed.0050141

Denny, George, and Michael Young, 2006. An evaluation of an abstinence-only sex education curriculum: An 18-month follow-up. *Journal of School Health* 76(8): 414–422.

Donnellan, M. Brent, Kali H. Trzeniewski, Richard W. Robins, Terrie E. Moffitt, and Avshalom Caspi, 2005. Low self-esteem is related to aggression, anti-social behavior, and delinquency. *Psychological Science* 16(4): 328–335.

Duffy, Michelle K., Jason D. Shaw, and John M. Schaubroeck, 2008. Envy in organizational life. In Smith, Richard H. (ed.), *Envy: Theory and Research*, 167–189. Oxford: Oxford University Press.

Dvorsky, George, 2013. Why Freud still matters, when he was wrong about almost everything. http://io9.gizmodo.com/why-freud-still-matters-when-he-was-wrong-about-almost-1055800815

Easterlin, Richard, 1973. Does money buy happiness? *The Public Interest* 30(3): 3–10.

Edelman, Benjamin, 2009. Markets red light states: Who buys online adult entertainment? *Journal of Economic Perspectives* 23(1): 209–220.

Efrat, Kalanit, and Aviv Shoham, 2013. The theory of planned behavior, materialism and aggressive driving. *Accident Analysis and Prevention* 59: 459–465.

Einholf, Christopher J., 2007. Empathic concern and prosocial behaviors: A test of experimental results using survey data. *Social Science Research* 37: 1267–1279.

Einholf, Christopher J., 2011. The link between religion and helping others: The role of values, ideas and language. *Sociology of Religion* 72(4): 435–455.

Eissa, Gabbi, and Rebecca Wyland, 2016. Keeping up with the Joneses: The role of envy, relationship conflict, and job performance in social undermining. *Journal of Leadership & Organizational Studies* 23(1): 55–65

Emergency Physicians Monthly, 2009. Transporting morbidly obese patients. http://epmonthly.com/blog/transporting-morbidly-obese-patients/.

England, Paula, and Shelly Ronen, 2015. Hooking up and casual sex. In James D. Wright (ed.), *The International Encyclopedia of the Social and Behavioral Sciences*, 2nd ed. Amsterdam: Elsevier Publishing Co.

Eskow, R. J., 2016. Six signs our culture is sick with greed. *AlterNet*, January 4, 2016. Available on January 15, 2016, www.alternet.org/economy/6-signs-our-culture-sick-greed on.

Esser, Marissa B., Sarra L. Hedden, Dafna Kanny, Robert D. Brewer, Joseph C. Gfroerer, and Timothy S. Naimi, 2014. Prevalence of alcohol dependence among US adult drinkers, 2009–2011. *Prevention of Chronic Disease* 11(November): 1–11.

Evans, Robert G., Morris L. Barer, and Theodore R. Marmor, 1994. *Why Are Some People Healthy and Others Not?* Hawthorn, New York: Aldine de Gruyter.

Felson, Richard B., 1991. Blame analysis: Accounting for the behavior of protected groups. *The American Sociologist* 22:1(Spring): 5–23.

Felson, Richard B., 2002. *Violence and Gender Re-examined*. Washington, DC: American Psychological Association.

Ferguson, Priscilla Parkhurst, 2006. *Accounting for Taste: The Triumph of French Cuisine*. Chicago, IL: University of Chicago Press.

Fierro, Inmaculada, Claudia Morales, and F. Javier Alvarez, 2011. Alcohol use, illicit drug use, and road rage. *Journal of Studies on Alcohol and Drugs* 72(2): 185–193.

Finer, Lawrence B., 2007. Trends in premarital sex in the United States, 1954–2003. *Public Health Reports* 122: 7–78.

Fischer, Agneta H., and Ira J. Roseman, 2007. Beat them or ban them: The characteristics and social functions of anger and contempt. *Journal of Personality and Social Psychology* 93(1):103–115.

Fiske, Susan T., 2012. *Envy Up, Scorn Down: How Status Divides Us*. New York: Russell Sage Foundation.

Flodmark, C. E, C. Marcus, and M. Britton, 2006. Interventions to prevent obesity in children and adolescents: A systematic literature review. *International Journal of Obesity* 30: 579–589.

Foster, Gwendolyn Audrey, 2012. Capitalism eats itself: Gluttony and coprophagia from *Hoarders* to *La Grande Bouffe*. Available at http://filmint.nu/?p=5799.

Foster, John Bellamy, and Fred Magdoff, 2009. *The Great Financial Crisis: Causes and Consequences*. New York: Monthly Review Press.

Frank, Robert H., 2011. *The Darwin Economy: Liberty, Competition, and the Common Good*. Princeton, NJ: Princeton University Press.

Freud, Sigmund, 1917. Mourning and melancholia. In the *Standard Edition of the Complete Psychological Works of Sigmund Freud*, Volume XIV (1914–1916): On the History of the Psycho-Analytic Movement, Papers on Metapsychology and Other Works, pp. 237–258.

Frommer, Martin S., 2007. On the subjectivity of lustful states of mind. *Psychoanalytic Dialogues* 16(6): 639–664.

Furedi, Frank, 2011. *On Tolerance: A Defense of Moral Independence.* London and New York: Continuum International Publishing Group.

Gentile, Haley, 2015. The perpetually angry activist: Emotions and social change in news media. *Sociology Lens.* September 30, 2015. https://thesocietypages.org/sociologylens/2015/09/30/the-perpetually-angry-activist-emotions-and-social-change-in-news-media/.

Glassner, Barry, 2010. *The Culture of Fear: Why Americans Are Afraid of the Wrong Things: Crime, Drugs, Minorities, Teen Moms, Killer Kids, Mutant Microbes, Plane Crashes, Road Rage, & So Much More,* 10th anniversary edition. New York: Basic Books.

Godfrey, Sarah, 2004. Massive burial: The heavy cost of funerals for the obese. *Washington City Paper,* April 16. www.washingtoncitypaper.com/articles/28423/massive-burial.

Goodwin, Leonard, 1973. *Do the Poor Want to Work? Social Psychological Study of Work Orientations.* New York: The Brookings Institution.

Grant, Adam, 2016. Why I taught myself to procrastinate. *The New York Times,* January 16, 2016. www.nytimes.com/2016/01/17/opinion/sunday/why-i-taught-myself-to-procrastinate.html?_r=0.

Gray, Kurt, Adrian F. Ward, and Michael I. Norton, 2014. Paying it forward: Generalized reciprocity and the limits of generosity. *Journal of Experimental Psychology: General* 143(1): 247–254.

Grubbs, Joshua B., Julie J. Exline, Kenneth I. Pargament, Joshua N. Hook, and Robert D. Carlisle, 2015. Transgression as addiction: Religiosity and moral disapproval as predictors of perceived addiction to pornography. *Archives of Sexual Behavior* 44: 125–136.

Hald, Gert M., and Neil M. Malamuth, 2015. "Pornography." In James D. Wright (ed.), *The International Encyclopedia of the Social and Behavioral Sciences.* Amsterdam: Elsevier Publishing Co.

Hamermesh, D. S., and J Slemrod, 2005. *The Economics of Workaholism: We Should Not Have Worked on This Paper.* National Bureau of Economic Research (NBER) Working Paper Series. Cambridge, MA: NBER.

Hardin, Garrett, 1968. The tragedy of the commons. *Science* 162(3859): 1243–1248.

Harrison, Trevor W., 2007. Anti-Canadianism: Explaining the deep roots of a shallow phenomenon. *International Journal of Canadian Studies* 35: 217–239.

Harvard Medical School, 2009. What causes depression? *Harvard Health Publications,* June 9, 2009. www.health.harvard.edu/mind-and-mood/what-causes-depression.

Heather, Nick, 1992. Why alcoholism is not a disease. *The Medical Journal of Australia* 156(3): 212–215.

Hesz, Alex, and Bambos Neophytou, 2010. *Guilt Trip: From Fear to Guilt on the Green Bandwagon.* New York: John Wiley & Sons.

Hill, Sarah E., and David M. Buss, 2008. The evolutionary psychology of envy. In Richard H. Smith (ed.), *Envy: Theory and Research,* 60–70. Oxford: Oxford University Press.

Huey, Laura, Danielle Hryniewicz, and Georgios Fthenos, 2014. 'I had a lot of anger and that's what kind of led me to cutting myself': Employing a social stress framework to explain why some homeless women self-injure. *Health Sociology Review* 23(2): 148–158.

Inciardi, James A., 1986. *The War on Drugs*. Palo Alto, CA: Mayfield.

Iveniuk, James, and Edward O. Laumann, 2015. Heterosexuality. In James D. Wright (ed.), *The International Encyclopedia of the Social and Behavioral Sciences*, 2nd ed. Amsterdam: Elsevier Publishing Co.

Janowitz, Morris. 1978. *The Last Half-Century: Societal Change and Politics in America*. Chicago, IL: University of Chicago Press.

Jemmott, John B., Loretta S. Jemmott, and Geoffrey T. Fong, 2010. Efficacy of a theory-based abstinence-only intervention over 24 months: A randomized controlled trial with young adolescents. *Archives of Pediatric and Adolescent Medicine* 164(2): 152–159.

Juth, Vanessa, Joshua M. Smyth, and Alecia M. Santuzzi, 2008. How do you feel? Self-esteem predicts affect, stress, social interactyion and symptom severity during daily life in patients with chronic illness. *Journal of Health Psychology* 13(7): 884–894.

Kahan, Dan M., and Eric A. Posner, 1999. Shaming white-collar criminals: A proposal for reform of the Federal sentencing guidelines. *Journal of Law and Economics* 42(1): 365–392.

Kahneman, Daniel, Jack L. Knetsch, and Richard H. Thaler, 1986. Fairness as a constraint on profit seeking: Entitlements in the market. *The American Economic Review* 76(4): 728–741.

Kamp, David, 2008. Whether true or false, a real stretch. *New York Times*, December 30. www.nytimes.com/2008/12/31/dining/31diam.html.

Karraker, Amelia, John DeLamater, and Christine R. Schwartz, 2011. Sexual frequency decline from midlife to later life. *The Journals of Gerontology, Series B: Psychological Sciences and Social Sciences* 66(4): 502–512.

Kasperkevic, Jana, 2014. Food stamps: Why recipients are haunted by stigmas and misconceptions. *The Guardian*. Available at www.theguardian.com/money/2014/apr/17/food-stamps-snap-coordinators-challenges.

Kass, Sarah A., 2014. Don't fall into those stereotype traps: Women and the feminine in existential therapy. *Journal of Humanistic Psychology*, March 11. http://jhp.sagepub.com/ content/early/2013/03/08/0022167813478836.abstract.

Kaufman, Scott Barry, 2012. Pride and creativity: How is pride related to creative achievement? *Psychology Today*. www.psychologytoday.com/blog/beautiful-minds/201207/pride-and-creativity.

Kelling, George L., Michael Julian, and S. Miller, 1994. *Managing 'Squeegeeing': A Problem Solving Exercise*. New York: NYPD.

Kemp, Simon, and Friedel Bolle, 2013. Are egalitarian preferences based on envy? *Journal of Socio-Economics* 45: 57–63.

Kenway, Jane, and Johannah Fahey, 2010. Is greed still good? Was it ever? Exploring the emoscapes of the global financial crisis. *Journal of Education Policy* 25(6): 717–727.

Kinniburgh, Colin, 2014. Beyond "conflict minerals:" The Congo's resource curse lives on. *Dissent Spring*. www.dissentmagazine.org/article/beyond-conflict-minerals-the-congos-resource-curse-lives-on.

Kohler, Pamela K., Lisa E. Manhart, and William E. Lafferty, 2008. Abstinence-only and comprehensive sex education and the initiation of sexual activity and teen pregnancy. *Journal of Adolescent Health* 42: 344–351.

Kopelman, Shirli, Weber, Mark J., and Messick, David M., 2002. Factors influencing cooperation in commons dilemmas: A review of experimental psychological research. In E. Ostrom et al., (Eds.), *The Drama of the Commons*. Washington, DC: National Academy Press.

Koss, Mary P., 2000. Blame, shame and community: Justice responses to violence against women. *The American Psychologist* 55(11): 1332–1343.

Kreutziger, Sarah, Richard Ager, Evelyn Harrell, and James D. Wright, 1999. The Campus Affiliates Program: Universities respond to troubled times. *American Behavioral Scientist* 42(5): 827–839.

Kunz, Jenifer, 2015. The effectiveness of virginity pledges: The demographic debate rages. *National Social Science Conferences Proceedings*. New Orleans: Professional Development Conference. www.nssa.us/journals/pdf/NSS_Proceedings_2015_New_Orleans.pdf#page=82.

Lambert, Craig, 2007. The science of happiness. *Harvard Magazine*, January–February. http://harvardmagazine.com/2007/01/the-science-of-happiness.html.

The Lancet, 2013. The third national survey of sexual attitudes and lifestyles. *The Lancet* 382(9907): 1781–1855. Available at www.thelancet.com/journals/lancet/issue/vol382no9907/PIIS0140-6736(13)X6059-3.

Lauderdale, Diane S., Kristen L. Knutson, Lijing L. Yan, Paul J. Rathouz, Stephen B. Hulley, Steve Sidney, and Kiang Liu, 2006. Objectively measured sleep characteristics among early middle-aged adults: The CARDIA study. *American Journal of Epidemiology* 164(1): 5–16.

Leach, Colin Wayne, 2008. Envy, inferiority and injustice: Three bases of anger about inequality. In Smith, Richard H. (ed), *Envy: Theory and Research*, 94–116. Oxford: Oxford University Press.

Lee, Barrett A., & Chad R. Farrell, 2003. Buddy, can you spare a dime? Homelessness, panhandling, and the public. *Urban Affairs Review* 38: 299–324.

Leka, Jona, Alastair McClelland, and Adrian Furnham, 2013. Memory for sexual and nonsexual television commercials as a function of viewing context and viewer gender. *Applied Cognitive Psychology* 27(5): 584–592.

Lemert, Edwin M., 1997. *The Trouble with Evil: Social Control at the Edge of Mortality*. New York: SUNY Press.

Levesque, Roger J. R., 2014. Envy. In Levesque (ed.), *The Encyclopedia of Adolescence*, 846–847. New York: Springer Verlag.

Levin, Jack, 2011. The invisible hate crime. *Pacific Standard Magazine*, March 1, 2011. www.psmag.com/politics-and-law/the-invisible-hate-crime-27984.

Liazos, Akexander, 1972. The poverty of the sociology of deviance: Nuts, sluts and perverts. *Social Problems* 20(Summer): 103–120.

Link, Bruce, and Jo Phelan, 2001. Conceptualizing stigma. *Annual Review of Sociology* 27: 363–385.

Lustman, Michele, David L. Wiesenthal, and Gordon Flett, 2010. Narcissism and aggressive driving: Is an inflated view of the self a road hazard? *Journal of Applied Social Psychology* 40(6): 1423–1449.

Lyman, Stanford M., 1978. *The Seven Deadly Sins: Society and Evil*. New York: St. Martin's Press.

Mallett, Robyn K., 2012. Eco-guilt motivates eco-friendly behavior. *Ecopsychology* 4(3): 223–231.

Mann, Michal, Clemens M. H. Hosman, Herman P. Schaalma, and Nanne K. de Vries, 2004. Self-esteem in a broad-specttrum approach for mental health promotion. *Health Education Research* 19(4): 357–372.

Mariani, John, 1991. *America Eats Out*. New York: William Morrow.

Marmot, Michael, and Richard G. Wilkinson, 2005. *Social Determinants of Health*, 2nd ed. Oxford: Oxford University Press.

Marsden, Sara J., 2013. Supersize my funeral: How the obesity epidemic in the U.S. is impacting on the funeral industry. www.us-funerals.com/funeral-articles/funerals-for-oversize-people.html#.VroSG_krJhE.

Massey, Douglas S., 2007. *Categorically Unequal: The American Stratification System*. New York: Russell Sage Foundation.

Matuska, Kathleen M., 2010. Workaholism, life balance, and well-being: A comparative analysis. *Journal of Occupational Science* 17: 104–111.

McAlinden, Anne-Marie, 2005. The use of 'shame' with sexual offenders. *British Journal of Criminology* 45(3): 373–394.

McCall, Patricia L., and Joshua A. Hendrix, 2015. Crime trends and debates. In James D. Wright (ed.), *International Encyclopedia of the Social and Behavioral Sciences*, 2nd ed. Amsterdam: Elsevier Publishing.

McKeever, Brice S., 2015. *Public Charities, Giving, and Volunteering*. Center on Non-Profits and Philanthropy. Washington, DC: The Urban Institute. Recovered at www.urban.org/ sites/default/files/alfresco/publication-pdfs/2000497-The-Nonprofit-Sector-in-Brief-2015-Public- Charities-Giving-and-Volunteering.pdf.

Morell, Parker, 1934. *Diamond Jim: The Life and Times of James Buchanan Brady*. New York: Simon and Schuster.

Myers, B. R., 2011. The moral crusade against foodies. *The Atlantic*, March 2011. www.theatlantic.com/magazine/archive/2011/03/the-moral-crusade-against-foodies/308370/.

Nafei, Yasser, 2009. *Corporate Dictatorship: The Evil behind the Collapse of the World's Economy*. Naperville, IL: Prothics Consulting, Inc.

National Institute on Aging, 2016. *Growing Older in America: The Health and Retirement Study*. Washington, DC: National Institute on Aging, US Department of Health and Human Services.

National Institute on Alcohol Abuse and Alcoholism, 2016. *Alcohol Facts and Statistics*. Washington, DC: NIAAA.

National Institute on Drug Abuse (NIDA), 2015. *Drug Facts*, June 2015. Washington, DC: NIDA.

Nielsen, S. J., and B. M. Popkin, 2002. Patterns and trends in food portion sizes, 1977–1998. *Journal of the American Medical Association* 289: 450–453.

Nock, Steven L., Laura A. Sanchez, and James D. Wright, 2008. *Covenant Marriage: The Movement to Reclaim Tradition in America*. New Brunswick, NJ: Rutgers University Press.

Northrup, Chrisanna, Pepper Schwartz, and James Witte, 2013. Sex at 50-plus: What's normal? *AARP Magazine*, February 2013. www.aarp.org/home-family/sex-intimacy/info-01-2013/seniors-having-sex-older-couples.html.

O'Connor, Justen P., and Trent D. Brown, 2010. Riding with the sharks: Serious leisure cyclist's perceptions of sharing the road with motorists. *Journal of Science and Medicine in Sport* 13: 53–58.

OECD, 2014. Obesity update. Available at www.oecd.org/health/Obesity-Update-2014.pdf.

Ostrom, Elinor, James Walker, and Roy Gardner, 1994. *Rules, Games, and Common-Pool Resources*. Ann Arbor, MI: University of Michigan Press.

Owen, Neville, Phillip B. Sparling, Genevieve N. Healy, David W. Dunstant, and Charles E. Matthews, 2010. Sedentary behavior: Emerging evidence for a new health risk. *Mayo Clinic Proceedings* 85(12): 1138–1141.

Pearson, David, Michelle Minehan, and Rachael Wakefield-Rann, 2013. Food waste in Australian households: Why does it occur? *Locale: The Australasian-Pacific Journal of Regional Food Studies* 3: 118–132.

Perry, Samuel L., 2016. Does viewing pornography reduce marital quality over time? Evidence from longitudinal data. *Archives of Sexual Behavior* 45 (forthcoming).

Persico, John, 2013. The 4th of Gandhi's seven social sins: Commerce without morality. https://agingcapriciously.com/2013/05/09/the-4th-of-gandhis-seven-social-sins-commerce-without-morality/.

Piff, Paul K., Michael W. Krause, Stephane Cote, Bonnie Hayden Cheng, and Dacher Keltner, 2010. Having less, giving more: The influence of social class on prosocial behavior. *Journal of Personality and Social Psychology* 99(5): 771–784.

Piff, Paul K., Daniel M. Stancato, Syephane Cote, Rodolofo Mendoza-Denton, and Dacher Keltner, 2012. Higher social class predicts increased unethical behavior. *Proceedings of the National Academy of Sciences* 109(11): 4086–4091.

Plante, Thomas G., 2013. Guilt isn't all bad. *Psychology Today.* www.psychologytoday.com/blog/do-the-right-thing/201309/guilt-isn-t-all-bad.

Poulsen, Franklin O., Dean M. Busby, and Adam M. Galovan, 2013. Pornography use: Who uses it and how it is associated with couple outcomes? *The Journal of Sex Research* 50(1): 72–83.

Powell, Caitlin A. J., Richard H. Smith, and David Ryan Schurtz, 2008. *Schadenfreude* caused by an envied person's pain. In Smith, Richard H. (ed.), 148–166. *Envy: Theory and Research.* Oxford: Oxford University Press.

Power, Julie, 2014. Obesity makes pallbearing too dangerous. *The Sydney Morning Herald,* August 3. www.smh.com.au/nsw/obesity-makes-pallbearing-too-dangerous-20140716-ztowm.html.

Puhl, Rebecca M., and Chelsea A. Heuer, 2010. Obesity stigma: Important considerations for public health. *American Journal of Public Health* 100(6): 1019–1028.

Regnerus, Mark, 2007. *Forbidden Fruit: Sex and Religion in the Lives of American Teenagers.* Oxford: Oxford University Press.

Resnick, Stella, 2012. *The Heart of Desire: Keys to the Pleasure of Love.* New York: John Wiley & Sons.

Richards, Jay W., 2009. *Money, Greed, and God.* New York: Harper Collins.

Richards, Jay W., 2012. *The Eight Biggest Myths about Wealth, Poverty and Free Enterprise.* The Discovery Institute: Center on Wealth, Poverty and Morality. Available at www.discovery.org/a/19601.

Roca, Carlos, and Dirk Helbing, 2011. Emergence of social cohesion in a model society of greedy, mobile individuals. *PNAS* 108(28): 11370–11374.

Rossi, Peter H., and Katharine C. Lyall, 1976. *Reforming Public Welfare: A Critique of the Negative Income Tax Experiment.* New York: Russell Sage Foundation.

Rossi, Peter H., Mark W. Lipsey, and Howard Freeman, 2004. *Evaluation: A Systematic Approach.* Thousand Oaks, CA: Sage Publications.

Saad, Lydia, 2014. The "40-hour" workweek is actually longer—By seven hours. Available at www.gallup.com/poll/175286/hour-workweek-actually-longer-seven-hours.aspx.

Sahoo, Chandan Kumar, and Sitaram Das, 2011. Employee empowerment: A strategy towards workplace commitment. *European Journal of Business and Management* 3(11): 46–55.

Sansone, Randy A., Charlene Lam, and Michael W. Wiederman, 2010. Road rage: Relationships with borderline personality and driving citations. *International Journal of Psychiatry in Medicine* 40(1): 21–29.

Sansone, Randy A., Justin S. Leung, and Michael W. Wiederman, 2012. Driving citations and aggressive behavior. *Traffic Injury Prevention* 13(3): 337–340.

Sansone, Randy A., and Lori A. Sansone, 2010. Road rage: What's driving it? *Psychiatry* 7(7): 14–18.

Santelli, John, Mary A. Ott, Maureen Lyon, Jennifer Rogers, Daniel Summers, and Rebecca Schleifer, 2006. Abstinence and abstinence-only education: A review of U.S. policies and programs. *Journal of Adolescent Health* 38: 72–81.

Sargeant, Adrian, and Lucy Woodliffe, 2007. Gift giving: An interdisciplinary review. *International Journal of Nonprofit and Volunteer Sector Marketing* 12(4): 275–307.

Schieman, Scott, 2010. The sociological study of anger: Basic social patterns and contexts. In Potegal, Michael, Gerhard Stemmler and Charles Spielberger (eds.), *International Handbook of Anger*, Chap. 19. New York: Springer.

Schoenborn CA, and PF Adams, 2010. Health behaviors of adults: United States, 2005–2007. National Center for Health Statistics. *Vital Health Statistics* 10(245): 1–132.

Schrank, David, Bill Eisele, Tim Lomax, and Jim Bak, 2015. *2015 Urban Mobility Scorecard*. College Station, TX: Texas A&M University: The Texas A&M Transportation Institute.

Schumaker, John F., 2004. In greed we trust. *New Internationalist*, Magazine Issue 369. Available on December 29, 2015, http://newint.org/columns/essays/2004/07/01/greed/.

Seltzer, Leon F., 2012. Greed: The ultimate addiction. *Psychology Today*. Available on December 29, 2015, www.psychologytoday.com/blog/evolution-the-self/201210/greed-the-ultimate-addiction.

Sezer, Ovul, Francsa Gino, and Michael I. Norton, 2015. Humblebragging: A distinct- and ineffective-self-presentation strategy. Harvard Business School Working Paper 15–080.

Shapiro, Ben, 2005. *Porn Generation: How Social Liberalism Is Corrupting Our Future*. Washington, DC: Regnery Publishing.

Shimazu, Akihito, Wilmar B. Schaufeli, and Toon W. Taris, 2010. How does workaholism affect worker health and performance? The mediating role of coping. *International Journal of Behavioral Medicine* 17: 154–160.

Shipler, David, 2005. *The Working Poor: Invisible in America*. New York: Vintage.

Shrestha, Nipun, Katrina T. Kukkonen-Harjula, Jos H. Verbeek, Sharea Ijaz, Veerle Hermans, and Soumyadeep Bhaumik, 2016. Workplace interventions for reducing sitting at work. *Cochrane Database of Systematic Reviews*, March 17. http://onlinelibrary.wiley.com/doi/10. 1002/14651858.CD010912.pub3/abstract.

Simmons, Roberta G., 1991. Presidential address on altruism and sociology. *The Sociological Quarterly* 32(1): 1–22.

Simmons, Robin W., and Kathryn Lively, 2010. Sex, anger and depression. *Social Forces* 88(4): 1543–1568.

Sinclair, Upton, 1906. *The Jungle*. New York: Doubleday, Jabber and Co.

Skolnikoff, Jessica, and Robert Engvall, 2013. *Young Athletes, Couch Potatoes, and Helicopter Parents: The Productivity of Play*. Lanham, MD: Rowman & Littlefield.

Smith, Richard H. (ed.), 2008. *Envy: Theory and Research*. Oxford: Oxford University Press.

Smith, Richard, 2014. What is the difference between envy and jealousy? *Psychology Today*, January 3, 2014. www.psychologytoday.com/blog/joy-and-pain/201401/what-is-the-difference-between-envy-and-jealousy.

Smith, Richard, 2015. The important distinction between benign and malicious envy. *Psychology Today*, January 11, 2015. www.psychologytoday.com/blog/joy-and-pain/201501/the-important-distinction-between-benign-and-malicious-envy.

Smith, Richard H., David J. Y. Combs, and Stephen M. Thielke, 2008. Envy and the challenges to good health. In Smith (ed.), *Envy: Theory and Research*, 290–314. Oxford: Oxford University Press.

Smith, Tom W., Jaesok Son, and Benjamin Shapiro, 2015. *Trends in Psychological Well-Being: 1972–2014*. Chicago, IL: National Opinion Research Center.

Snir, Raphael, and Itshak Harpaz, 2006. The workaholism phenomenon: A cross-national perspective. *Career Development International* 11(5): 374–393.

Snowdon, Christopher, 2015. *Selfishness, Greed and Capitalism: Debunking Myths about the Free Market*. London: The Institute of Economic Affairs.

Stack, Steven, Ira Wasserman, and Roger Kern, 2004. Adult social bonds and use of Internet pornography. *Social Science Quarterly* 85: 75–88.

Standage, Tom, 2006. *A History of the World in Six Glasses*. New York: Walker Publishing Company, Inc.

Stratton, Leslie S., 1996. Are 'involuntary' part-time workers indeed involuntary?" *Industrial and Labor Relations Review* 49(3): 522–536.

Streuber, Brittany, Laura Meade, and Shaelyn M. Strachan, 2015. Understanding the role of guilt and shame in physical activity self-regulation. *Journal of Exercise, Movement and Sport* 47(1), no pages given.

Suranovic, Steve, 2011. Is greed the problem with capitalism? *Liberty*, April 19, 2011. Available on January 5, 2016, http://libertyunbound.com/node/541.

Sussman, Steven, 2012. Workaholism: A Review. *Journal of Addiction Research and Therapy* 6(1): 1–18.

Sutherland, Jean-Anne, 2010. Mothering, guilt and shame. *Sociology Compass* 4(5): 310–321.

Szalavitz, Maia, 2014. We try more drugs than anyone else, and nine other ways addiction is different in America. *Pacific Standard Substance*, July 4, 2014. www.psmag.com/health-and-behavior/try-drugs-anyone-else-9-ways-addiction-different-america-85093.

Taflinger, Richard F., 1996. *Taking Advantage: The Sociological Basis of Greed*. February 10, 2018. http://public.wsu.edu/~taflinge/socgreed.html.

Tai, Kenneth, Jayanth Narayanan, and Daniel J. McAllister, 2012. Envy as pain: Rethinking the nature of envy and its implications for employees and organizations. *Academy of Management Review* 37(1): 107–129.

Tangney, June Price, Jeff Stuewig, and Debra J. Mashek, 2011. Moral emotions and moral behavior. *Annual Review of Psychology* 58: 345–372.

Thoits, Peggy A., and Lyndi N. Hewitt, 2001. Volunteer work and well-being. *Journal of Health and Social Behavior* 42: 115–131.

Tierney, John, 2011. Envy may bear fruit, but it also has an aftertaste. *The New York Times*, October 10, 2011. www.nytimes.com/2011/10/11/science/11tierney.html?_r=0.

Tomiyama, A. J., J. M. Hunger, J. Nguyen-Cuu, and C. Wells, 2016. Misclassification of cardio-metabolic health when using body mass index categories in NHANES 2005–2012. *International Journal of Obesity*, Prepublication preview available online on February 4, 2016. www.nature.com/ijo/journal/vaop/naam/abs/ijo201617a.html.

Trenholm, Christopher, Barbara Devaney, Ken Fortson, Lisa Quay, Justin Wheeler, and Melissa Clark, 2007. *Impacts of Four Title V, Section 510 Abstinence Education Programs: Final Report*. Princeton, NJ: Mathematica Policy Research, Inc.

Trimarchi, Maria, 2012. What happens when depression is turned inward? Available at http://health.howstuffworks.com/mental-health/depression/questions/depression-turned-inward.htm.

Tyler, Tom R., Lawrence Sherman, Heather Strang, Geoffrey C. Barnes, and Daniel Woods, 2007. Reintegrative shaming, procedural justice, and recidivism: The engagement of offenders' psychological mechanisms in the Canberra RISE drinking-and-driving experiment. *Law and Society Review* 41(3): 553–586.

Umberson, Debra, Kristi Williams, and Kristin Anderson, 2002. Violent behavior: Measure of emotional upset? *Journal of Health and Social Behavior* 43(2): 189–206.

Valor-Segura, Immaculada, Francisca Exposito, and Miguel Moya, 2014. Gender, dependency and guilt in intimate relationship conflict among Spanish couples. *Sex Roles* 70: 496–505.

Veenhoven, Ruud, 2015. Happiness: History of the concept. In James D. Wright (ed.), *International Encyclopedia of the Social and Behavioral Sciences*, 2nd ed. Amsterdam: Elsevier Publishing.

Veiga, John F., David C. Baldridge, and Lívia Markóczy, 2014. Toward greater understanding of the pernicious effects of workplace envy. *The International Journal of Human Resource Management* 25(17): 2364–2381.

Venzin, Elizabeth, 2014. How does low self-esteem negatively affect you? *World of Psychology*. http://psychcentral.com/blog/archives/2014/03/01/how-does-low-self-esteem-negatively-affect-you/.

Wacquant, Luic, 2008. *Urban Outcasts: A Comparative Sociology of Advanced Marginality.* Malden, MA: Polity Press.

Waite, Linda J., 2015. Sexuality over the life course. In James D. Wright (ed.). *The International Encyclopedia of the Social and Behavioral Sciences*, 2nd ed., 840–845. Amsterdam: Elsevier Publishing Company.

Wang, Youfa, and May A. Beydoun, 2007. The obesity epidemic in the Unites States—Gender, age, socio-econmic, racial/ethnic and geographic characteristics: A systematic review and meta-regression analysis. *Epidemiologic Reviews* 29: 6–28.

Wang, Long, Deepak Malhotra, and J. Keith Murnighan, 2011. Economics education and greed. *Academy of Management Learning and Education* 10(4): 643–660.

Wang, Long, and J. Keith Murnighan, 2011. On greed. *Academy of Management Annals* 5(1): 279–316.

Warburton, Wayne A., and Craig Anderson, 2015. Aggression, social psychology of. In James D. Wright (ed.), *The International Encyclopedia of the Social and Behavioral Sciences*, 2nd ed. Amsterdam: Elsevier Publishing.

Ward, Catherine, and Irene Styles, 2012. Guilt as a consequence of migration. *International Journal of Applied Psychoanalytic Studies* 9(4): 330–343.

Weber, Max, 1905. *The Protestant Ethic and the Spirit of Capitalism.* The usual reference is to the version published by Scribner's in 1958 (translation by Talcott Parsons).

Weil, Andrew, 1972. *The Natural Mind: A New Way of Looking at Drugs and the Higher Consciousness.* Boston, MA: Houghton Mifflin.

White, Mel, 1994. *Stranger at the Gate: To Be Gay and Christian in America.* New York: Plume Books.

White, Michael, 2001. *Rivals: Conflict as the Fuel of Science.* London: Secker and Warburg.

Willer, Robb, Fancis J. Flynn, and Sonya Zak, 2012. Structure, identity, and solidarity: A comparative field study of generalized and direct exchange. *Administrative Science Quarterly* 57(1): 119–155.

Williams, Walter E., 2001. The virtue of greed. *Capitalism Magazine*, January 2001. Available on January 15, 2016, http://econfaculty.gmu.edu/wew/articles/99/nature-of-greed.htm on.

Wright, James D., 2009. The founding fathers of sociology: Francis Galton, Adolphe Quetelet, and Charles Booth; or: What do people you probably never heard of have to do with the foundations of sociology? *Journal of Applied Social Science* 3(2): 63–72.

Wright, James D., 2016. *Social Problems, Social Issues, Social Science: The* Society *Papers.* New Brunswick, NJ: Transaction Publishers.

Wright, James D., and Joel A. Devine, 1994. *Drugs as a Social Problem.* New York: Harper Collins.

Wright, James D., Amy M. Donley, and Sara Strickhouser, 2018. *An Ungrateful Wretch: Food Insecurity in America* (forthcoming).

Wright, James D., and Peter H. Rossi, 1986. *Armed and Considered Dangerous: A Survey of Felons and Their Firearms.* Hawthorne, NY: Aldine Publishing Co.

Wu, Bao-Pei, and Lei Chang, 2012. Envy: A social emotion characterized by hostility. *Advances in Psychological Science* 20(9): 1467–1478.

Wuthnow, Robert, 1994. *God and Mammon in America.* New York: Free Press.

Yang, Zhiyong, Narayan Janakiraman, and Morgan, K. Ward, 2015. Moral responsibility and paying it forward: The effects of social distance and queue length on paying forward generosity. In Kristin Diehl and Carolyn Yoon (eds.), *NA—Advances in Consumer Research* Volume 43, 270–275. Duluth, MN: Association for Consumer Research.

Yaniv, Gideon, 2011. Workaholism and marital estrangement: A rational-choice perspective. *Mathematical Social Sciences* 61: 104–108.

Young, Lisa R., and Marion Nestle, 2002. The contribution of expanding portion sizes to the US obesity epidemic. *American Journal of Public Health* 92: 246–249.

INDEX